High Culture, Popular Culture

Australian Cultural Studies
Editors: John Tulloch and Terry Threadgold

High Culture, Popular Culture

The long debate

Peter Goodall

ALLEN & UNWIN

To my father, and in memory of my mother

First published in 1995

Allen & Unwin Pty Ltd
9 Atchison Street, St Leonards, NSW 2065 Australia

National Library of Australia
Cataloguing-in-Publication entry:

Goodall, Peter, 1949– .
  High culture, popular culture: the long debate.

  Bibliography.
  Includes index.
  ISBN 1 86373 833 9.

  1. Popular culture—Australia. 2. Australia—
  Intellectual life. I. Title. (Series: Australian
  cultural studies).

306.4850994

Set in 11/12 Adobe Garamond by DOCUPRO, Sydney
Printed by SRM Production Services Sdn Bhd,
Malaysia

10 9 8 7 6 5 4 3 2 1

SERIES EDITOR'S FOREWORD

Nowadays the social and anthropological definition of 'culture' is probably gaining as much public currency as the aesthetic one. Particularly in Australia, politicians are liable to speak of the vital need for a domestic film industry in 'promoting our cultural identity'—and they mean by 'cultural identity' some sense of Australianness, of our nationalism as a distinct form of social organisation. Notably, though, the emphasis tends to be on Australian *film* (not popular television); and not just *any* film, but those of 'quality'. So the aesthetic definition tends to be smuggled back—on top of the kind of cultural nationalism which assumes that 'Australia' is a unified entity with certain essential features that distinguish it from 'Britain', the 'USA' or any other national entities which threaten us with 'cultural dependency'.

This series is titled 'Australian Cultural Studies', and I should say at the outset that my understanding of 'Australian' is not as an essentially unified category; and further, that my understanding of cultural is anthropological rather than aesthetic. By 'culture' I mean the social production of meaning and understanding, whether in the interpersonal and practical organisation of daily routines or in broader institutional and ideological structures. I am *not* thinking of 'culture' as some form of universal 'excellence', based on aesthetic 'discrimination' and embodied in a pantheon of 'great works'. Rather, I take this aesthetic definition of culture itself to be part of the *social mobilisation of discourse* to differentiate a cultural 'élite' from the 'mass' of society.

Unlike the cultural nationalism of our opinion leaders, 'Cultural Studies' focuses not on the essential unity of national cultures, but on the meanings attached to social difference (as in the distinction between 'élite' and 'mass' taste). It analyses the construction and mobilisation of these distinctions to maintain or challenge existing power differentials, such as those of gender, class, age, race and ethnicity. In this analysis, terms designed to socially differentiate people (like 'élite' and 'mass') become categories of discourse, communication and power. Hence our concern in this series is for an analytical understanding of the meanings attached to social difference within the *history* and *politics* of discourse.

It follows that the analysis of 'texts' needs to be untied from a single-minded association with 'high' culture (marked by 'authorship'), but must include the 'popular' too—since these distinctions of 'high' and 'popular' culture themselves need to be analysed, not assumed.

Peter Goodall's *High Culture, Popular Culture* makes the long process of construction of these distinctions his central focus. He argues that the assumed contemporaneity of the high culture/popular culture conflict in much cultural studies writing misses its long history. Importantly, Goodall insists that 'For most of its history, the discourse of culture has been about making choices', that the distinctions between high and popular culture cannot avoid debates about what constitutes the 'aesthetic', and that the history of institutional forms (for instance, the history of the growth of Australian television) cannot be separated from this—or from the related struggle between élitist and populist discourses. In particular, Goodall blames the historically uninformed hostility to 'high art' and the resulting obsession with contemporary popular culture for the failure to develop a comprehensive (and yet more defined) study of culture 'based on a broad grasp of the social dimension of art in both its production and consumption'. The 'vital mistake' of English studies in not following the direction of Richard Hoggart and Raymond Williams, and its ensuing formalism, has only added to this failure to breathe new life into the field. For Goodall, 'Whatever the rights and wrongs of these kinds of struggles . . . a Cultural Studies which can find no place now for high art—for what most people think of, after all, when they hear the word "culture" used on its own—or for English, is a fatally weakened project.'

Peter Goodall draws our attention here to the institutionalised conflict of reading formations within academia itself, and to the losses—especially of the 'aesthetic'—which have resulted. He asks us to read Raymond Williams' well known definition of culture as 'ordinary' as itself polemical and contestive, in the context of the historical moment of modern élitism. Now, through the 1970s, 1980s and 1990s, that moment has changed; and with it, Goodall insists, the polemical need for Williams' early, undifferentiated concept. The book argues that 'neither an undifferentiated (and intellectually ungraspable) notion of culture . . . nor an uncritical populism . . . offers a way forward'. The *history* of the struggle to define culture— and in defining making distinctions and divisions—is one way forward offered by this book.

Culture, as Fiske, Hodge and Turner say in *Myths of Oz*, grows out of the divisions of society, not its unity. 'It has to work to construct any unity that it has, rather than simply celebrate an achieved or natural harmony.' Australian culture is then no more than the temporary, embattled construction of 'unity' at any particular historical moment. The 'readings' in this series of 'Australian Cultural Studies' inevitably (and polemically) form part of the struggle to make and break the boundaries of meaning which, in conflict and collusion, dynamically define our culture.

JOHN TULLOCH

CONTENTS

PREFACE

This book is an attempt to trace in an accessible and readable form the broad intellectual context of one of the most enduring and complex debates about culture: between culture as art and culture as way of life; between high culture and popular culture, that is, between culture as the possession of an élite and culture as a phenomenon of the people as a whole. This is more than a matter of theory; it is a matter of history and public consciousness and policy: there are few areas of our daily lives which are not touched by it in some way. Although the debate has its origins elsewhere and in the past, it is of particular relevance to the history of Australia, which, like all post-colonial societies, has struggled with questions of its identity, but which has interpreted them to a peculiar extent in terms of a conflict between élitist and populist definitions of its culture.

While most of the material in this book is already available piecemeal, scattered through many publications by many authors, it has not been collected together in one place before, collated and juxtaposed, and focused on Australia. The advantages of looking at this debate in a broad framework are obvious; the disadvantages (especially to the writer) are equally so: selective knowledge, painting with too broad a brush, dilution of expertise, over-reliance on secondary sources. Nevertheless, the book has been written in the conviction that a broad understanding of this area is necessary to people working in both English and Cultural Studies today—that it might defuse some of the tension between them—and that the value of this will outweigh the occasional lapse of subtlety.

This topic was first suggested to me by John Tulloch and he gave support and good advice in getting it off the ground. Elizabeth Weiss of Allen & Unwin has been a thoughtful and encouraging editor. Jane Goodall has furnished moral and intellectual support throughout—although she cannot be blamed for the book's failings—and the quality of her own work has been a source of inspiration. Many of the ideas in the book were tried out on Jonathan Goodall—not always with his knowledge—and his comments were always helpful. I thank my colleagues in the School of English, Linguistics, and Media at Macquarie University for providing the kind of intellectually diverse and mutually supportive environment that Cultural Studies needs, and I thank the University for granting me a period of leave to complete the book.

INTRODUCTION: FROM HIGH CULTURE TO BEER CULTURE

Culture and cultures

On the day in early 1994 when I heard the reporter on the Australian Broadcasting Corporation's current affairs program '7.30 Report' speak about 'Australian beer culture'—he was discussing patterns of consumption of low alcohol beer—I began to fear that the word 'culture' might have entered a terminal phase of uselessness. I have nothing against beer, of course, nor the discussion, serious or otherwise, of its production and consumption; but the glib use of a word with such a history as 'culture' in connection with it is very disconcerting.

In recent times, 'culture' has become one of the most common words in all kinds of public discourse, constantly on the lips of journalists and politicians, not to speak of academics from almost all disciplines of the Humanities. 'Police culture', 'welfare culture', 'enterprise culture', 'research culture'—there seems almost no limit to its applicability in almost any context. At the same time it has become an increasingly empty term. The more frequently it is used, the more regularly it seems to need another word to prop it up and define its field of reference. Is this because *qua* culture, there is almost nothing in common between the police force, the welfare services, business and the universities? The word promises much in these contexts but delivers little; it poses as a noun but it is really an adjective. In the examples I have given, 'culture' itself hardly means more than 'group behaviour', 'practice' or 'shared assumptions'.

The other side of this is that while 'culture', defined in context by another term and spelt in lower case, is used more and more to mean less and less, 'Culture', standing on its own and spelt (on occasions) with a capital *C*, is used less and less but seems to mean something more and more specific—for those rash souls game enough to use it at all in this way, that is. While 'culture' seems to take place everywhere, 'Culture' seems to happen only at the Sydney Opera

House. Its context nowadays effectively confines its field of significance to 'high art'.

Compounding this is the tendency in the Humanities to reduce drastically the role of aesthetics. In *Outside Literature* (1990), Tony Bennett urges its complete abandonment in the context of Cultural Studies, but even in a book about new forms of the discipline of English, *Rewriting English* (1985), Batsleer et al. see aesthetics as nothing more than a mystification of what is really only the mundane exercise of personal taste:

> Literary criticism confers on this quite normal activity something of the intensity, exclusiveness and intolerance of a religious sect. It lifts it out of the everyday circumstances of reading and conversation and claims for it, in the name of some shibboleth such as 'beauty', 'significance' or—absurdly—'life', the status of a transcendent ethical value. (Batsleer et al., 1985, p. 29)

The judgement of relative value is thus, to all intents and purposes, the same as personal preference. Popular art seems to have fared even worse than this: there was not even a tradition of practice to withstand it. Although there have been attempts to evolve poetics and aesthetics for popular art—David Bordwell's *Classic Hollywood Cinema* (1985), Pierre Bourdieu's work (1980, 1984), Peter Brooks's study of *Melodrama* (1976), for example—the dominant theme in the study of popular culture in Australia has been 'resistant reading', which in its cruder forms is not an aesthetics at all, but an oppositional *practice*, upending the traditional categories of judgement about art, finding value in what was formerly dismissed as trash, sometimes because it is trash.

In some ways this displacement of the so-called 'aesthetic' view of culture by the so-called 'anthropological' view is the Whig view of Cultural Studies. The democratisation of a narrow view of culture as art, the province of the few, seems to parallel the forward march of democracy and liberalism in society as a whole. Unfortunately, like the Whig view of history, it is not always a reliable interpretation of the facts.

Sacred sites and unvisited graves

One of the purposes of this book is to restore a longer historical perspective to the study of culture. In this I am resisting the trend in Cultural Studies to use the term as synonymous with '*Contemporary* Cultural Studies'. Simon During says as much in the introduction to his *Cultural Studies Reader*: 'Cultural Studies is, of course, the study of culture, or, more particularly, the study of *contemporary* culture' (During 1993, p. 1, author's emphasis). There are several reasons for this trend—the authority of the Birmingham Centre for Contemporary Cultural Studies, founded in 1963, being one of the most persuasive—but there are still good reasons for resisting it. The main one is that the study of culture was not invented in the early 1960s or the late 1950s: there is a powerful body of writing about culture, still strongly influential and relevant, going right back to the eighteenth century, if not beyond. Yet while it is inconceivable that this literature would have been ignored by people like Richard Hoggart who founded the Birmingham Centre or Raymond Williams who wrote extensively about it in *Culture and Society* (1957), one of the seminal texts of Cultural Studies, it is increasingly ignored by modern students and modern courses. These texts look like sacred sites, but they are, in reality, unvisited graves.

If we look at the subject of culture in a historical way, from this longer perspective, then three things emerge immediately. The first is that 'culture' as a subject and as a social issue is not the invention of our own time. On the contrary, the farther we go back to the eighteenth century the more culture, its nature and composition, is the central issue in the Humanities. Furthermore, it was not really until the 1920s and 1930s—the period of modernism in the English-speaking world in other words—that 'culture' became another word for 'high art'. This is a consequence of many factors; one of them is the professionalising and specialising of English in the University and the downgrading by the mid-1930s of the broader educational aims for English of the Newbolt Report of 1921. That much sneered at report, which envisaged English as the foundation of a system of popular education, is illuminated throughout by a broad sense of the nature of English culture. To go back further, Matthew Arnold's *Culture and Anarchy* (2nd edn 1875) makes almost no mention of literature or art, popular or otherwise. Arnold's focus is always on the broadly social—in fact the central issue Arnold deals with is the proposed disestablishment of the Church in Ireland. While Williams's description of culture as the 'whole way of life' of a people was first used in *The Long Revolution* (1961), this way of conceiving of culture is quintessentially a nineteenth-century one—as Williams would have been the first to concede.

The second is that from the beginning of the discussion of culture in the eighteenth century, there has been a debate about the relative status and merits of its parts. Although, as a general principle, the farther one goes back towards the eighteenth century the more broadly culture is defined, that does not mean that anything goes. Although Arnold took it for granted that culture was a phenomenon on a large scale, comprising much more than art—indeed he laments the way in which culture in his own time had become so much a matter of what is read—he would have found it inconceivable that all parts of the social could be viewed as equally cultural. The other side to the breadth of Arnold's vision of culture is his conviction about what it is and what it is not. He is a convinced centralist: culture is general, total, metropolitan, classical. Underlying all of it is a sense of culture's lofty nature and aspirations: it is the pursuit of the *best* that has been thought and said, it is a quest for 'our total perfection' (Arnold 1960, p. 6). For Arnold, there is no conflict between an aesthetic and an anthropological view of culture: the essence of culture is the way it interrelates these different dimensions of our lives. Culture is the social dimension of art. The moment that culture becomes important as a theme, then it becomes important to discriminate within it: between what is good and what is bad, between what is important in a tradition and what is not, between what is central and what is peripheral. For most of its history, the discourse of culture has been about making choices.

The third is that culture always becomes a burning issue in times of perceived change and conflict: it is in moments of change, of course, that it becomes important to reflect on what is good and worth preserving in a society, what is centrally meaningful to its experience and its civilisation. Williams identified the Industrial Revolution as the dynamic social context for the origins of speculation about culture in Britain. One can, I think, go further than this and say that the long debate about culture, about high culture and its other, has been a way of addressing the question of the role of the machine in our society and the nature of art in an industrial society. The word 'mechanical' is one of the central pejorative terms in the debate about high culture and popular culture—Arnold uses it this way himself. If there is to be an end to the debate, it may well arrive in the post-industrial society of today and tomorrow. Already the contemporary discourse of art and *technology* seems to be a very different matter.

Coincidence of opposites: overview of the book

The first three chapters provide a broad historical overview of the use of the word 'culture', predominantly in the English-speaking world and, in particular, the struggle between élitist and populist definitions of it. In chapter 1 I locate the origins of the term in the eighteenth century, setting it in the broad context of the European Enlightenment, and connecting it particularly with the development of a philosophy of aesthetics, the rise of nationalism and the industrialisation of Britain. From the collocation of these factors in this period derives that perception of a fundamental antipathy between industry and culture. The expansion of the middle class created by this industrialised society enlarged the reading audience, but for the first time divided and stratified it, with two classes of writing produced by two types of writer—creating in effect a high culture and a popular culture. The dissolution of society implied by this becomes one of the central concerns of nineteenth-century writing. Although 'culture' is a much broader concept and category than 'art'—it is more a question of morality and social policy than aesthetics—it does not form the basis for a liberal view of society. Culture is a centralising, unifying, homogenising concept for Matthew Arnold; individualism—the root of English philistinism for him—is at heart its opposite.

Chapter 2 looks at the evolution of mass society in the twentieth century and the accompanying fear of cultural decay. This is not a narrowly English concern and the work of writers like F. R. and Q. D. Leavis is set in a more broadly European context than is usually the case. For all of these writers, the foundational idea is the minority nature of culture—F. R. Leavis's first pamphlet was published by the 'Minority Press'. The survival of a society's culture for all depends upon the influence of a small cadre of artists and thinkers, and yet in the modern world their position is constantly threatened by the debased standards of mass art. This kind of critique of mass culture has continued to be a feature of cultural criticism from both the political left and right throughout the twentieth century. I see

modernism continuing and developing that concern with the stratification and categorisation of the text and culture which is the legacy
of nineteenth-century criticism. This attitude—what makes one text
different from, better than, more critically interesting than another—
links several kinds of critical practice which might at first seem very
different and are usually treated so: various attempts made in the
context of Cambridge English to differentiate literary value; formalist
distinctions between literary and non-literary language; conservative
descriptions of the 'classic'; Lukács's distinctions between realism and
naturalism; Kermode's idea of the 'surplus signifier'; Barthes's distinction between the writable and readable text; Eco's distinction between
the open and closed text. Even those works which see status and
category imposed from without, by the (changing) judgements of
society rather than intrinsic features of the text, collaborate in this
practice of stratification and categorisation and, sometimes, valuation.
This habit of mind leads inevitably to models of culture which are
hierarchical.

Chapter 3 examines some examples of twentieth-century thought,
from within modernism itself and in postmodernism, which have
sought to abrogate, make redundant or change the nature of this
hierarchising of critical practice. One of the forms this has taken is
through the disestablishment of some of the most rigid of traditional
cultural antitheses: between art and technology, and between art and
all forms of consumerism, especially advertising. Another form has
been in the development since the Second World War of various
kinds of populist literary and cultural theory: in the development of
a counter-aesthetics of 'pop' in America, and in the influence of
French sociologies of 'everyday life'. The latter, in particular, has
stressed the active rather than the passive nature of the consumption
of mass culture—thereby deconstructing one of the most fundamental
modernist distinctions between art and non-art. This kind of cultural
populism has been influential in the development of Cultural Studies
everywhere in the 1980s—especially, I argue, in Australia—but it has
also been increasingly widely criticised as a model for cultural analysis.

The last three chapters examine particular sites of contestation
between cultural models. In chapter 4 I interpret the fundamental
association between cultural analysis and nationalism in an Australian
context. The discussion of the cultural identity of white Australia,
more than other nations, has polarised starkly between populist and

élitist models. The former model has, until the last thirty years, been the dominant one—epitomised in a succession of mainly masculinist myths such as the 'currency lad', the bushman and the larrikin of the 1890s, the digger of the First World War, the Bondi life-saver of the inter-war years, and the ocker of more recent times—but it should not be allowed to dominate the analysis of Australian culture. The weakness of this populist nationalism is, on the one hand, a sentimentalisation and whitewashing of Australian working-class life and, on the other hand, a curious insensitivity to and undervaluation of Australian 'high culture': the achievements of colonial culture, including federation, the impressive expansion of many branches of the 'public sphere' from the 1930s onwards, including that most maligned of decades, the 1950s. An especially striking phenomenon is how often these antithetical models have collaborated. The bush myth was not the creation of shearers themselves but of an urban bohemia; the ocker was created as a popular icon by performers and writers like Barry Humphries, an antipodean aesthete if there ever was one, within the context of the Australian film new wave of the 1970s. In the 1990s, I see the current Prime Minister, Paul Keating, as continuing and typifying the features of this kind of 'coincidence of opposites'.

Much of modernist cultural theory is predicated on an anxiety about the influence of the new media of mass communication developed in the twentieth century: print journalism, film, broadcasting on radio and television. Yet these were never simple instruments of populism. The graphic, tabloid style of the popular press quickly influenced and ultimately transformed the style of the quality press as well; within a surprisingly short time there developed a canon of film art, capable of generating the same level of critical engagement as other art forms. Both the BBC and the ABC attempted to establish themselves as bulwarks of high cultural resistance rather than agents of decay. It is television—the most recent of these forms, first broadcast in Australia in 1956—that has seen the most unsettling and unresolved struggle between élitism and populism, between addressing minority or mass audiences. The struggle to achieve a television 'art' comparable to that of the cinema has been fought in a context of its poor technical quality, its over-commitment to an aesthetic and poetics of naturalism, and the demands for 'ratings' that such an expensive medium of production inevitably creates. In chapter 5

I argue that there has been very little development of such a television art and high culture in Australia.

A renovated 'English'

The guiding principles of this book are formation and interrelationship, producing a view of culture perhaps best epitomised in the ancient rhetorical notion of art as a 'coincidence of opposites'. Yet, although 'culturalism' is fundamental to the development of English as an academic discipline in the twentieth century, and English, in its turn, the basis from which much work in Cultural Studies in the 1950s and 1960s grew, especially in Britain, English and Cultural Studies seem doomed in the 1980s and 1990s to become oppositional discourses. Recently published anthologies and readers of Cultural Studies include almost nothing that is recognisably part of a common mission with English: the work is overwhelmingly anthropological in its view of culture, oriented towards the mass media, hostile in its view of high art or even of art at all as a category, shallow in its historical field of reference—the notion that one could have a cultural study of a period before the twentieth century or which dealt sympathetically with the literary canon seems unimaginable.

Chapter 6 argues for a new rapprochement between the study of high culture and the study of popular culture and for an increased contribution of the discipline of 'English' to Cultural Studies. There were several moments in the development of English when it could have—and in my view should have—gone in the direction of Cultural Studies: the language and socio-historical strands in nineteenth-century medieval studies (very underrated in histories of English as a discipline and quite invisible in histories of Cultural Studies), departments formed under the influence of Cambridge English in the 1920s and 1930s, the early work in Cultural Studies itself in the late 1950s. In all cases, the opportunity for the development of a comprehensive study of culture, based on a broad grasp of the social dimension of art, in both its production and consumption, was lost. The vital mistake was, in my view, not following the sense of direction that writers like Richard Hoggart and Raymond Williams gave to the study of culture in the late 1950s. By and large English chose the route of formalism—what is nowadays often called the 'old' New Criticism—rejecting the chance to use a wider definition of culture and art to breathe new life into the culturalist focus that English had had since the work of the Leavises in the 1930s, but which had increasingly marginalised itself through its narrowness of focus and—quite frankly—its bigotry. Within this mixture of formalism and narrow high culturalism there was little for students of popular culture to do except find a home somewhere else.

Whatever the rights and wrongs of these kinds of struggles, it seems to me, however, that a Cultural Studies which can find no place now for high art—for what most people think of, after all, when they hear the word 'culture' used on its own—or for English, is a fatally weakened project. Raymond Williams's famous comment in the early 1960s that 'culture is ordinary'—one of the critical bases of modern cultural studies—needs to be read in its polemical context, as an intervention in the reigning modernist notion that culture is the contribution of the few in any society, especially the mass society of the twentieth century. One of the problems of Williams's work, and by extension one of the problems of Cultural Studies, is that he never thoroughly revised his early work in the changed conditions of the 1970s and 1980s. There is, however, evidence in his late work of misgivings about a wholesale populist direction for Cultural Studies. In 'The Future of Cultural Studies', published posthumously in 1989, he speaks thus:

> It is necessary . . . to analyse serials and soap operas. Yet I do wonder about the courses where at least the teachers . . . have not encountered the problems of the whole development of naturalist and realist drama . . . so that the tension between that social history of forms and these forms in a contemporary situation . . . can be explored with weight on both sides. (Williams 1989a, p. 159)

The book argues finally that neither an undifferentiated (and intellectually ungraspable) notion of culture—such as Grossberg et al.'s 'study of all the relations between all the elements in a whole way of life' (Grossberg et al. 1992, p. 14)—nor an uncritical populism, such as has threatened to become the house style of Australian Cultural Studies, offers a way forward.

'A PURSUIT OF OUR TOTAL PERFECTION': THEORIES OF CULTURE IN THE EIGHTEENTH AND NINETEENTH CENTURIES

The emergence of the debate about high culture and popular culture

There is no more basic misconception in the study of culture than to see the debate about popular culture and its social effects as simply the product of our own times, the consequence of living in an era in which the media can be seen to have both democratised the audience but debased the standard of art. Even if we understand culture in the narrow sense of performed texts, then it is clear that cultures of the people at large, as distinct from small minorities of them, are as old as human civilisation. In his book *Literature, Popular Culture and Society*, Leo Löwenthal points to, amongst other examples, the difference between esoteric and exoteric religious practices in the ancient world and the carnival festivities of medieval Europe. In a similar way, in *Rabelais and His World*, Mikhail Bakhtin theorised pre-modern culture in the West as structured fundamentally by plurality, difference and conflict; for every solemn moment, ritual, text, or act in the life of society there was a corresponding disruptive, popular one, the two bonded like the sides of a coin.

On the other hand, Löwenthal makes the important qualification that it is only in the modern era that the *relationship* between these two cultures within the one society has become controversial. An important moment for him is the crisis in seventeenth-century France at the end of what is often called the 'Age of Faith'. The intellectual protagonists in this conflict are the philosophers Montaigne and Pascal. For Montaigne, leisure, an escape into diversified activities, is a solace against the overwhelming sense of isolation produced by this loss of faith, but for Pascal, adumbrating a persistent worry in this debate, this leisure is a dangerous thing, and unhappiness results from an inability to stay quietly in one's own sphere: 'the attitude towards leisure which, for Montaigne, guarantees survival means self-

1

destruction for Pascal' (Löwenthal 1968, p. 4). Whereas Löwenthal can see in Montaigne a precursor of the box-office manager of our own times, Pascal is clearly a forerunner of the modernist fear and dislike of popular culture. As we shall see, many of Pascal's kinds of fears were taken up later. Q. D. Leavis, for example, saw popular fiction in 1932 as reading to be done in 'the face of lassitude and nervous fatigue', by people who could not bear peace and quiet, for it is 'only the exceptional character that can tolerate solitude and silence' (Q. D. Leavis 1965, pp. 49, 55).

Many discussions of this subject see the second half of the eighteenth century as a watershed. There is good reason to see modern thinking about culture as linked inextricably to those social and intellectual changes of the European 'Enlightenment'. Several of the most abiding issues in the debate about culture seem to emerge naturally out of the concerns of this era: a contest between the claims of unity and coherence, on the one hand, against plurality and difference, on the other, which is perhaps the underlying battle between classicism and romanticism; the conflict in society between culture and technology, and the nature of art in this new industrial society; culture and national identity in an age of national consolidation and imperial expansion. From another perspective, it was the period in which modern speculation about the nature of beauty and the whole domain of experience which lies outside reason or ethics was born. According to Roger Scruton, Immanuel Kant was the first philosopher since Plato to give aesthetics such a prominent role (Scruton 1982, *passim*), and since his time it has been accorded a high priority in western thought. Yet in the form of the Industrial Revolution, the period witnessed the profoundest challenge to those same notions. For D. H. Lawrence, the worst offence of industrialism in English culture was its criminal ugliness. In this time was born not just the notion of high culture but of popular culture also. Although antiquaries had been interested in the lives and art of the 'people' for a long time, the notion of popular culture—the idea that the stories, songs, ceremonies etc. of the people are all part of a whole, expressing the 'spirit' of a nation which informs its life from every angle—was first theorised in this period. It is usual to trace this way of looking at popular culture to the German historian, J. G. Herder; it was he who, for example, first used the word 'cultures' in the plural and coined the term *Volkslied*, 'folksong'. The word 'folklore' was coined a little later, by the English antiquarian, William Thoms, in 1846.[1]

Anthropology, in the form of the discovery of other cultures, became a major area of study in the nineteenth century. While differences in the quality of work, canons of taste and discriminations between audience groups will doubtless always exist, there is good reason to see the understanding of 'culture' as a problem to be a feature of modern industrial society. From a local viewpoint, the modern debate about culture is coextensive with the history of European settlement in Australia; our society is very much a product of it.

Aesthetics, art and culture

By 1830, according to Raymond Williams in *Culture and Society*, the central concern in writing about culture was 'beauty'. The essence of art is its ability to reveal aspects of beauty, not just in the limited sense of describing beautiful things, or using beautiful words and images, but its ability to reveal on a profounder metaphysical level aspects of universal beauty and truth—the Greek vase at which Keats marvels provokes the reflection in 'Ode on a Grecian Urn' that '"Beauty is truth, truth beauty,"—that is all / Ye know on earth, and all ye need to know'. The beauty of the world is the most powerful evidence for the existence of God's grand design.

The primacy of the aesthetic dimension of art and culture was achieved in a very short time, considering that the modern use of the term 'aesthetic' derives from Kant's mentor, Alexander Baumgarten, whose *Aesthetica* was only published in 1750. Baumgarten used the term, however, in a much wider sense than we are used to, to describe the whole domain of experience which lies outside of the sphere of reason; it is thus to do with perception and sensation, with the apprehension of things rather than thoughts. The realm of the aesthetic is thus, in the words of Terry Eagleton, 'the most gross and palpable dimension of the human' (Eagleton 1990, p. 13). More immediately relevant are those essays on 'taste'—for example those produced by Oliver Goldsmith, Joshua Reynolds, Hugh Blair, and David Hume—which are a particular feature of the later eighteenth century. Of similar importance is the speculation on the nature of the imagination and its role in the production of art which became a central theme in European Romanticism. For Goethe, the function of art is to stimulate 'productive imagination'. Wordsworth, likewise, distinguished between true art, which stimulates the imagination, and cheap art, which merely blunts the mind.

Although there is a wealth of writing about art, aesthetics, and the creative process in this period—the German philosopher Schelling is particularly important for the development of English poetry at this time, for example—for me the most important text in the development of the modern aesthetics of art is Kant's *Critique of Judgement*, published in 1790 towards the end of his life. Despite the fact that his study does not really deal with 'art' at all in the main, but with 'natural beauty', the beauty of the natural world, almost all attempts to evaluate art or to describe the special nature of its functioning in the next two hundred years seem to owe something to it—this is certainly the view of Pierre Bourdieu and those writers who have tried to evolve an aesthetic of popular culture in opposition to it. From Kant derive such fundamental ideas as the distinctive nature of aesthetic pleasure, bypassing sense experience and reliant on a detachment from the object which gives the pleasure; the notion that the study of art is a special kind of knowledge, not readily theorised; the importance of form in the production of art and sensitivity to it on the part of the 'consumer'; the central role of originality and the special nature of genius in the creation of true art.

For Kant, aesthetics is a faculty of judgement which *mediates* between understanding (pure reason) and ethics (practical reason). As a kind of judgement it is very special in that it has both subjective and objective aspects. The judgement of beauty is subjective in that beauty is clearly not an attribute of the object in the way that heat is objectively an attribute of fire. It is necessarily grounded in the personal experience of pleasure, not in concepts. There can be no *a priori* grounds for attributing beauty to an object. Despite the attempts of philosophers like Batteux, Lessing, and Winckelmann to provide universal principles for the classification and judgement of works of art, to find objective criteria for beauty in art, Kant is firm that there are no objective rules of taste. On the other hand, claims for beauty are not made merely on a personal basis. When I say that something is beautiful I mean something more than merely this seems beautiful to me. The communicability of the mental state of the aesthetic experience is fundamental. In talking about beauty, one is attempting to distinguish some quality which may meet with the agreement of others. There is an essential connection between beauty and rationality—only a rational being can experience beauty—yet the mechanism of this rational process seems very complex. It is always personal experience which is the basis of the judgement of beauty— beauty is the one thing we can never take on trust without seeing it for ourselves—yet, logically, how can a judgement, something which demands universal agreement, be based on experience which is always personal? Kant's definition of the beautiful—'that which pleases universally, without a concept' (Kant 1957, p. 392)—contains a paradox at its heart. It is no wonder the rest of us have found the going so tough.

Pleasure is a crucial concept here, but the special nature of aesthetic pleasure is that it is independent of sensuous value, even in some ways opposed to it. Kant's argument is a series of subtle but unbridgeable antinomies: 'that which pleases' must be distinguished from 'that which gives pleasure', 'disinterestedness' from 'the interest of the senses'. Aesthetic pleasure must be distinguished from pleasures such as food and drink. Its distinctiveness is that while it is immediate like other pleasures, it is also 'contemplative', involving reflection upon its object. This contemplation involves attending to the individuality of the object, as the particular thing that it is, not as an instance of a universal. Aesthetic judgement abstracts from every 'interest' of the observer. The moral or sensory value of the object is irrelevant. Aesthetic judgement is an end in itself, not a means to some other end.

The experience of beauty, the aesthetic judgement, is fundamentally different from the feeling of charm or the emotion an object can stimulate: '[that] taste that requires an added element of charm and emotion for its delight, not to speak of adapting this as the measure of its approval, has not yet emerged from barbarism'.[2] The pleasure which beauty brings is a pure one, like a pleasure purified of pleasure as Pierre Bourdieu says. This pleasure is closely linked to a sense of form: 'not what gratifies in sensation but what pleases by means of its form' (Kant 1957, p. 396). This sense of form is both disinterested and detached: it has nothing to do with the charming of the senses and nothing to do with 'life' in any broader, practical or ethical sense. Beauty does have a purpose; in responding to form we respond to a purposiveness, but it is a purposiveness which is entirely self-reflecting, as Kant says rather cryptically, a kind of 'purposiveness without a purpose' (Kant 1957, p. 397). When we look at a beautiful painting we respond to the purposiveness of its form, but our sense of its purpose is of something entirely free from the constraint of rules and principles.

Kant's sense of the artist grows out of these ideas. Beauty is created by the artist of genius, and Kant's definition of genius is a talent for producing that for which no definite rules can be given: 'originality must be its first property' (Kant 1957, p. 418). It is impossible to describe scientifically how the artist produces the beautiful products that he does, how this original genius operates. It follows no rules (or at least does not make it obvious how the rules are being followed) yet, like nature itself, it has the power to lay down the rules for others to follow. The artist's genius is fundamentally opposed to the spirit of imitation and hence to learning in its more usual sense, which for Kant is largely imitation, on a simple or complex level as the case may be.

Industrialism and the division of culture

'Aesthetics' was only one of a whole group of words coined, re-used or 're-signified' in the second half of the eighteenth century. But whereas Germany was slow to industrialise—the small city of Königsberg in Prussia in which Kant spent his whole life is so far north-east that it is not even in modern Poland but in Russia, renamed after one of Stalin's henchmen—one of the fundamental insights of Williams's influential book, *Culture and Society*, is that 'culture' as a term and a problem was first conceptualised in England during the Industrial Revolution. Several keywords in the debate—art, class, culture, democracy, industry—were first used, or used with a new sense of the possibilities of their meaning, at this time. Words which were formerly used in a rather neutral, unspecific way, were now used in a pointed, contentious way, as elements in a developing controversy. The meaning of 'industry', for example, changed from individual diligence to manufacturing institutions; 'art' changed from meaning the bodies of knowledge or skills belonging to all kinds of practices to the imaginative arts, a special kind of truth. The contentiousness of these terms is a reflection of the conflict in society as a whole. For Williams, England in the late eighteenth century is a place of contrasts, especially between the old, feudal England and the new, industrial, one. Although the word 'industrialism' was not coined until 1833 by Thomas Carlyle in *Sartor Resartus*, industry is seen from early on in this period by many writers as the most powerful threat to English culture. Manufacture, and the philosophy of Utilitarianism which is so often associated with it, lead to ugliness and the loss of human feeling. The view of Robert Owen, that industry will provide the opportunity for a new moral world, that increase in wealth will lead the people to culture—a foreshadowing of the Marxist attitude to the machine—is very much the minor partner in this debate. The notion that there is a fundamental antipathy between the machine, technology in general, and culture, or, to see it from the other side, that popular culture is in some way essentially bound up with technology and, for that reason, is not true culture, is one of the most powerful and long-lasting elements in this whole debate.

With the emergence of this new society, its culture divided by industrialism, comes a powerful series of changes in the reading public and its literature. At the most basic level, the population increased dramatically. It has been calculated that while the population of Europe had never exceeded 180 million at any time before 1800, between 1800 and 1914 it grew to 460 million.[3] There was a vast increase in the size of the reading public after 1740. This enlarged reading public was not distributed evenly throughout society however, but was concentrated in the middle class, a class associated with the wealth brought into being by industrialisation. This greatly enlarged readership, including for the first time a significant number of women, formed a new kind of relationship with its authors; instead of a relationship of patronage, reader and author entered into what is essentially a market relationship. The author becomes a professional selling his product to an audience of consumers. Some writers seem to have accepted and even relished this new situation. Walter Scott, for instance, early came to see writing as a legitimate business and emphasised what Löwenthal calls 'the pre-stabilised harmony between books which sell well and the healthy tastes of the reading public', quoting Scott's own view that 'those who have been best received in their own time have also continued to be acceptable to society' (Löwenthal 1968, pp. 35, 36). But it is obvious that Scott's views were not shared by many other 'serious' novelists. In this period another powerful theme in the high culture–popular culture debate is born, as long lasting as the theme of the machine, that there is an irreconcilable conflict between high art and success in the market place. Indeed, commercial failure comes to be seen as a hallmark of the serious work of art, guaranteeing its authenticity. In a later stage of the argument, this becomes one of the main reasons why it must be funded by the state.

One of the central ideas of Q. D. Leavis's *Fiction and the Reading Public* (1932) is that after 1760 there comes a stratification of the literate public which had not existed before: between 'highbrow' and 'lowbrow' readers—she uses these terms quite unashamedly—between novelists themselves, and between novelists and their readers. Prior to this time—so her argument goes—there was only one *literary* culture; the culture of the mass of the people was a culture of the folk, expressed in essentially oral terms. Although these cultures were quite separate, the power of the literary culture paradoxically derived from the vigour of the oral one; words like 'homely' and 'plain' and phrases like 'vital oral discourse', 'art of conversation', are commonly used and are always terms of praise. John Bunyan's seventeenth-century allegory, *The Pilgrim's Progress*, is an heroic exemplar in this model of culture. It is the most popular work of its age, deriving its power from a basis in the spoken culture of the people, 'from the soil' (p. 99), yet it is unashamedly 'highbrow' in other ways, on the side of learning against ignorance. Pre-industrial society was thus an 'organic society' in the sense of being a unified whole whose parts functioned together. The single, unified, literary culture, and the educational system which propagated it, was unashamedly élitist and quite uncompromising in its standards. If the people wanted to participate in it, they could only do so as the result of great personal efforts; there was no possibility of the literate culture levelling down to meet them half way. As Q. D. Leavis says, the records of self-made scholars in this period are very impressive: 'having learnt to read they would straightway read the seventeenth and eighteenth-century classics' (Q. D. Leavis 1965, p. 14). Access and participation never worry her. The fascinating question of how Shakespeare's textually dense plays were understood let alone appreciated by a genuinely popular and largely uneducated audience is brushed aside: 'they had to take the same amusements as their betters, and if *Hamlet* was only a glorious melodrama to the groundlings, they were none the less living for the time being in terms of Shakespeare's blank verse' (Q. D. Leavis 1965, p. 85). The result of all this for Q. D. Leavis is that seventeenth-century journalism was of far higher quality than anything after. There was no distinction of quality between journalism and literature in the seventeenth century, with the consequence that lower middle-class culture in 1700 was finer in every way than its equivalent in the twentieth century.

This unified literary culture began to break into two conflicting parts in the second half of the eighteenth century; this is, in essence, the origin of the divide between high culture and popular culture. For Q. D. Leavis the extension of literacy and the creation of new reading publics is not one of the great humane achievements of the eighteenth century but the beginning of a catastrophe. She sounds the cry depressingly familiar whenever the extension of education is proposed, that more will inevitably mean worse. This newly extended reading public does not struggle to join the élite literary culture as in the seventeenth century, but demands a debased literature of its own with which it can more easily cope. Writers are only too willing to oblige. Q. D. Leavis compares the *Tatler* or the *Spectator* of the early eighteenth century with the *Idler* after 1760: 'the one talking at his ease to a circle of friends and the other consciously raising his voice for the benefit of a public assembly' (Q. D. Leavis 1965, p. 130).

This debased literary culture grew on two fronts. The major innovation was in the number of journals, magazines, and newspapers produced. The average daily sale of newspapers—always one of the villains in this debate—doubled between 1753 and 1775. Löwenthal estimates that between 1730 and 1780 there was at least one new magazine per year for the London public. In a more recent book, *The Printed Image and the Transformation of Popular Culture: 1790—1860*, Patricia Anderson has traced the spectacular growth into the next period as well, focusing on the new technology of illustrated magazines. For the first time it became possible to reproduce cheaply illustrations other than woodcuts. Various factors contributed to this flood of literature: reductions in the paper tax, the development of mechanised paper-making (1803), the steam-powered press (1814), multiple-cylindered stereotype printing (1827). By the middle of the nineteenth century the extent of printed literature was seen commonly as a kind of wonder of the modern world and Anderson has referred to the new, inexpensive printed picture—especially important in an era when literacy was not universal—as 'the first medium of regular, ongoing, mass communication' (Patricia Anderson 1991, p. 3).

The other major area of development was the novel. Obviously, prose fiction existed before the eighteenth century, but the novel as we have come to understand it, in its mixture of introspection, sentiment and middle-class realism, is very much the creation of this period. Samuel Richardson's *Pamela*, published in 1740, is conventionally cited as the first novel in English. The growth of the novel in the following years is quite prodigious. The already existing book clubs were transformed into the circulating library—Löwenthal dates the first one in 1740 significantly—to keep pace with the demand. Audiences were built in other ways as well, not just through a growth in publishing and the book trade generally, but through the reviewing of novels in the newspapers. Considering the amount of work that Q. D. Leavis did on the novel, one might expect this to be viewed as a positive development, but in fact she puts this new form squarely in the enemy camp: 'a taste for novel-reading as distinct from a taste for literature is not altogether desirable' (Q. D. Leavis 1965, p. 132). It is true that some novels, a small minority, pass the test for her and are admitted to high culture. The yardstick seems to be that the novel which is high art is a challenging intellectual experience, whereas the novel which is part of the debased popular culture deals only in emotional responses. The circulating libraries specialise in novels of the latter kind, a 'clumsy call for tears, pity, shudders, and so forth' (Q. D. Leavis 1965, p. 134). The distinction can be exemplified in a comparison between two novels of the period: 'whereas to read *Tristram Shandy* is a bracing mental exercise, *The Man of Feeling* represents only a refined form of self-indulgence' (Q. D. Leavis 1965, p. 135). The choice of texts is very significant: although Laurence Sterne's *Tristram Shandy* is often held up as a kind of pure form of the novelist's art, it is in fact quite untypical of the English novel as a mode. It often has a special role in this kind of argument because it can be read more like poetry. Samuel Taylor Coleridge's view, expressed in his *Lectures on Shakespeare and Milton*, was that the reading of novels 'produces no improvement of the intellect but fills the mind with a mawkish and morbid sensibility' and that while they improve the heart 'they vitiate the taste' (Q. D. Leavis 1965, p. 137). It is as if the novel really belongs in the camp of popular culture rather than high art. One of the things that makes Virginia Woolf's novel *To the Lighthouse* part of high culture is that it requires that the reader 'should have had a training in reading poetry' (Q. D. Leavis 1965, pp. 223, 231).

In the eighteenth century itself, the growth of a broader reading public did not immediately lead to gloomy forecasts of the decline of taste or to a sense of inevitable conflict between two cultures. At the beginning there was even a certain amount of optimism about the educative potential of the magazine. The slightly later development of the illustrated magazine in the 1830s followed a similar path of early optimism. The first of the illustrated magazines, Charles Knight's *Penny Magazine*, published first in March 1832, was sponsored by the Society for the Diffusion of Useful Knowledge. The first issue proposed to 'enlarge the range of observation [and] add to the store of facts' (cited in Patricia Anderson 1991, p. 53). It not only took its moral and educative role seriously—Hogarth was one of the etchers most frequently used—but aimed to inculcate aesthetic values through a careful popularisation of high culture. Paintings and sculpture were reproduced extensively and all the evidence suggests that for many of its working-class readers this was their first and most important encounter with the world of 'art'. The magazine was very successful in its early years and found a genuinely wide readership amongst the lower middle and working class. Knight's aims of bringing culture to the working class were widely admired and Anderson's book contains many moving testimonials from working people. Its educative role fitted in well with the self-improvement plans of many of its readers, their genuine thirst for knowledge and art. It is worth remembering that the pressure for Sunday opening of the British Museum came from working people, the sort of people who bought the *Penny Magazine*, who could not visit it at other times.

Such optimism was, however, short-lived for the most part. Knight's very project of spreading a taste for art to the people was criticised. He encountered a powerful lobby committed to the exclusiveness of art appreciation. Anderson describes the attacks on his work from newspapers like the *Morning Chronicle* which believed that art could not be removed from the domain of the privileged few. As the magazine faltered within a few years, the bulk of the illustrated magazines became ever more crass and sensational. The history of the illustrated magazine from 1845 to 1860 makes depressing reading. While some of the magazines retained a commitment to moral uplift none took up the cause of 'art' in the way that Knight's had. On the other side, art retreated to what Knight described as its 'long reign of exclusiveness' (cited in Patricia Anderson 1991, p. 110). In the novel the seriousness of the ideas and the weight given to moral improvement were not powerful arguments of literary quality and the whole concern with content rather than form becomes part of a classic argument against their aesthetic worth. Moreover, in many cases the moral improvement itself was not a straightforward matter. Henry Fielding satirised the specious morality of *Pamela* in *Shamela*, and in many novels the 'uplifting' value from one point of view was inextricably linked with a trashiness of sensibility and style from another. One of the most popular forms of fiction in this new era, the Gothic novel, provoked much criticism of violence and excess in literature and on the stage. Wordsworth's Preface to *Lyrical Ballads* (1800) contains a sustained attack on the degrading nature of the Gothic romance.

By the end of the eighteenth and the beginning of the nineteenth centuries, the nature of the debate about high art and popular art had taken shape in a way that we are still familiar with. In this period writers themselves noted the manipulative factors in entertainment and the new role of business intermediaries. Goethe described the restlessness and passivity of the new audience for literature, its conformism, and the role of newspapers in producing it. Writers themselves began to develop a sense of belonging to one camp or the other, as hacks for the new popular culture or as serious writers for a minority. Raymond Williams notes in *Culture and Society* the frequent hostility in the early nineteenth century of 'serious' writers towards the reading public. At the same time as writers first became aware of the financial reality of working in a new era of commodity production, there arose a kind of conflicting discourse about high art and the solemn mission of the writer. Goethe's differentiation between the work of art which occupies the imagination as distinct from the work that only exercises the senses, based on a distinction fundamental in Kant's work, is an early version of one of the most enduring differences drawn between high culture and popular culture. There was much speculation about whether people naturally desire what is 'good' in culture and what the mechanism of aesthetic pleasure consists of. One of the problems is whether the serious artist can have anything to do with this new popular audience at all. In his prelude to *Faust*, Goethe wondered (rhetorically) whether the artist should make concessions to popular taste. The Romantic view of the artist, especially in its more extreme German manifestation, sees the artist and the intellectual élite generally as a group with a mission which it betrays when it plays up to the people by producing inferior work. The function of art, as distinct from philosophy, religion or science, is to stimulate the productive imagination. Inferior art is not just a betrayal of this solemn mission by the writer, but actually hinders the imaginative process for the reader.

This kind of split between highbrow and lowbrow culture took place elsewhere. It has been traced in American culture, for instance, by Lawrence Levine, although he dates the change to around 1850 rather than the late eighteenth century. His work is interesting because it confirms the drift of Q. D. Leavis's thinking, and her evidence, although its scheme of values is in many ways quite the opposite. Levine's fundamental assumption is that 'the perimeters of our cultural divisions have been permeable and shifting rather than fixed and immutable' and his hypothesis is that before about 1850 a 'rich, shared public culture' (Levine 1988, p. 8) existed in America, which later fragmented. While these beliefs are compatible with Leavis's approach, he differs in assigning the blame for this fragmentation neither to the people themselves nor to the supposed manipulators of mass culture but rather to the self-appointed guardians of high culture. His book is a rich source of evidence of how the people at large had parts of their culture expropriated by minorities and sectional interests. For example, before the middle of the nineteenth century, the theatre was a genuinely popular cultural institution. In frontier cities it was usually the first and most important institution to be founded. It performed a social and cultural function in the early nineteenth century akin to the movies in the early twentieth century: 'it was a kaleidoscopic, democratic institution presenting a widely varying bill of fare to all classes and socioeconomic groups' (Levine 1988, p. 21). Central to this mixed repertory was Shakespeare's plays; they were not a supplement to the 'popular' theatre but a vital and integral part of it. His work was genuinely popular in the most obvious senses of the word. Not only was he widely enjoyed but his work seemed to 'fit' American culture in an extraordinary way. His plots lent themselves easily to the popular melodramatic style; his poetry, especially the more oratorical sides of it, seemed in accord with the central place the spoken word had in early nineteenth-century American life. The audience of the nineteenth-century American theatre was as heterogeneous as the Elizabethan one. Levine likens its atmosphere to a modern sports match, with the audience noisy, partisan and emotional. Likewise, there was no caste system of actors; the Shakespearean actors took part in all the other items on the bill.

After about 1850 Levine discerns a profound change. Not everyone was pleased with the mixed audience in the theatre, especially the mixed audience for English literature's crowning genius. There were conscious moves to differentiate—even, in a sense, to segregate—plays, audiences, theatres, actors and acting styles. Much of this was done in the name of 'improving the standards' of Shakespearean production: restoring the original text and purifying it of later accretions, moving towards less declamatory and more introspective acting styles, trying to foster a less rowdy style of audience reception, encouraging the 'study' as distinct from the acting of Shakespeare's plays. Levine's name for this process is 'sacralisation': an author whose work had spoken easily, immediately and compellingly to a wide audience—albeit at times inauthentically—was gradually transformed into the remote figure of an immortal genius, the creator of sublime poetry in an archaic language, too difficult for ordinary tastes. Whatever the improvement in the quality of productions and however necessary the raising of the standards of Shakespearean study, the evidence is compelling that Shakespeare was simply produced far less and that the theatre declined as an institution of popular culture, a trend that accelerated with the coming of vaudeville and then the movies.

Similar transformations can be observed in other aspects of nineteenth-century American culture. Opera suffered a similar fate to Shakespeare. Music in general followed a similar course. In the first part of the century there was little distinction between the world of the 'orchestra' and the world of the 'band': composers wrote for both, musicians worked for both, and concerts were a blend of musical styles and genres. Gradually the process of sacralisation changed the understanding of the nature of music: it came to be seen as divine in origin, revealing eternal but difficult truths accessible only to the few, with a conductor like a priest presiding over an orchestra of committed artists. If the process of sacralisation had worked only on high art it would not have been so bad, but there was another side to this process of artistic discrimination by which other kinds of music and the whole ethos of the amateur musical world was deprecated—in a sense, to continue Levine's religious metaphor, demonised. Music which is not of the highest standard or not performed in the best possible way is simply not worth it. Popular music is even worse than bad music; its performance is an offence to the fragile hold which really great art has in the world. The word 'amateur' itself gradually came to be synonymous with 'bad workmanship'. The result is much the same as with Shakespeare: 'parlor' music was almost destroyed; in popular culture the concert musician, especially the conductor, became the very type of all that is remote, condescending and absurd. A typical instance for Levine of the revenge of popular culture can be seen in the Marx Brothers film, *A Night at the Opera*, where Groucho interrupts the performance of *Il Trovatore* to lead the orchestra in a rendition of 'Take Me Out to the Ball Game'. If it were not such a good joke it would be tragic.

This sense of two classes of creative artist, working from within and for two opposing cultures, is continued and indeed exaggerated in Victorian England, until there is almost no dialogue between them. For Q. D. Leavis, in the world of the novel, Charles Dickens on the one hand and George Eliot on the other are the exemplars of the two cultures. But Dickens and George Eliot are still 'near neighbours' (Q. D. Leavis 1965, p. 169). The real chasm between the cultures opened up later on. She sees Edward Bulwer Lytton as the prototype of the modern best-seller. For the first time he exemplifies the novelist consciously 'writing-down' to his readership in a way that earlier 'popular' novelists like Scott never would have. The conscious exploitation of emotion and crude instinct becomes one of the hallmarks of popular culture for Q. D. Leavis; the Northcliffe newspapers of the twentieth century work upon the same 'herd instinct' (Q. D. Leavis 1965, p. 185). This is not simply a feature of lower-class culture though. The public schools had exalted rugby over reading and conspired to make intellectual pursuits inherently suspicious and unmanly. Muscular Christianity had had a similar coarsening effect on the spirituality of English life. On the other hand, under the influence of French writers like Flaubert, there develops a contrary tendency toward a sense of the novel as a work of art. The difficult novels of Henry James are perhaps the supreme achievement in this kind of contrary process. Another manifestation of this is the 'Art for art's sake' philosophy of the 1890s. Where, for all their differences, George Eliot and Dickens had been near neighbours, by the end of the nineteenth century 'there is an unbridged and impassable gulf between Marie Corelli and Henry James' (Q. D. Leavis 1965, p. 169).

Victorian views of 'culture'

One of the differences that Löwenthal notices in the development of this debate in Europe is that in England, in contrast to Germany, the question of taste and standards is much more than a question about art. Popular writing is only one manifestation of a whole syndrome of changes in the cultural life of the nation; it is a manifestation of a complex interplay of social and cultural forces. According to Raymond Williams, the idea of 'culture' enters decisively into English thinking from Coleridge onwards. It is usually defined in a broad and inclusive way as the 'whole life of the people' and the debate about high culture and popular culture is less a debate about particular texts and more a debate about the cultural life of society as a whole. Reading practices may be a crucial aspect of this view of the culture of the nation, but it is not the only one; indeed one complaint heard more and more often is that reading has taken over culture, displacing the oral culture of the folk, and now has to do duty for a whole range of social practices that it could formerly ignore. Again, it is a version of the 'more means worse' school of thought in education.

Nothing more clearly illustrates this generalising tendency in thinking about culture than Matthew Arnold's *Culture and Anarchy*, published in 1869 and revised for a second edition in 1875. As a poet himself, Arnold was not of course insensitive to the importance of reading and literature, although he often expressed the kind of regretful misgivings about reading and books bearing too much of the burden of English culture that I have just been describing: 'how much, in our present society, a man's life of each day depends for its solidity and value on whether he reads during that day, and, far more still, on what he reads during it (Arnold 1960, p. 6).[4] Even in this quotation it is possible to see how the essential features of the argument are less a question of aesthetics and more a question of morality, the solidity and value of everyday life. *Culture and Anarchy* is the work not only of an important poet but of a man who was for 35 years one of Her Majesty's Inspectors of Schools and an important voice in the development of a national system of state education, the son of Thomas Arnold, the great headmaster of Rugby School portrayed, idealised, in *Tom Brown's Schooldays*. From the outset culture is seen in broad terms and as a fundamental part of our lives. Culture is our help in the present difficulties, in the time of anarchy alluded to in the title—how often culture becomes a burning issue in times of real or perceived social upheaval! All the positive epithets that Arnold applies to culture bear witness to this generalising, totalising tendency: 'total perfection', 'general', 'harmonious', 'full', 'the main current', 'national'. What is not a feature of this culture is 'incomplete', 'provincial', and 'one-sided'. Although, doubtless, there is a canon of literary works in dispute somewhere, the foreground of the book is political, in a broad sense and sometimes a narrow sense as well, and the examples of the debate about culture in action in chapter 6 are such contemporary political issues as the disestablishment of the Church in Ireland, the Inheritance Bill, and the Deceased Wife's Sister Bill.

Culture is to do with the whole of our lives:

> all the love of our neighbour, the impulses towards action, help, and beneficence, the desire for removing human error, clearing human confusion, and diminishing human misery, the noble aspiration to leave the world better and happier than we found it,—motives eminently such as are called social,—come in as part of the grounds of culture, and the main and pre-eminent part. (Arnold 1960, pp. 44–5)

Although 'social' is a keyword here, it would be misleading to think that Arnold understands 'culture' as something essentially practical; even in the quotation, it is not the 'action', 'help' or leaving the world a better place, but the 'impulses' towards them which are characteristic—Arnold's word is the 'grounds'—of culture. On the contrary, it is important to understand that culture for Arnold is first and foremost something mental, a habit and quality of the mind, a process of thought. Elsewhere in the book he vigorously attacks the English passion for 'doing' rather than thinking (or 'being') as typical of that materialistic, middle-class culture that he deplores as

'Philistine'. Culture can be, moreover, a desire for the things of the mind for their own sake, unconnected to any moral or social improvement. It is easy to see here how we have come to lay so much stress on the intrinsic worth of high cultural works and to see any attempt, on the part of government or whatever, to apply them and make them 'useful' in a direct way, as proof of an uncomprehending philistinism.

This 'inwardness' of culture makes it like religion; culture becomes a secular counterpart of the kingdom of God, to be discovered within us. The development of the discipline of English in the university has frequently been seen as a secular alternative to theology, developed in the increasingly agnostic society of later Victorian England. Like religion, culture for Arnold has a strongly moral dimension. Its aim is no less than 'perfection': 'it is a study of perfection' (Arnold 1960, p. 45). Not just perfect in this or that area of behaviour or knowledge—here again there is a danger in seeing culture as about doing things—but a perfection which is both inward, to do with what one is rather than what one does, and which is general and 'harmonious', a word which carries a lot of weight in a society threatened with anarchy: 'harmonious perfection, general perfection, and perfection which consists in becoming something rather than in having something, in an inward condition of the mind and spirit, not in an outward set of circumstances' (Arnold 1960, p. 48). This kind of perfection is something greater than the moral perfection pursued within the traditions of English puritanism, best exemplified for Arnold in the contemporary non-conformist churches. The quest for religious perfection, while no doubt laudable, is only perfection in part. It relies for its achievements on victories which are essentially outward, it is characterised by conformity, and a conformity to outward law and circumstance. Its zealotry is in fact one of its biggest drawbacks, fundamentally of a different temper from that harmoniousness characteristic of culture, called by Arnold 'sweetness and light'.

This perfection of our being—our culture—is to be achieved in the ways in which we use our minds to reflect upon the world around us. Contrasted with the conformism and zealotry which lie at the heart of puritan views of perfection—what Arnold calls in a shorthand 'Hebraism'—it is characterised by vitality and freedom of thought and it strives to see things freshly and as they really are—called

'Hellenism' in the same shorthand. Its enemies could be seen to be those things which, albeit for good reasons of morality, lie at the heart of Hebraism: rigid and conventional habits, untested assumptions, clichés, and 'stock notions'. Without these new mental habits our culture is doomed to stagnation:

> [culture is] a pursuit of our total perfection by means of getting to know, on all matters which most concern us, the best which has been thought and said in the world; and through this knowledge, turning a stream of fresh and free thought upon our stock notions and habits, which we now follow staunchly but mechanically. (Arnold 1960, p. 6)

Put like this one can, I think, see the beginnings of a whole tradition of liberal and humanist thinking about culture. It is also just as clearly the beginnings of a system of education, in English particularly but in the Humanities generally, in which the role of culture is to foster free thought.[5] Although we might now be more cautious about being able to see things as they really are, the whole liberal thrust of Arnold's thinking has gone deep into our society.

At the same time, there is a contradictory discourse at work in Arnold's book as well. Arnold is not in fact at heart a liberal at all; in reality the liberals (in both small *l* and capital *L* terms) were, amongst others, the non-conformists he was attacking. For all its rhetoric of liberalism, its easy talk of the free play of thought, Arnold's 'culture' has a strongly authoritarian spirit to it. Most of the fresh thoughts go towards attacking liberal political policy, for example. The book begins and ends with Arnold's resistance to moves to disestablish the Church in Ireland. It is not just his rejection of certain aspects of Victorian liberalism (as it is more usually defined) which it is important to note. His view of culture is fundamentally authoritarian in character, stressing the importance of the national picture, the role of the metropolis in controlling the province. The sweetness and light of culture, the free play of thought, is meaningless unless developed within the framework and order of the law, which, as Arnold says in the conclusion to *Culture and Anarchy*, is sacred. The harmony which it is the job of culture to create is not the result of a consensus of the parts, worked through with compromise, but the surrender of the autonomy of marginal elements to the authority of the centre. Religious dissenters practising within those non-conformist churches cannot aspire to the perfection of culture, not just because their zealotry is at odds with the sweetness and light of Hellenism but because non-conformism by its very nature has separated itself from the national church and rejected its authority. People who practise within it are doomed to an existence 'not in contact with the main current of the national life' (Arnold 1960, p. 14).

For culture to be perfect, it must not only be general, it must be of the State. It cannot be based on a kind of Protestant 'individual light'; the passion of the English for personal rights and individualism is in this view a perennial hindrance to the development of culture. Indeed, one could go so far as to say that individualism is at heart the opposite of high culture. In chapter 2 of the book, entitled 'Doing as One Likes', Arnold deplores the fact that the central feature of English life is 'the assertion of personal liberty' (Arnold 1960, p. 74); indeed England lacks the very notion of the 'state', and the worship of personal freedom is an anarchical tendency, leading to 'relaxed habits of government' (Arnold 1960, p. 79). In chapter 5, individualism is seen as the root of the present troubles. Although he worked long—and nobly—for better public education, Arnold also worried at its too great diversity and its worship of pluralism.

Culture for the many or for the few?

In *Culture and Anarchy*, we can see focused some of the most important elements of the debate about culture as it had developed from the middle of the eighteenth century. In a context of profound social change brought about by the industrialisation of Europe—leading to an increase in population and new social groupings, the expansion of overseas empires, the creation of new literary forms and a massive increase in the production of literary texts to meet the demands of an expanded reading public—a rich tradition of thought developed around the interconnected and sometimes conflicting themes of art, aesthetics, nationalism, and the nature of social life and change. Although it is possible to see 'art theory' as in many ways an ancient topic, as one can see 'social theory' as well, this was perhaps the first time that the social dimension of art—how art is produced in society and what its social effects are—had been addressed so consistently as a separate question. From a more particularly English tradition of thought, Arnold inherited a view of culture, going back at least as far as Coleridge, as something more than a question of aesthetics or the composition of an artistic canon. It is a view of culture best summed up in Raymond Williams's phrase, 'the whole life of a society'.[6]

This view of culture is inherently a liberal one; it ought to lead naturally to a respect for all aspects of a society's life, including the cultural life of all the people, not just the art of a small section of it. But, almost because it is such an inclusive definition, because so much seems to come within its purview, it creates a kind of anguish about culture which pulls in a contradictory way towards conservatism. Implicit and explicit within much of the work both influencing and influenced by Arnold, there develops a conviction that not all parts of this broadly defined culture are qualitatively the same, indeed that the development and vigour of some parts actively threaten others. In many ways, this conservative, 'classicising' cultural view, rather than the liberal, has been the stronger part of the legacy of Arnold's work in the twentieth century. It is this aspect of his thought which underlies the militancy of much 'modernist' angst about the threat to cultural life and standards. Instead of culture residing in the whole of a society it turns out to reside within a very small part of it, whose job now becomes to ensure the ascendency of its views against the majority.

TWENTIETH-CENTURY THEORIES OF HIGH CULTURE AND MASS CULTURE

The era of mass society and the decay of culture

In British and Australian cultural studies it has become commonplace to see high culture and its dominant position in the English curriculum in schools and universities as a product of the work of F. R. Leavis and his circle at Cambridge from the 1930s. Because Leavis's own work is known to have been greatly influenced by Arnold, there is a danger, however, in seeing the whole process of thought about high and popular culture at that time as an exclusively English phenomenon, a problem of uniquely English social and cultural traditions.

In fact, Leavis's writing in the 1930s—especially those books with the word 'culture' in the title—is better seen as a strand in modernist thought more generally, a European rather than a narrowly British or anglophone body of work. It may seem surprising to locate the Leavises within the wider framework of European modernism, or indeed to see them as modernists at all, but in this area of thought— and it is, of course, only one aspect of the complex phenomenon of modernism—this is where they clearly belong. While there are important English precursors of the modernist fear of the masses and the decline of culture other than Arnold—for example the novels of George Gissing at the end of the nineteenth century—the real authority figures in this debate are mostly European. In his book *The Intellectuals and the Masses* (1992), John Carey emphasises the fundamental role in thinking about the 'masses' of the work of Friedrich Nietzsche. Another key work is Gustave Le Bon's, *The Crowd*, first published in French in 1895. Sigmund Freud's study of group psychology (called more revealingly in German *Massenpsycholgie*), with a first chapter dealing in detail with Le Bon's work, was published in 1921. Of particular importance, however, to the generation which survived the First World War is the great two-volume work by

Oswald Spengler, *Decline of the West*, first published in German in 1922, but available in English translation by 1928. The essential themes of Spengler's work, the twin evils of urbanisation and mechanisation, leading to the development of megalopolis and the decay of culture into a formless, inorganic mass, can be traced explicitly and implicitly in many of the writings about culture in the late 1920s and 1930s. Within a year or two, many of the key texts in the European debate about culture, almost all of them containing the same apocalyptic, gloom-laden fears of a cultural decline and a world overrun by mass culture, were written: Clive Bell's *Civilization* (1928), dedicated to Virginia Woolf; Karl Jaspers's *Man in the Modern Age*, first published in German in 1931 and translated into English in 1933, which sees the modern age as re-enacting the fate of imperial Rome, a society destroyed through a surfeit of what amounts to popular culture (although it is not framed quite as nakedly as this); José Ortega y Gasset's *Revolt of the Masses*, first published in Spanish in 1930 and translated into English in 1932; F. R. Leavis's *Mass Civilization and Minority Culture* (1930) and (with Denys Thompson) *Culture and Environment* (1933). John Dover Wilson's edition of Arnold's *Culture and Anarchy* in 1932 was the first in over fifty years. There is, moreover, endless cross-referencing and repetition between the works: H. G. Wells's *The Shape of Things to Come* (1933), for example, was dedicated to Ortega y Gasset. At a broader level, other literary and critical movements seem to be shaped by comparable value systems. A case could be made, for instance, for seeing the development of New Criticism in America and the work of I. A. Richards, *Principles of Literary Criticism* (1924), and William Empson, *Seven Types of Ambiguity* (1930), in England as interventions in a related spirit into the debate about what makes the products of high art distinctive. The work of the Frankfurt School on popular culture from the 1930s, while coming from the opposite end of the political spectrum, also bears many striking similarities to this general thrust of modernist thinking about culture. Keith Hancock's brilliant and influential study of Australian society and culture, *Australia*, published in 1930, while offering many local inflections that I shall deal with in chapter 4, is also clearly a part of this way of thinking.

Perhaps the clearest exposition of this line of thought can be found in Ortega y Gasset's *Revolt of the Masses*. Although, according to Ortega, the idea of a mass culture has been around for a long time—he cites the fear back as far as Hegel's that 'the masses are coming' (Ortega 1932, p. 54)—it is only in recent times that in Europe the masses have acceded to 'complete social power'. This is a clear echo of Le Bon's view that the coming era, the modern era, is the era of the crowd. In this respect, Europe has become much more like America, although Ortega rejects as simplistic the widespread view that contemporary Europe has suffered from too much American influence and become 'Americanised'. What has happened to Europe has happened for reasons which are intrinsic to its own history—but it so happens that these developments coincide with the most marked feature of American life for the last two centuries. America is still as powerful a negative model in the modernist analysis of culture as it was for Arnold or Tocqueville in the nineteenth century.

In Ortega's view, the distinctive characteristic of modern life is its 'plenitude'. In every aspect of our existence we are confronted with a new sense of fullness. We have more of everything; there are more people on the earth; we live longer; we know more about the world, both historically and geographically; we have many more outlets for pleasure; there are more things to buy. Many of these things are obviously good, but there is a price to pay, and that price has been paid by our 'culture'. The population has not just increased but been radically transformed in nature. In particular, that part of it which we have traditionally called 'the masses', that part which is outside the aristocracy for Ortega, has come to see itself and its social role in new ways. In essence, the masses are born *not* to rule; by definition, the masses cannot and should not direct their own existences; they need the guidance of superior intellects, and yet everywhere in Europe they are coming into power and demanding that their opinions be heard. They have even claimed possession of those areas, like culture, formerly the exclusive domain of minorities. The plenitude which seems superficially so attractive conceals a deep threat to the future of our civilisation. When everything seems possible, then the worst of all is also possible. Ortega's view of contemporary Europe is haunted by the fear not just of decadence but of unspeakable barbarism, and both Fascism and what is called in the English translation either 'syndicalism' or 'Bolshevism' are living proof of the dangers of the ascendency of mass man and his 'culture'.

What are the features of 'mass man'? Although Ortega's conception is based at some level on class, and minority values are more likely to be found within the upper class than elsewhere, mass man is not simply another name for the proletariat, the lower orders, or whatever. If anything, Ortega locates mass man within the bourgeoisie. It is the nature of the citizen's life, his mind and culture, which determines the categories. One sole individual, if he lives and thinks in a certain way, can be mass man. The essential distinguishing feature of mass man is his lack of distinction; he is Mr Average, totally ordinary and unspecial. Ortega's name for the mind of mass man is 'commonplace'. What makes this commonplaceness threatening in this new world, however, is that mass man has ceased to be ashamed or indifferent to this and now exults in it and seeks to propagate it in society: 'the characteristic of the hour is that the commonplace mind, knowing itself to be commonplace, has the assurance to proclaim the rights of the commonplace and to impose them wherever it will' (Ortega 1932, p. 18). It is particularly dangerous in that mass man has taken to proclaiming this ascendency through direct action rather than the traditions of liberal democracy. This direct action favours violence, 'lynch law'; it is appropriate for him that lynch law comes from America, 'the paradise of the masses' (Ortega 1932, p. 116). This penchant for violent solutions has provoked by way of response the shocking expansion of the police force in the modern world. All aspects of the state have increased dramatically in the modern state, crushing human aspiration. Fascism is thus typically a society of mass men.

Mass man defies the hopes of liberals in that he cannot realistically be educated out of his commonplaceness, even if he wished to be. There is thus an unbridgeable gulf formed between the culture of the civilised minority—Ortega says that 'society' is an inherently aristocratic concept—and the culture of mass man. The excess population of Europe in the last two hundred years cannot be saturated with high culture; there is only so much of it to go around, and it depends for the maintenance of its quality on the small number of people who absorb it. One of the strongest themes in all modernist writing on culture is the conflict between, as F. R. Leavis puts it in one of his first publications, mass civilisation and minority culture. Over and over again, it is asserted that the maintenance of culture is the responsibility of the very few—if these people are not in positions of power, then a society's culture will decay and vanish. Even in the sciences, one can find examples of this powerful myth. In a note, Ortega cites the view of Hermann Wely that 'if ten or twelve specified individuals were to die suddenly, it is almost certain that the marvels of physics today would be lost forever to humanity' (Ortega 1932, p. 52n.).

When Ortega talks about mass man's lack of education, he means particularly lack of a liberal education. He is not talking about the illiterate hordes exactly. A mass man can be highly educated in certain spheres and yet not be able to transcend this mass-ness. In fact, certain kinds of technical specialism are quintessentially characteristic of mass man. Specialism is attacked as a whole tendency in society and its education—chapter 12 is revealingly entitled 'The Barbarism of Specialisation'. Of all specialisms, science—with its 'technicism', as it is slightingly described, at its heart—is both the most characteristic and the most dangerous. Opposed to this is knowledge of the general scheme of things, what is often dismissed by the technicists as dilettantism. In particular the modern age is one in which there is a lack of 'understanding' in a broad sense, an insight which is often based on a knowledge of history, something which Ortega sees as particularly lacking, even amongst those who in other respects are very 'cultured'. Without this understanding of history, one may be fatally deluded in particular into thinking that civilisation is an inevitable concomitant of any society: robust, self-supporting, and self-sustaining. In fact, history teaches us the opposite, that culture is fragile. The plenitude which is the experience of modern life, the life of mass man, is not understood by him, nor is it valued; in his mixture of passionate desire and ingratitude, mass man is like a spoilt child, not working for the plenitude which surrounds him but outraged when it is lost. It is the peculiar fate of experimental science that much of its truly great progress has been achieved through the efforts of people who are not in Ortega's terminology either educated or cultured, 'mediocre' men as he calls them. His most graphic term for them is the 'learned ignoramus'. Mass man is a primitive in the heart of his own civilised world.

It is important in this context to point out the role played by 'mass woman' as well. The connection of women with literary culture generally, but especially with popular fiction, is notable from the beginning of the expansion of the reading public in the eighteenth century. They emerged in significant numbers as writers in that period, and have remained so, and women also became a new and commercially valuable target audience as consumers, for novels especially. One fictional example of the specific connection with popular culture which is often cited is Gustave Flaubert's novel, *Madame Bovary* (1857): one of Emma Bovary's greatest pleasures is the consumption of pulp literature.

What is new in the modernist era is the attempt to gender mass culture as feminine in a wholesale way. Andreas Huyssen has drawn attention to the role Nietzsche plays in this. For Nietzsche, woman is one of the most pernicious threats to the development of the artistic genius of the male. This kind of other side to the romantic view of the artist can be easily traced in literature. The number of plots in which the aspirations of a high-minded man are frustrated by his silly wife is far too long to list: some examples might be Mr and Mrs Lydgate in George Eliot's *Middlemarch* (1872), Thomas Hardy's *Jude the Obscure* (1896), D. H. Lawrence's *Sons and Lovers* (1913). It has remained a favourite theme long after the end of modernism proper; indeed, it is particularly common in the late 1950s and early 1960s: George Johnston's *My Brother Jack* (1964), John Osborne's *Look Back in Anger* (1956), Stan Barstow's *A Kind of Loving* (1960). There is more than a little of it in the way Charles and Diana have been mythologised: he with his water colours, chamber music, solitude and deep thoughts, she with her shopping, pop music, and dining at McDonalds. More broadly, Andreas Huyssen has pointed out that the 'fear of the masses in this age of declining liberalism is always also a fear of woman, a fear of nature out of control, a fear of the unconscious, of sexuality, of the loss of identity and stable ego boundaries in the mass' (Huyssen 1986, p. 52). In the late nineteenth century it is a commonplace to find mobs, the proletariat and the *petite bourgeoisie* characterised in terms of an essentially female threat: hysterical, uncontrollable, all-enveloping. This kind of discourse runs throughout Le Bon's *The Crowd*. Nor has this way of thinking been universally resisted by feminists. Ann Douglas's *The Feminization of American Culture* (1978) laments the way in which the 'toughness' and robustness of nineteenth-century American intellectual life was sentimentalised and debased through the increasing influence of the clergy and of women, creating a culture which exalted the average and the emotional, in which melodrama was a dominant art form—

leading directly to twentieth-century mass culture, so her argument
runs. It is a particularly agonising thesis for a self-proclaimed feminist
like Douglas to have to argue.[1]

When D. H. Lawrence visited Australia in the early 1920s he
found it 'the most democratic place I have *ever* been in', but 'the
more I see of democracy the more I dislike it'. Material progress for
the working person had brought the inevitable destruction of the
inner life: 'your real inner life and your inner self dies out and you
clatter around like so many mechanical animals'.[2] Although the more
overtly radical and democratic ethos of the development of Australian
society provided a different context for the reception of these kinds
of views, many local writers voiced similar kinds of fears about the
direction of social change. Frederic Eggleston, for example, expressed
a dislike of the new breed of populist politician. He saw the principled
statesmen of the past (of both parties) swamped by the 'utilitarian
demands of democracy' (Rowse 1978, p. 109), and replaced by
narrow, sectarian demogogues. The epitome of this changed scene
was the wartime Prime Minister, W. M. (Billy) Hughes, who had
opportunistically changed his political allegiance from Labor to
Nationalist, subsequently tried to impose a kind of socialism on the
Nationalist party, and then, while winning votes at home by his
populist policies, had brought disgrace to Australia in the international arena by his posturing and chauvinism at the Paris Peace
Conference in 1919. While a master of *Realpolitik* and a skilled hand
at parliamentary invective, in Eggleston's view he was a shallow man,
who had 'consistently neglected the imponderable elements of human
nature'.[3] The likelihood that such people would increasingly dominate
public life was a frightening thought. Keith Hancock expressed similar
concerns later in the decade. While he saw the strengths of the
democratic heritage of Australian history, he was alive to their dangers
as well: 'the passion for equal justice can so easily turn sour into a
grudge against those who enjoy extraordinary gifts and the aspiration
for fraternity can so easily express itself by pulling down those lonely
persons who are unable to fraternise with the crowd' (Hancock 1930,
pp. 56–7). Despite his sense of the distinctively democratic temper
of Australian culture, he was worried not just by the crowd's fraternal
threat to more solitary souls but, like Ortega, by the spectre of Mr
Average, especially when he is minded to assume control: 'What class,
what tradition is there that can hold the state against the assault of

numbers . . . if . . . the machinery of state exists for the "divine average", then the majority controlling this machinery becomes, after all, a master class' (Hancock 1930, p. 54).

Although Ortega points up the horrors of Fascism in his book, seeing them as the product of the changes in society in modern times, it is hard to resist making comparisons between the scorn for the masses and the racial and ethnic policies of Fascist regimes later in the decade. One of the sad conclusions of Carey's *The Intellectuals and the Masses* is that Hitler's views were not wildly anomalous in their time but are widely echoed in many writers of the period. Many writers fantasised about extinguishing the masses. H. G. Wells, for instance, in his *Modern Utopia* (1905), could see no social improvement possible unless the population was controlled, especially the 'low-quality' populations of Asia and Africa. Carey sees the main problem in *When the Sleeper Wakes* (1899) as the 'mass of lowgrade humanity such as inhabits the underground' (Carey 1992, p. 123). Society can be saved only by the elimination of this people of the abyss. One of the most memorable visualisations of this idea is in the 'Undercity' occupied by the workers in Fritz Lang's film *Metropolis* (1926). Even George Orwell, in *The Road to Wigan Pier* (1937), uses the metaphor of modern industrial life as an existence underground, of 'having got down into some subterranean place where people go creeping round and round, just like blackbeetles, in an endless muddle of slovened jobs and mean grievances' (Orwell 1979, p. 15). Carey wonders whether Charles Darwin's explanation of the process of evolutionary selection in *On the Origin of Species* (1859) had rendered the belief in human equality—the basis of liberalism— untenable, although it should be pointed out, less pessimistically, that both Orwell and Lang hoped in their different ways for a rapprochement between the classes in a new common culture.

British writing about culture in the 1920s and 1930s

The writing about culture which was produced in England, especially in Cambridge, in the late 1920s and early 1930s developed against the background of these views. There is more than one strand to it. That strand associated with I. A. Richards—from which derives 'practical criticism', the central methodology in the study of high art in English—does not really address popular culture in a central way, although Richards's pronouncements are always powerfully influential when they are made, such as the belief that there has been a noticeable decline in the standards of the best-seller in our time which Q. D. Leavis repeats in the preface to *Fiction and the Reading Public*. Richards's work is part of a wider attack in the 1920s on traditional aesthetic theory through a rigorous study of the nature of language and the process of communication. The other strand, associated with the work of F. R. Leavis and his circle at Cambridge—including the work of his wife, Q. D. Leavis, on the reading public of popular fiction that I have already discussed—their publications and the journal *Scrutiny*, is much better known in this debate about culture and its relationship to literary education in school and university.

Fundamental to the work of both the Leavises is the belief in the minority nature of high culture. F. R. Leavis's first pamphlet, whose title drew attention to the contrast between *Mass Civilization and Minority Culture*, was published by the Minority Press. All that is valuable in a civilisation's culture is the work of a few people, a small portion of the total population. A culture grows through the *original* work of a tiny number of people. Outside that group, there is another, wider, although still very small, group which, while not contributing in an original way to this culture, can appreciate the creative work done in it. For both Arnold and Leavis, one of the basic responsibilities of the critic, as distinguished from the creative artist, is to maintain the flow of ideas in society, the intellectual culture which the true creative artist draws on. But, in relation to the social whole, this group is still frighteningly small, although its importance is great and its role in the survival of culture crucial. In the words of the Australian poet and critic Vincent Buckley, influenced by Leavis, thirty years later: 'only a tiny minority asks itself the central questions about the destiny of all' (Buckley 1957, p. 2).

Outside this élite world of high art and its appreciative and knowledgeable audience, there was in former days the living culture of the people, an oral folk culture of an organic community. In much modernist writing about culture this is the romanticised other to mass culture, to be found in pre-industrial village life, the old 'feudal' ways of the agrarian south for the American New Critics, in the pastoral radicalism of the shearers in nineteenth-century Australia, or, in more exotic terms, amongst primitive societies. For the Jindyworobak poets in Australia in the late 1930s and early 1940s, the Aborigines provided a vivid example of a unity of culture and environment to set against the alienation of modern industrial society. The organic community in its various guises—pre-industrial village life, primitive society, Aboriginal culture in Australia—is a popular counterpart to the 'undissociated sensibility' that T. S. Eliot perceived in the élite culture of seventeenth-century poetry. For commentators on the left in this way of thinking, the other of the spoiled industrial society of the 1930s is a mythologised working-class community life, usually as it existed in some legendary past, in some period of full employment, before the First World War or whatever. Orwell's *The Road to Wigan Pier* (1937) is a typical example of this. On the one hand there is graphic description of the degradation of living on the dole: the famous vision of the woman poking a stick up a blocked drain-pipe, for example, or the tripe shop where Orwell lodged. Part of Orwell's purpose was, of course, to show southern middle-class readers of the Left Book Club what life on the dole in the north was really like. On the other hand, there is much sentimentality about 'working-class interiors as I knew them in my childhood' and romance about the noble bodies of the miners working beneath the ground. Orwell's long history of trying to 'cross over' to the working class—the ending of *The Road to Wigan Pier* urges the middle class to join them in their struggle—is constantly complicated by a triangular struggle between the quest for objective standards of truth in reporting, modernist revulsion at the swarming hordes, and left-wing sentimentality about the unspoiled working-class community of the past. Orwell's book is a conscious and unconscious attempt to exorcise the modernist horror of the lives of the masses and be objective about the mythology of working-class community life which often strangely accompanies it.

The profound change in modern times, as Q. D. Leavis, Ortega and others say with different points of emphasis, is that this organic community has broken down and in its absence the people have demanded a right of entry to the literary high culture. Because the people as a mass are unable to appreciate high culture with its high aesthetic standards and rigorous intellectual requirements, a debased literary culture has been provided to cater for their needs. The living culture of the organic community has been destroyed by 'motor-coach, wireless, cinema, and education' (Leavis and Thompson 1962, p. 1). All about them F. R. Leavis and Denys Thompson see 'taste and sensibility assailed by films, newspapers, advertising' (Leavis and Thompson 1962, p. 2). The machine in all its forms is a principal culprit—a tradition of thought running like a thread from the Industrial Revolution, through Matthew Arnold and into the days of Spengler and Ortega. It has led to mass production—the people who support this are 'inhuman' according to Leavis and Thompson—and thus, in an inexorable progression, to standardisation and the lowering of the public taste. We should also notice the curious negative role played here by education as well. As I mentioned above, the great achievements in education in the nineteenth century such as the *Education Acts* of 1870 and 1902 were far from unqualified blessings for writers like Q. D. Leavis. Few modernist writers were in favour of universal education and many regarded the attempts of working people to educate themselves as little more than pathetic, leading to a lifetime of frustration and alienation. Leonard Bast, in E. M. Forster's *Howard's End* (1910), would have been better off working in the open air on a farm, but instead he ruined his health working in an office in the city, hopelessly pursuing the world of culture in his spare time. Clerks and their aspirations to culture are a particular object of scorn in much of this writing. When the time came later on to increase the participation rate in higher education as well, few academics looked with pleasure on the greater numbers of students enrolling. Most saw the inevitable equation that more would mean worse. In Australia, for example, John Anderson, professor of Philosophy at Sydney University, remarked that the government did not understand that 'the greater the number of people held to be capable of higher education, the lower this "higher" education must be' (Anderson 1952, p. 18). He criticised the notion of Commonwealth scholarships for university students which were introduced by the Labor government during the Second World War. Cultural values can only be maintained at the expense of inequality; indeed inequality must sometimes be defended: the upholders of high cultural and intellectual standards must be prepared to 'attack progressivist and egalitarian dogma and to uphold privilege' (John Anderson 1952, p. 15). The newspapers, one of the most sinister developments in the later phases of the Industrial Revolution, are a source of some of the deepest attacks on standards—as they were for Arnold—'mechanising' thought and levelling down culture. Advertising is another enemy, more powerful than ever in the modern environment and another example of technology, in the sense of the scientific practice of applied psychology, at work in culture. In this context, Carey cites the formation as far back as 1893 of a journal called *A Beautiful World: The Journal of the Society for Checking the Abuses of Public Advertising*. It is, by a cruel irony for Leavis and Thompson, one of the few art forms which have really flourished in the modern world.

Yet what in the end distinguishes Richards, and Leavis and his group, from Spenglerian doom-watchers like Ortega and the cruder fantasies of modernism, is a residual faith in the power of education. Even so, it is still not always clear just how many people will be able to benefit. Leavis spent his entire working life as a don at Cambridge, although Denys Thompson made a career as a schoolmaster. It is probably safe to assume that neither saw their educational projects as applying across the board. For Richards, the arts provide examples of values and organisation to counter the chaos of life in the mass culture of the modern world. Richards is much more clearly focused on what the 'culture' of mass man actually consists of than Ortega; he is alive, for example, to the influence (albeit baleful) of commercial art and the cinema in the mid-twenties. Whereas the cinema exploits stock responses, the experience of reading great literature provides us with models, not just of beauty but of experience finely organised. In this, the study of high art is a kind of training-ground for life itself, 'in that capacity for organisation which is man's only profitable response to his altered and dangerous condition' as Raymond Williams summarises it (Williams 1958, p. 249). It is not too difficult to see in this a rehearsal in modernist guise of the culture and anarchy theme of Arnold's book.

The resistance to mass culture which will come from education will not in any case be from the narrow education of the elementary schools set up by the reforms of the nineteenth century, but a new liberal education, with the subject of 'English' at its core. An education in the great books of English high culture is more important now than ever before because it is the only substitute for the loss of the living culture of the organic community. A comparison of traditional folk song with modern popular music, for example, will show up the cheapness and emotionalism of popular culture. Education must resist the blandishments of advertising in particular. Leavis and Thompson recommend the practical criticism of good prose as a way of getting to the lies and deceit of advertisements. Reading the criticism of this period one could be forgiven for thinking that English was established as a school subject with the principal aim of countering advertising.

The critique of mass culture from both political right and left

Although some of these ideas now seem quaint, they formed the basis of English teaching and the views of high culture and popular culture for nearly fifty years, until well into our own times. As a teacher, Denys Thompson was the author, sometimes co-author, of many widely used school textbooks of English. His books, with just the kinds of exercises in them that I have cited, were still used extensively when I was at secondary school in England in the 1960s. The views which he had expounded with Leavis in the early 1930s were still being published in books like *Discrimination and Popular Culture* (1964), the outcome of a National Union of Teachers conference, held in October 1960, on the theme of 'Popular Culture and Personal Responsibility', with the aim of examining 'the impact of mass communications on present-day moral and cultural standards' (Thompson 1964, p. 7). The themes, the familiar line-up of friends and enemies, seem to have changed little in thirty years: the machine has led to a lowering of standards through mass production, the resultant decline in quality concealed by the dazzling production values, enhanced by advertising, that technology can bring. Education plays the vital role of teaching children how to discriminate, by providing fine examples of music, art, and literature 'against which the offerings of the mass media will appear cut down to size' (Thompson 1964, p. 20).

The mass culture critique has remained a powerful lobby through-out the world. One of the writers in Australia who has had most to say in this vein over a considerable period of time is Clement Semmler, who combined a career in the Australian Broadcasting Corporation with a life as reviewer and man of letters. Unlike many of the mass culture commentators, he was actively involved in its production as well as being a stinging critic of some of its worst excesses. A persistent theme of his is the connection between the increase in living standards and the decline in standards of culture. He even has a formula to express this idea in all its brutality:

$$(60 - 20) + ACL + OUE = \text{kitsch.}$$

The lowering of the working week by twenty hours plus the abolition of child labour and the increased opportunities for universal education have led inexorably to the worsening of culture, to 'kitsch'.

At least the formula has the virtue of brevity and of saying what many people thought but few were game enough to express. Semmler cites G. M. Trevelyan's view, expressed in his *Social History*, that 'modern popular education has produced a vast population able to read but unable to distinguish what is worth reading' (Semmler 1963, p. 7). All the usual villains are here: modern technology, advertising, American influence. Mass culture is nothing but a parasitic growth on high culture. The particular local relevance is that the oft-noted casualness of the Australian character has shown itself especially lacking in resistance to the attack from mass culture.

Ironically, considering the anti-American attitudes of writers in the Arnoldian tradition, some of the most powerful criticism of mass culture has come from America itself. The first footnote in Semmler's book, for instance, is to the influential book of essays edited by Bernard Rosenberg and David M. White, *Mass Culture: the Popular Arts in America*. Dwight McDonald, one of the contributors to the volume, sums up mass culture thus: 'Mass culture is imposed from above. It is fabricated by technicians hired by businessmen; its audience are passive consumers, their participation limited to the choice between buying and not buying' (McDonald 1957, p. 55). It was McDonald who coined the term 'midcult' to characterise that section of the community which attracted particular odium from this school of criticism, who, for example, knew enough about art to enjoy the odd popular symphony but who were not sufficiently serious-minded to enjoy 'real' classical music—presumably Bach or Schoenberg. The midcult sector borrows unthinkingly or opportunistically what it wants or likes from high art but refuses to identify its interests openly or totally with high culture in its struggle against the masses.[4]

This trend in publication shows little signs of abating; indeed the evidence suggests that books which come out with these sorts of views are good sellers. One sign of the popularity of this kind of discriminatory understanding of culture was the extraordinary success of Allan Bloom's *The Closing of the American Mind*, published in America in 1987. It is a passionate denunciation of much of American popular culture. It was seized upon in many quarters as a defence of traditional values in the academy, perceived as being under threat from various quarters, including the growing trend towards a 'commercialisation' of education. Unfortunately, one of the traditional values the book does not uphold is generalising from a careful use of evidence. Fundamental to the book is Bloom's belief in the existence of *absolute* values of taste and truth. In fact, it opens with the assertion that the only thing which today's ignoramuses know when they first come to university is that such standards do not exist and that truth is relative. Besides its popular success, Bloom's book was positively reviewed in the Australian media and well received in the academy. A more considered version of some of the same points—although at times expressed in even less temperate language—is James B. Twitchell's *Carnival Culture: the Trashing of Taste in America*, published in 1992. Twitchell's book aims to be a study of the aesthetic character of the 'vulgar'—an interesting project—but much of the book consists of the same vilification of the people and their tastes that is familiar from modernism, despite the fact that Twitchell believes that public taste has declined most spectacularly in the last twenty years, particularly from 1960. What most people want to see is trash. The category of 'art' is under attack not just from the trash which has its origins in the modern cult of show business, but through the abandonment by intellectuals of their role as 'gate-keepers' of the standards of public taste. The word 'vulgar' has become almost meaningless in modern culture so rapidly have standards of taste dropped and the process of discrimination been abandoned: 'we are rapidly approaching the point where there will be no border between lower Aesthetica and upper Vulgaria' (Twitchell 1992, p. 23).

As I pointed out in the case of Arnold, it is easy for liberal declarations about art and culture to conceal a conservative agenda. What is more surprising, at least at first glance, is the way in which the criticism of popular culture coming from the political left in this period and afterwards should have come to conclusions which are similar in many ways. On the other hand, as Andrew Ross (1989, p. 22) says, the Trotskyist left was the natural home in many ways for high culture intellectuals. Trotsky himself was deeply sceptical about attempts to create a proletarian culture, a *proletkult* to rival the claims of traditional art. Like many others on the left in his tradition, he was high-minded and suspicious of native populist American culture.

'Culture' became a major sphere of interest for the first time for the whole of what is often called 'western Marxism' and in particular for that part of it associated with the Frankfurt School for Social Research: Theodor Adorno, Leo Löwenthal, Georg Lukács, and Herbert Marcuse in particular. A theme running through their work is the idea of popular culture as 'false consciousness'. Whereas true literature lays bare the reality of social conditions and individual experience, mass culture is mechanically produced to deceive and lull the people into acceptance. In this tradition, the products of popular culture are like a drug, depriving the individual of all power to resist the manipulation of consumer society. Marcuse adds an ethical dimension to this in his distinction between true and false needs, the role of mass culture being to satisfy the latter.

As Tony Bennett has pointed out, for a Marxist there is a paradoxical aspect to this mode of analysis. Traditional Marxist aesthetics conceives 'both aesthetic objects and the subjects of aesthetic judgement as being marked by the processes of their historical formation' (Bennett 1990, p. 123). In its crudest form this is the source of the notorious base–superstructure model of culture, which has haunted Marxist literary and cultural analysis, in which the forces of production, principally economic, make up the base from which the superstructure of a society's culture is produced. In seeking to avoid this reductive paradigm of cultural production, with its narrow economism, the writers of the Frankfurt School saw the text of true art as marked by its ability to transcend the circumstances of its social production. It is simultaneously both produced by them and yet able to be analytical and critical of them. For Bennett, this is the central and (for him) unresolvable contradiction of Marxist aesthetics: 'that artistic practices are socially determined, and that Art is not' (Bennett 1990, p. 146).

Lukács finds a kind of reconciliation by means of an important distinction between 'naturalism' and 'realism'. While it is axiomatic that the human being is a social animal, it is only in the naturalist text that social conditions are seen to be all-determining of consciousness and character. Naturalism thereby presupposes, in effect, that reality has a static condition which human beings have no control or capacity to change. For this reason, Lukács sees the socially alienated, solitary and anxiety-ridden desperates of the modernist novel as (somewhat paradoxically) the heirs of nineteenth-century naturalism. The essence of realism, on the other hand, is not just its conception of history as changing and dynamic or its belief in the social nature of the human condition but its faith that human beings are agents in that process of change. The distinctiveness of high art lies in its peculiar historical self-awareness. Realism is more than a faithful recreation of history—indeed, in some ways the more faithful this is, especially at a superficial level of historical detail, the more it lays itself open to the underlying weakness of naturalism, the conviction that things must be as they are. The great realist writers do not just portray individual characters or stories or exact historical detail but a complex marriage of both of them, achieving in their characterisation especially an evocation of the most significant 'types' of the era. The most impressive characters of this kind of art are those who thus stand in a kind of symbolic relationship to their society, expressing the 'dialectic between man-as-individual and man-as-social-being' (Lukács 1963, p. 75). In Lukács's view, the realist writer must strive to portray the nodal points of this dialectic—where they are at their most vivid and their most 'typical'—understanding the underlying trends in the historical development of an era, 'in that area where human behaviour is moulded and evaluated, where existing types are developed further and new types emerge' (Lukács 1963, p. 56). Although literature is a relatively autonomous sphere of practice, the high points of its art are not those which are the finest exemplars of style but those texts which create 'types' in this sense and identify the emergent and developmental forces of social change.

During the Second World War, the Frankfurt Institute decamped to America. Although Marcuse became something of a guru figure to the generation of rebellious American students of the 1960s, Adorno's stay in America was a bitterly unhappy one. He seems to have disliked almost every aspect of American life and to have developed a particular antipathy to its distinctive contributions to twentieth-century popular culture—popular music, jazz, films, television, for instance. He remained unmovedly European: a splendid example of the strengths and weaknesses of the most traditional type of German intellectual, of formidable intellectual resources and skills, qualified in fields beyond Marxism and philosophy such as music, and yet, for all the breadth of his learning, at the same time cripplingly narrow and uncompromising.

The fundamental antipathy between high art and 'industrially' produced consumer art is basic to Adorno's work. In a letter to Walter Benjamin, another member of the Frankfurt School, in 1936, he referred to them in a famous line as 'torn halves of an integral freedom, to which, however, they do not add up' (Adorno 1991, p. 2). The industrial nature of mass art, its mechanical mass-production, in both literal and figurative senses, in the course of making profit and its consequent surrender to consumerist values, is what distinguishes it fundamentally from the popular art of the past. The 'culture industry'—a phrase first used by Adorno and Max Horkheimer in their book, *Dialectic of Enlightenment* in 1948—has transferred the profit motive to cultural forms, with profit now sought directly, not indirectly as in the past. Culture has, in effect, become one more kind of commodity and abdicated its true role in society, to be a critical voice.

Central to all high art for Adorno is its vision of what he calls the 'good life'; not in the escapist sense of Hollywood fantasy, but in the sense of a vision of what the world might be, founded on a grasp of how the world actually is, how it operates and on what basis it is structured. This sense of the good life is what makes high art, including much bourgeois art, radical and disruptive to consciousness. In contrast, the products of the culture industry are designed to hide the good life behind a veil of fantasy, in their course reinforcing the belief that what exists is the only reality: 'culture cannot represent either that which merely exists or the conventional and no longer binding categories of order which the culture industry drapes over the idea of the good life as if existing reality were the good life, and as if those categories were its true measure' (Adorno 1991, p. 90). Modern mass culture propagates to the people a system of social values, for example, which reflects almost unchanged the ideology of middle-class life of a much earlier period. In particular the culture industry confuses reality by making unlike things appear like, by treating particulars as if they were universals, a feature which he calls 'subsumption'. The so-called 'traditional values', the very phrase concealing the conflict and struggle which always exists over social and ethical value, become the norms of authoritarian and hierarchical society. The image of pure womanhood in early popular culture for example, the result in Adorno's view of conflict between concupiscence and the internalised Christian ideal of chastity, is now presented in popular culture as the natural state of women and their chastity as a value per se.[5] Mass culture aspires to a shared experience and in the process de-emphasises real class differences. This kind of repressive integration in conceptual matters is the counterpart to Fascism in social policy. Ultimately, people feel that there is no alternative to the status quo. The culture industry thus effects an act of 'anti-enlightenment', attacking rationality, replacing consciousness with conformity.

Some of the most important work in this field was done by Marcuse, easier to read than Adorno and destined for wider circulation, and important for many reasons, including the fact that he continued writing into the 1960s, where some of his most influential late work forms an interesting bridge to postmodernism, which has sought to reverse many modernist ideas about popular culture. For Marcuse, high art deals in uncertainties; it is about the basic conflict between appearance and reality. This, amongst other things, is why it is anathema to totalitarian regimes. Mass culture, on the other hand, seeks to suppress conflict and to deal in certainties. As a consequence, it denies the reality of a world based on social conflict. It becomes impossible to distinguish between the mass media as 'instruments of information and entertainment, and as agents of manipulation' (Marcuse 1964, p. 8). One of the distinctive features of advanced capitalism has been its ability to incorporate culture into the established order. For example, high culture was formerly the expression of a conscious alienation from the world of business and industry. Its literature was full of outsiders: artists, prostitutes, rebel-poets, fools, devils, leading in fact to the paradox that the bourgeois order's literature was hostile in essence to the spirit of business. Literature was an oppositional discourse within the establishment's own art. In the society of advanced capitalism, the antithetical role of art has been neutralised and it has been absorbed into the materialistic culture and lost its truth value. The kinds of social undesirables formerly represented in literature have been utterly transformed into such characters as the vamp, beatnik, gangster, neurotic housewife; they are 'no longer images of another way of life but rather freaks or types of the same life, serving as an affirmation rather than negation of the established order' (Marcuse 1964, p. 59).

Modernist definitions of high art, literariness, and the 'classic'

At the opposite end of the debate are two recently published books: Harriet Hawkins's *Classics and Trash* (1990) and Antony Easthope's *Literary into Cultural Studies* (1991). While both authors come from traditional university English literature backgrounds, their books strive to bring out the essential similarities between the texts of high culture and popular culture rather than their irreconcilable differences. There are several strands to Hawkins's argument. At bottom, she sees the attempt to distinguish rigidly between the two cultures as a tradition of critics and of the academy rather than a real division in the minds of authors. Authors have found it much easier to move between the worlds of high art and popular art in their work than critics would assume was possible. Critics have been similarly one-eyed, if not plain dishonest, in their understanding of the historical process by which works become naturalised in one culture or another. The decline in standards of reading and textbook lists in the university portrayed by writers like Bloom is not historically accurate; in Hawkins's view the presence of Shakespeare on reading lists in America, for instance, has little to do with the influence or standards of the Ivy League. Shakespeare entered American culture through his reception on the popular stage. It was genuine popular taste which made Shakespeare a force in American culture. The image of generations of students in the past drilling their way through the plays is simply an illusion.

Far from being a battleground, literary history is in fact full of a rich intertextuality of high and popular culture. In the twentieth century this intertextuality seems particularly striking. As an example, Hawkins points out the many variations on the Faustus story in twentieth-century art, ranging from the art novel to the popular film: Thomas Mann's *Doktor Faustus,* Klaus Mann's film *Mephisto,* other films such as *Bedazzled, Cabin in the Sky* and *Angel Heart.* From its origins, the film has used screenplays based on novels derived from what we might think the alien world of high culture. Sometimes the interrelationships are very surprising, like the similarity between the wicked stepmother in Disney's *Snow White and the Seven Dwarves* and Lady Macbeth. In preparing for the role of Richard III, Laurence Olivier used the theatrical entrepreneur, Jed Harris, as a model. When a cartoonist used the same man as an inspiration for the Big Bad Wolf, an uncanny resemblance developed between Olivier's great creation and the cartoon figure. In many ways, Hollywood at its most popular was also very attuned to the world of high culture: Hawkins's book begins with a study of the subtle interplay between Shakespeare's *Tempest* and the film *The Maltese Falcon.* At the less sublime end, one might note the line attributed to Cecil B. De Mille: 'Give me any couple of pages from the Bible and I'll give you a picture' (Hawkins 1990, p. 118).

Not only have critics falsified the complex interplay of high art and popular art in the practice of authors and performers, they have failed to see this interplay at work in the way audiences actually read. The customary divisions between high culture and popular culture have little to do with the reality of reading experience. In her chapter, 'From *King Lear* to *King Kong* and back', she argues that it is often the experience of reading the texts of popular culture which provides the foundations—intellectual, moral, spiritual, and aesthetic—for reading the texts of high culture: the experience of seeing the film, *King Kong,* makes possible an engagement with the issues of the play, *King Lear,* not vice versa. Not only does much high drama contain elements of soap, they sometimes constitute its 'life'; without the lurid and sensational basis of the plot, *Measure for Measure* would not just be a dull play to watch but our whole reading of it, the nature of its impact upon us, would be changed.

Antony Easthope comes to similar sorts of conclusions in his comparison of the plots of Conrad's great novella, *Heart of Darkness* (1902), and Edgar Rice Burroughs's *Tarzan* (1914), works written at roughly the same time. At the levels of pure plot and ideology there is not a great deal to choose between them. What makes for a difference between the two texts and what is more generally the nature of the difference between high art and popular art is what Easthope calls 'textuality'. Hawkins arrives at a similar mode of differentiation in her book. In a nutshell, *Heart of Darkness* is a more complex work than *Tarzan.* The nature of this complex textuality is a mixture of things: *Heart of Darkness* has an inwardness, a psychological depth, a high ratio of reflection to action that *Tarzan* does not have. The most important differences are more to do with the nature of the narrative itself, however. *Heart of Darkness* works towards the resolution of a narrative enigma; it has a double plot structure; its meaning is deferred rather than made immediate and, when it does come, is multi-levelled and plural. Its style lends itself more to the abstract rather than the concrete, to the figurative rather than the literal, to connotation rather than denotation, to a pervasive irony. It is a densely verbal text, inherently suited to that kind of close reading in which everything is assumed to be significant, called by Easthope, suggestively, 'modernist reading'.

Easthope's work belongs, consciously or not, to a broad tradition of thought about the the nature of the high art text. Doubtless he is right in seeing it as foregrounding certain kinds of qualities, like complexity, polysemy, irony, density of verbal texture, which we think of as quintessentially modernist. Not all the writers or critics that we associate with modernism rejected popular culture outright, and even for several of those who did, the identification and articulation of those qualities which made the art text what it is or what constituted its 'literary' nature, was a vital project. At Cambridge in the 1920s, Richards was convinced of the need for a new theory of literary value—something which could, moreover, be communicated to students in the university—to meet the onslaught of mass culture. He based his ideas of the capacity of great poets to attain supreme levels of self-control and understanding, of intellectual poise and the capacity of art to produce 'wholeness of mind', on a mixture of literature, philosophy, psychology and neurology.

Richards's strange views are not accorded much attention now but the work of another group active in the period and shortly before has had a profound effect on our understanding of the nature of the art text. One of the abiding concerns of the work deriving from the Moscow linguistic circle during the First World War, is the definition, not so much of what constitutes high art in broad terms, as the more local and specific question of the nature of literary language. In a subtle variation on the content and style, or plain style and high style dichotomies, the basis of art is seen to lie in its 'artfulness'. Literary language functions in such a way as to draw the reader's attention to the effects of words beyond the purely communicative. The writer's ability to draw the reader's attention to the aesthetic effect of language, the literary text's power to draw attention to itself, to the way it works, is called, variously, 'baring the device' or 'foregrounding the utterance'. Nor does literary language draw attention to itself simply for its own sake—this is something more than another version of 'Art for art's sake'—it has the power to make us see reality in new ways, to 'defamiliarise' the object of perception. This mode of understanding literary language has been so influential because it can harmonise with other views of the way art operates, sometimes with views which come from quite different, even antithetical, traditions. On the one hand it has clear affinities with Cambridge practical criticism as devised by Richards and its later development in American New Criticism, with their close focus on the text itself—usually poetry—and how it works, to the exclusion of 'extraneous' material such as the social conditions of the text's production. Quite at the other extreme, the concept of the defamiliarising nature of art is compatible with a wide range of Marxist literary criticism, especially with cultural study which comes from the Frankfurt tradition and which stresses the capacity of real art to look beneath the surface nature of things, to resist the sense of things as they are, even in Althusserian terms to defamiliarise ideology.[6]

Another version of this can be seen in the work of T. S. Eliot on the nature of the 'classic', to be found in various places but particularly in 'Tradition and the individual talent' (1919) and especially as updated by Frank Kermode in his book, *The Classic* (1975). In attempting a description of the classic, both writers are trying to account for that complex textuality which is a feature of great literature, of the high cultural text. The principal manner in which the classic manifests that complexity is in its ability to generate meaning, especially in its capacity to mean something important and relevant even to a culture very different from the one in which it was originally written, in particular a later one. The power of the classic to generate meaning is indefinite. In this it has a power, in effect, to dissolve history. As a model or criterion, the notion of the classic is based on the assumption that the ancient can be relevant to a contemporary situation. History becomes a kind of unity. The classic is always, in effect, modern, and the modern work of importance is in its turn a renovation of the classic.

Kermode and Eliot differ, however, in their understanding of the mechanism of this generation of meaning and in their notions of what kinds of meaning are possible. For Eliot the classic is a product of the metropolis and a witness to the power of a 'central' authority and tradition. He is very like Arnold in this aspect of his thought. The classic demonstrates the singleness of the high cultural tradition. This single, unified, continuous tradition of which the classic text is an individual instance is yet preserved from ossification by its ability to incorporate new works into it. The new work is not only influenced by the tradition but in the manner of its incorporation subtly redefines the nature of the tradition itself. The tradition of classics is thereby not merely preserved but perpetually renovated by new work. It is a literary version of the old political idea of *translatio imperii*, of the ability of the (Roman) Empire to refashion itself in changed environments, transformed and yet mystically ever the same.

Although Kermode responds to these same qualities, he stresses the plurality of meaning that the classic text can generate far more than the centrality, singleness and unity of the tradition of meaning. This emerges in a discussion of an article by Q. D. Leavis, which he greatly admires, on Emily Bronte's novel, *Wuthering Heights*. Leavis had subtly distinguished the many different ways in which the reader could respond to the novel and find meaning within it: as high art, as Gothic romance, as melodrama etc. But for her these different modes of signification are not equal alternatives but form a definite hierarchy—we shall arrive at the true spirit of the novel, its classic status as high art, by discarding some of these modes and holding on to others. Where Kermode differs from Leavis, and of course where he differs from Eliot, is in seeing these distinct modes of meaning as having equal claim on our attention. Leavis is concerned with what is timeless in the classic; Kermode with how different generations, and different readers within the same generation, read and construct different meanings. The heart of the difference between Kermode's idea of the classic and that of the modernist generation of Leavis and Eliot is that the new view is tolerant of plurality, whereas the old view wanted centrality and authority.

Kermode calls this power of the classic text to produce a plurality of meaning the 'surplus signifier': 'one may speak of the text as a system of signifiers which always shows a surplus after meeting any particular restricted meaning' (Kermode 1975, p. 135). Although Kermode acknowledges his source for this term in the work of the anthropologist Claude Lévi-Strauss, it bears similarities to the work of several other writers and groups of writers in the twentieth century.

It is analogous to the idea of 'dissemination' in Jacques Derrida's work, for example. While no text can have meaning outside of a context, its meaning is not limited to one context; it is never just a communication between one individual and another. At a simple level, a text, a letter say, can be read meaningfully by someone other than the person to whom it was written, for whom it was intended. What Derrida terms this 'spillage' of meaning entails that the text can be taken up in a fresh context, something quite beyond what the author had intended. This process happens indefinitely, and a text has the potential for endless inscription and re-inscription. But whereas for Derrida all written communication demonstrates this surplus of meaning, for Kermode it is a feature of the classic text alone and it is the one which ensures its survival from generation to generation. A comparable distinction is the one drawn by Roland Barthes between the 'readable' and 'writable' text. The readable text is one which has a strong authorial presence and which forces a pattern of meaning on to the reader; if this pattern of significance is not accepted then the text becomes, in a real sense, meaningless. The writable text, on the other hand, is one which offers the reader a role in this construction of meaning. This is effected by various means: making the narrator's role and expressed views ambiguous, avoiding strong narrative closure. The difficulty is that Barthes associated what he calls the 'classic realist text', not with the writable but with the readable text. Although Barthes's method of discrimination bears some marked similarities to Kermode's, the results apply to the opposite group of texts. Another theory which seems closely associated is Umberto Eco's distinction between the 'open' and 'closed' text, a paradigm based on similar differences as Barthes's work.

The status of the text as a function of social process

The opposite of this search for something in the text itself which produces its literariness, its classic quality or whatever, is to see this kind of stratification in art and culture as determined by social process. Literariness, or 'artistic quality' even, is not something texts have 'inside them' but a marker, a seal of approval as it were, conferred from without by society as a whole, in different times and places, or else by particular groups in society whose job it is to make these kinds of decisions. Raymond Williams (1981, *passim*) has discussed the use of 'signals' to designate the boundaries between what is art and what is not, or what is high culture and what is not. The concert hall is a guarantee that the music heard there will be of high quality even though, personally, one may not like it very much. A pile of bricks by the roadside is one thing but the same pile in an art gallery—a place where one is told works of art are to be found—demands to be looked at in a different way. Time and place of performance are powerful signals in this way. In the broadcast media, where place especially cannot function as a sign in the same way, the signalling is done with introductions, promotions, and reviewing. ABC promotions constantly alert us to the quality of the products about to go to air; some of them seem to win awards even before they are broadcast.

If one examines notions of what art is and is not, even within the relatively short time of the last couple of centuries, one cannot but be struck by the instability of the categories. One generation's pulp is another generation's high culture, and vice versa. For Coleridge, novel-reading was something which weakened the brain. Even for Q. D. Leavis, there are very few novels which are not as intellectually useless as going to the cinema—so the argument goes. When the cinema attained a kind of respectability, then it was the products of the broadcast media which were suspect. Despite the aspirations of John Reith of the BBC, the wireless was to many writers of the 1930s and 1940s—Orwell, for instance, despite his pioneering interest in popular fiction and in popular culture generally—one of the main agents of the often-observed great decline in standards. With, for a later generation, the acceptance of radio, television became the evil menace. Listening to the radio was somehow more of an active pursuit, akin in some mysterious way to reading, whereas television was passive. The things which Coleridge had attacked in the novel were now those most characteristic of television, and reading—especially the reading of novels—was now high culture. In our own time, we have come to subdivide television into quality networks like the ABC, and popular networks like the commercials, or, even more carefully, into those programs on the ABC which conform to its traditional standards and those which, by 'chasing ratings', are a betrayal to one section of mass culture or another.

It is not just whole genres and communication media which move between one level of culture and another but also individual texts. A whole tribe of literary critics, among them Richard Hoggart, an important figure in the development of Cultural Studies, testified in court that D. H. Lawrence's novel, *Lady Chatterley's Lover* (1928), was not a piece of popular trash but a work of literature. The power of the views of certain authorised sections of the community is vital in these sorts of cases. By applying the standards and practices of literary criticism, especially those characteristic of the university department of English, it could be established that *Lady Chatterley's Lover* was a work of art: it could be shown, for example, to form part of a recognised writer's *oeuvre*. One of the stages in the naturalisation of films as high art was the discovery of film directors whose role seemed analogous to that of the author. One could thereby *study* the films of John Ford or whoever in a manner not dissimilar to the way novels were studied in the university. The trouble with this process is that it is, in effect, almost endless. Laura Kipnis (1986, p. 27) laments the recent application of *auteur* theory to the makers of adverts and even to porn films.

Many texts lead a kind of double life as well; a text which is high art to one section of the audience may be popular art to another. 'Doctor Who' engages the attention of a mass audience, including sub-groups of 'fans' who follow the productions in a way which is both obsessively detailed and methodologically unsophisticated, and also sections of the academic community, who read the television texts in the kind of searching way that was once applied only to the novels of Henry James.[7] In *Bond and Beyond* (1987), Tony Bennett and Janet Woollacott show in great detail how the James Bond novels and films have sustained a range of different readings for different audience groups. In their thirty-year career, the Bond novels and films have gone through an extraordinary number of transformations: from genre to genre, actor to actor, audience to audience, changing from a small coterie publication, aimed at a certain section of the middle class, to a truly mass, international audience of film and television watchers. There is not just evidence that Fleming himself changed his style to reach different groups, nor only that the film producers consciously tried to mould the audience, but that different audiences emerged at different times independently, finding relevance in different aspects of the stories. In a way it could be argued that James Bond is a classic in Kermode's sense, a notion that would have amused Ian Fleming who, as Bennett and Woollacott make clear, had few aspirations to writing 'art'.

These kinds of observations can be seen as part of a project in the study of culture to shift interest away from the producer to the consumer, or in literary terms, from the author to the reader. One of the most detailed expositions of this approach in the field of popular literature has been the work of Umberto Eco (1979), again on the James Bond texts. For Eco, the Bond novel is not inherently a work of popular culture or high culture but becomes such according to the way in which it is read. The 'average reader', according to this view, derives pleasure from the recognition of a predictable plot, combined with a minimal amount of variation along fairly well-defined lines. On the other hand, the sophisticated reader derives pleasure from the novel's self-reflexive nature, from the recognition of internal parody and literary and cultural allusions. There is much to recommend this view and it accords well with the nature of the Bond 'phenomenon' detailed in all its ramifications by Bennett and Woollacott. Proving the existence of different audiences, and hence of different patterns of reading, is one thing, but that does not necessarily prove the existence of different popular and high cultural ways of reading the same text. In fact, Bennett and Woollacott dispute Eco's conclusions about the Bond novels and films. On the one hand they cite the view of an established novelist like Kingsley Amis, who disliked the increasing sophistication of the films, claiming that their jokiness and parody destroyed the novels' mythic power—perhaps a kind way of talking about their lack of sophistication. On the other hand, work on the way people actually read popular texts like soap operas has, if anything, made us aware of the complexity of response they generate. Far from being read in simple expectation of formula repetition of plot and ideas, many texts of popular culture are read for their parody and allusions, for what is in fact quite a complex intertextuality. Like most phenomena of popular culture, the Bond books and films can generate ways of reading which are not only either popular or sophisticated, but, as in the case of fan obsessions, both.

Modernist accommodations to the technology of mass culture

In much of the writing of the Frankfurt School about culture there is an interesting mixture of high modernism and adumbrations of its other. It could be argued, for example, that if Marcuse's analysis of the way art has formed an alliance with the world of advertising, money, and business were accepted and celebrated rather than deplored, then one could see the beginnings of a postmodern aesthetic rather than a modernist one. J. M. Bernstein has pointed out the ways in which the work of Adorno on the 'Culture Industry' anticipates (and rejects) much of postmodernism.[8]

On a larger scale, it has been argued by both Peter Bürger (1984) and Andreas Huyssen (1986) in their work on what they call the 'historical avant-garde', that from the start there were always strands and movements within modernism committed to the deconstruction of some of its most central antinomies: to the celebration of the machine and its influence on culture, to the willing embrace of popular and mass art and to their use in a war against high art and its institutions. This avant-garde within modernism was not simply interested in formal change in art for its own sake but committed to social change in a more total sense, to a cultural transformation which included both political radicalism and artistic innovation. The narrowing of the term 'avant-garde' to artistic change of a merely formal nature, and the suspicion in which it has come to be held on the left, happened, according to Huyssen, only after the 1930s.

Huyssen argues that a schizophrenic attitude towards the machine has existed since the late nineteenth century: between, on the one hand, a horror of technology and, on the other hand, an 'aestheticisation' of technics, a new sense of the beauty and spirituality of the machine. In modernist architecture especially, there is a kind of fetishisation of the technical, of the means of production. The problems of building are held to be fundamentally technical and scientific, never social or personal. At the same time that the motor car was destroying the organic society for one kind of modernist like F. R. Leavis, for the Futurists in Italy its sleek lines and, above all, the sheer speed of change and communication that it seemed to epitomise, were seen as sublime moments of a new aesthetic. In the ideas of some critics and designers it is even possible to effect an astonishing marriage between the ideologies of the peasant world of the organic society and the engineers of the new 'machine age'. The contempt for ornament and decoration which is one of the hallmarks of modernist style in design is the symbol of an uncorrupted mind which Adolf Loos attributes only to peasants and engineers. Marinetti, one of the leaders of the Futurists, saw the engineer as a kind of noble savage. To build without decoration 'is to build like an engineer, and thus in a manner proper to a Machine Age' (cited in Banham 1960, p. 97). The French architect, Le Corbusier, aimed to design houses as 'machines for living'. In the universal grammar of modernist architects like Mies van der Rohe, the 'factory' became the dominant metaphor in architectural language. When, in Evelyn Waugh's novel *Decline and Fall* (1928), it is planned to 'renovate' King's Thursday, a Tudor manor house unchanged and un-modernised since the days of Queen Mary, the modernist architect 'Professor' Otto Friedrich Silenus is called in and asked to build something 'clean and square'. He sees the 'human dimension' as the greatest problem facing modern architecture and bases his own aes-thetic model on the factory because it is designed to house machines rather than people. Much later, Andy Warhol called his New York studio, the 'Factory'. In less extreme forms, many modernist artists, designers and architects in particular, for instance in the work of the Bauhaus in Germany and De Stijl in Holland, felt the attraction of the machine and tried to effect a productive marriage between technology and craft.

A similar mixture can be found in the work of Walter Benjamin, a peripheral member of the Frankfurt School whose work is com-monly seen as fundamental to the contemporary study of the art of the mass media and the first recognition of its distinctive character. At the same time, it needs to be emphasised that there are several moments in Benjamin's 'The work of art in the age of mechanical reproduction', first published in 1936, where one can see the heritage of 'classical' modernist and Frankfurt School thought about popular culture. For example, towards the end of the essay, Benjamin laments the 'distractedness', the absent-mindedness, of the modern audience, carried to its extreme in the watching of film. As Benjamin himself comments, this is an aspect of an ancient lament that popular culture is only a form of entertainment, a distraction, whereas true art demands concentration and the engagement of the mind from the spectator. While this is subtly different from Marcuse's work, it is clearly part of a common heritage of thought.

For Benjamin, the fundamental change in the new era has been to sever the connection between art and authenticity. Formerly, the work of art, especially any work with a major visual component, could only be apprehended in its original form, in a close encounter between the work and the spectator: the painting could only be viewed in the gallery, the play could only be watched on the stage, the sonata could only be heard played by the pianist in the concert hall. This necessary condition of presence is a mark of the art object's authenticity and the source of its powerful 'aura'. The new age has not only enhanced through technological development the possibilities for the reproduction of original work—it could be argued that this always existed in some form—but has witnessed the birth of new art forms, principally the new visual media of film and photography, whose very essence is in their mechanical reproducibility. We can all distinguish ontologically between the Mona Lisa in the Louvre and a copy, however good, hanging on the living room wall, but what is the 'original' of a film or a photograph? In the new art forms, the basis of art in cult ritual has been eradicated; the requirement of the art object's presence, fundamental to ritual, has been eliminated. For Benjamin the question of whether film is or is not art has been superseded by the question of whether or not film has transformed the notion of what art is.

Mechanical reproduction of the art object changes the ways in which it may be perceived. It is able to bring out things not noticeable in the original. Art can be studied in a way formerly impossible. In the new arts a whole new dimension of detailed apprehension, study and re-study, opens up. Filmed behaviour, through its use of close-up, slow-motion or whatever, is inherently more accessible to study than behaviour on the stage. These new methods not only enlarge the object and make our understanding of it more precise, they change our understanding: 'the enlargement of a snapshot does not simply render more precise what in any case was visible, though unclear: it reveals entirely new structural formations of the subject' (Benjamin 1969, p. 236). Those engaged in performance for these new arts operate under different conditions and in new ways. On the one hand, there is a new potential for popular involvement; the film of real life, the documentary and documentary style of the Soviet film for instance, have made it possible for anyone to think of himself or herself as a potential film actor. On the other hand, the nature of the film actor's skill and the actor's relationship to the audience have changed markedly. The film actor does not perform to an audience at all in the strict sense, but to a camera. There is thus a second level of interpretation in the film actor's performance. The aura which had formerly enveloped the actor on the stage has vanished and been replaced by a build-up of star status outside the studio. Paradoxically, the greatest effects on the screen are obtained by 'acting' as little as possible. The film actor must first and foremost represent *himself* or *herself* to the audience rather than a character in a script.

Concomitant with these technical and performative changes there is a transformation in the relationship between the people and their culture. By destroying the condition of presence and bringing out things not noticeable in the original, art has effectively been detached from the domain of tradition. It has come to meet the beholder rather than the other way round; the cathedral can now be viewed, and in some instances viewed better, in the living room. This bringing things closer overcomes the uniqueness of reality. It promotes a directness and depth of apprehension formerly impossible: a 'direct, intimate fusion of visual and emotional enjoyment with the orientation of the expert' (Benjamin 1969, p. 234). At the same time it makes possible a sense of collective experience; the film meets the beholder half-way not just in the living room but in the cinema with hundreds of others. These features of the new cultural experience are connected with mass movements in the rest of the contemporary world, but their most powerful agent is, beyond dispute, the film.

The problem of the machine in culture is surely one of the most basic themes in the whole debate about culture and the interest (albeit cautious at first) in the role of technology in the arts, as distinct from outright rejection, is one of the things which marks a real turning-point. The work of Marshall McLuhan is a good illustration of this. His early work is steeped in the modernist ideology of agrarianism— the antipathy between the southern states of America and the mechanised north—which he inherited not just from the American New Critics but from his own boyhood in the north-west of Canada. At Cambridge he was further influenced by the organic pre-capitalist 'villagism' of the Leavisite group. As an academic, he was trained in the discipline of English literature, publishing on Renaissance poetry in the early part of his career. He is best remembered, however, for his work done in the field of mass media and mass communication, developed after the Second World War. His study of advertising, *The Mechanical Bride: the Folklore of Industrial Man* (1951)—the title is rather significant—contains some scintillating analysis of popular cultural products, in its way every bit as impressive as Barthes's *Mythologies*, written a little later in the same decade; but throughout McLuhan finds it hard to shake off the prejudices of high modernism: 'Ours is the first age in which many thousands of the best-trained individuals have made it a full-time business to get inside the collective mind. To get inside in order to manipulate, exploit, control is the object now' (McLuhan 1967, p. v). The machine, albeit ubiquitous in modern life, is there basically to rob us of our humanity, and throughout the book there is a suspicion of the influence of the machine on our culture and on our lives, even in their most personal moments: one of the most peculiar features of our world is the 'interfusion of sex and technology' (McLuhan 1967, p. 94).

Status and stratification in the analysis of culture

In this chapter I have used the term 'modernist' in ways which are both narrower and broader than usual: narrower in that I have been concerned with only one aspect of modernism, its attitude towards mass culture, and broader in that I have tried to identify this attitude beyond the historical confines of what is normally thought of as the 'modern' era. I have thus seen this aspect of modernism more as a habit of mind, discernible in both the 1890s and the 1990s, and occasionally mixed in with much else—ideas and beliefs drawn from very different traditions as in the work of the Leavises.

The most distinctive feature of modernist criticism of culture in the sense I am using it is its practice of questioning the status and stratification of the text and the culture which produces it, producing almost always, in consequence, a model of culture which is hierarchical. Although much modernist literary and art criticism is formalist in character, more concerned with style than content, modernist criticism of culture is not simply a matter of form and structure, category or genre. The central question it asks is what makes this group of texts, and the culture which produces them, distinctive, and this is almost inevitably a question with a judgement of relative value, either overt or covert, built in. Despite the abandonment of simple, unreflective notions of good and bad art—modernism was centrally concerned with the professionalisation of criticism—all sorts of other ways of discriminating and hierarchising culture and its products have crept in to take their place: the formalist distinction between literary and non-literary language, Eliot's concept of the classic, Adorno's sense of the fundamental antipathy between 'art' and industrially produced mass culture, Lukács's distinction between realism and naturalism, Eco's mode of distinction between the open and the closed text, Barthes's idea of the writable and the readable text. All of these theories, with varying results and degrees of sophistication, are strategies for discriminating the good, the worthwhile, the permanent, the meaningful or whatever in texts and culture and marking off its domain from that which is bad art, useless, ephemeral, or trivial. Even those approaches which see this task as the role of society rather than the critic, which see quality as determined by social process rather than as something inherent in the text itself, effect a result which is similar.

That result, a result which unifies the modernist criticism of culture in all its many variants, is that culture is a minority phenomenon, a small area of brightness and interest, however constructed, surrounded by a sea of blandness and indifference. What I have referred to as the 'mass culture critique' continued on both sides of the political divide long after the period of 'modernism', more strictly defined, was over; it is only in the last ten years that it has been significantly challenged and displaced. In many ways its practitioners on the left were more high-minded and unforgivingly intellectual than those on the right, although it is from the right that most of the criticism of mass culture in this mode continues to appear. Both Bloom's *The Closing of the American Mind* (1987) and Twitchell's *Carnival Culture* (1992) were best-sellers. Both assert as fundamental a belief in a hierarchy of art, taste and culture; that there are absolute values; and that academics have deserted their traditional role of gate-keeping, policing the cultural boundaries of a world which for Twitchell has been almost inundated by the 'vulgar'.

The move towards an accommodation with mass culture has been a feature of the art, literature and criticism of the last twenty years especially; it is part of the new aesthetic of the postmodern, and of a new style of populism, which I shall discuss in chapter 3. It must be pointed out, however, that there were always strands in modernism itself, from the nineteenth century in fact, which opposed the dominant line in cultural criticism, which aimed at the dethronement of the high art of the institutions, which embraced the democratic and revolutionary potential of a new kind of communication, which glorified the machine, so consistently held up as the principal source of the decay of culture. In the mid-twentieth century, Benjamin and McLuhan, in different ways, are obvious prophets of this new cultural aesthetic, but it might for the moment be worth stressing the less well known but just as important high modernist side of their work. Benjamin saw the film as having revolutionised the nature of art, but he also worried that the audience of film was an essentially passive one. The early McLuhan is full of forebodings about the new mechanical arts whose transformative powers he so revealingly analysed. It is just as important to see both Benjamin and McLuhan as the end of one tradition of cultural criticism as the beginning of another.

POSTMODERNISM AND CULTURAL POPULISM

From modern to postmodern in accounts of mass culture

Decades after it was written, McLuhan's work still reads well, despite the fact that one of the essential characteristics of the new world he sought to describe is its rapid change. More recent writers like Jean Baudrillard, who are now more celebrated, remain in his debt. One of his fundamental points is that the print-oriented intelligentsia, with its whole analytical training in *content*, is ill-equipped to deal with the new electronic age of global communication, based as it is on *form*: on 'multiple interfaces, its decentralising channels of communication, and its altered ratios of sense perception' (Ross 1989, p. 115). Nevertheless, as Andrew Ross says in *No Respect: Intellectuals and Popular Culture* (1989), despite the radical nature of this insight, it is still easy to see the whole modernist interest in the formal properties of the text and its concern with stylistic innovation. Like Baudrillard, McLuhan envisaged a new age, a world whose culture is dominated by the technology of electronic communication, but he retained a belief that technology could be controlled.[1]

It is hard to see him acquiescing in the poststructuralist concept of subjectivity as a phenomenon of textuality, especially of media texts, or to be happy with Baudrillard's idea of television as inaugurating a new stage of human consciousness, a new universe of communications, in which there is neither fiction nor reality but simply a realm of simulacra, where art is everywhere, but dead.

It is these deep-seated attitudes which mark off the early McLuhan, and to some extent the later, from the whole contemporary world of the postmodern. Leslie Fiedler (Fiedler 1975, *passim*) has said that only traditional culture sees the machine as an enemy. From a slightly different perspective, Arthur Kroker conceives of contemporary French thought as a 'creative . . . account of technological society. Refusing the pragmatic account of technology as freedom and eschewing a tragic description of technology as degeneration' (Kroker 1992, p. 2). This connection between technology and postmodernism has become one of the best studied aspects of contemporary culture and, to a greater or lesser extent, of modern artistic practice. The art of the mass media is by its nature technological, but technology has also found its way into what was formerly the preserve of high art as well. Australia has played a significant role in this. One of the most interesting examples is the work of the Melbourne-based performance artist, Stelarc. His work is based on a fundamental rejection of the body-machine or psyche-machine antithesis which lies close to the centre of the traditions of high art. At the Sculpture Triennial in Melbourne in 1993, his piece was a small metal sculpture, called 'Stomach Sculpture', self-illuminating and sound-emitting, which he swallowed and which was then viewed through an image projected on to a screen through an endoscope. In recent years, he has worked closely with scientists and engineers on the design and manufacture of a bionic arm and a virtual hand.

Two of the most commonly encountered statements about the postmodern are that it has finally naturalised the machine into culture and that it has effected a reconciliation between high culture and mass culture. The two themes are, of course, closely connected. Mass culture in the west is unthinkable without twentieth-century technology. If one adds to this the fear that the Arnoldian school of cultural theorists maintained about the dangers of American influence, then the celebration of American influence is also important. In Andreas Huyssen's view, in *After the Great Divide: Modernism, Mass Culture, Postmodernism* (1986), the postmodern is a quintessentially American phenomenon; it could not have been invented in Europe at any time.

The idea that postmodernism has changed the nature of the existing categories of high art and mass art, or even made them redundant, is associated particularly with the work of Fredric Jameson. Postmodernism, in this view, is not just a reaction against modernism's 'anxiety of contamination' (Huyssen 1986, p. vi) by mass culture, but is a response to the institutional ascendancy of modernism, its almost unchallenged occupation by the middle of the twentieth century of the realm of high art. What had once been radical, marginal, or simply plain shocking has long since become the official culture: modernism's paintings hang on the walls of museums and art galleries, its texts are set on university reading lists, its artists are well-subsidised by state and private foundations. In this view, postmodernism is an attempt to recover the oppositional status and discourse of the avant-garde of the 1920s. It has accomplished this, however, not by making its products ever more difficult and intellectually inaccessible but by crossing over into mass culture. Jameson refers to the postmodern fascination with:

> that whole landscape of advertising and motels, of the Las Vegas strip, of the late show and Grade-B Hollywood film, of the so-called paraliterature with its airport paperback categories of the gothic and the romance, the popular biography, the murder mystery and the science fiction or fantasy novel. (Jameson 1983, p. 112)

Whereas many writers in the past, even modernist writers like James Joyce, had 'quoted' from popular texts, in the process reinforcing the reader's sense of the stratification of culture, the postmodern directly incorporates them, gladly abdicating art's traditional responsibility to differentiate levels of culture. Thus—for the first time I would argue—a high culture of the intellectuals has been built from a genuinely mass culture of the people. In particular, Jameson has stressed the two-way link in postmodernism between art and consumer culture, demolishing one of the most powerful modernist binaries. The arts do not just incorporate the commodities produced by consumer society in the same manner as they incorporate other aspects of mass culture, but commodity production itself is now intimately connected with stylistic changes which derive from experimentation in the arts. Postmodernism feeds off consumer culture and symbiotically drives the style and advertising of commodity production.

Art, culture and consumerism

This sense of common cultural purpose and enterprise between consumerism, commodity production, advertising, and 'art' is certainly a long way from the traditional antipathy between culture and industry—or, to put it in other ways, between art and business, between creative quality and commercial success—which is one of the fundamentals in the whole culture debate. The modernist understanding of culture, the sense of its problematic, derives from an agonistic view of its relationship to the changed world of the Industrial Revolution. Nor is this simply a tradition emanating from the

Arnoldian right in the culture debate. From the beginning there is a resistance to consumption in left-wing thought which passes beyond an understandable antipathy to the products of capitalism to become a kind of moral puritanism, found in its most obvious manifestations in the concrete cities and cardboard shoes of eastern Europe and in the Mao suits of revolutionary China. But the resistance to consumerism goes deeper than this: as if 'that material basis of modern, civilised, rational political economy is structurally equivalent to that which is most inimical to modern consciousness' (Mitchell, 1986, p. 192). Hostility to mass production and the whole commercial world links the dominant views of culture from both right and left, particularly in the period of modernism's ascendancy in the first half of the twentieth century.

Certainly, one of the central changes in the 1980s has been the re-evaluation from both right and left of the role of consumption in culture. On the right this took a more predictable form in the replacement of older 'tory' high cultural values with a new form of right-wing thought, drawing, on the one hand, on a new economics, and, on the other, mixed with a new form of cultural populism. On the left as well, there was a need felt to respond in new ways to what was obviously a new culture. This can be seen occurring even before the collapse of the communist world in eastern Europe and the Soviet Union. As far back as the mid-1980s, Kathy Myers (1986, pp. 130ff) had admonished the left for failing to realise the force of consumerism in the lives of ordinary people, that consumption was not simply a 'reactive' process or even somehow outside of economics. It has been argued in this vein that shopping is not some degraded apology for what used to take place in the leisure time of the people, a poor compensation for the loss of their culture, but that consumption has become genuinely part of popular culture, a replacement for the loss of some of its traditional elements. There is even a kind of political liberation in consumption. The old distinction in left-wing thought between the useful and the useless commodity in particular has come under attack in postmodernism as part of a revaluation of the nature of the commodity itself. The older kind of feminist view of mass culture, as represented by works like Betty Friedan's *The Feminine Mystique* (1963), which sees consumer society as a process of seduction, leading women to forfeit their personhood, has been challenged by work which points to the enhancement of the relative status of women in consumer society and which rejects the notion of merely passive consumption. Lesley Johnson has traced this in an Australian context in *The Modern Girl: Childhood and Growing Up* (1993). The fashion industry, long the butt of some of the most virulent opposition from the left, is increasingly defended, by feminists in particular. Far from being a source of oppression and manipulation for women, it 'has become increasingly associated with strategies of resistance to fixed images of femininity' (Evans and Thornton 1989, p. 32). The publication of *New Times* in 1987–89, sponsored by *Marxism Today*, edited by two prominent members of the left, Stuart Hall and Martin Jacques, was an attempt to find ways of understanding, from the perspective of Marxism, new forms of living and new patterns of work and leisure in contemporary culture.

One of the profoundest changes in art's attitude to consumerism has been in advertising. For many writers in the modernist tradition, advertising epitomised the threat to culture. For the left it was socially useless, persuading people to buy commodities they did not need. For the Leavisite group it was the principal threat to culture, founded on deceit rather than truth, leading the public to respond like automatons; it looked like art but it was really a debased science, applying psychological research in a 'mechanical' way. Training a scepticism and resistance to it was the prime duty of education in the Humanities.

One of the things which changed was the artistic quality of the advertisements themselves. In the late 1970s, in his book on television commercials called, provocatively, *The Best Thing on TV*, Jonathan Price defended the artistic standards of television advertising. In comparison, most television programs look old-fashioned, under-funded, crudely produced, unpolished—badly acted, directed and edited in general. It is the television advertisement which has trained us to expect 'a new style of visual entertainment' (Price 1978, p. 1), based on textual density, symbolism, brevity and fast cutting. In this view, rather than being culture's other, advertising seems to have taken on most of the qualities of the modernist poem. In his study of advertising in the postmodern era, *The Consumerist Manifesto: Advertising in Postmodern Times* (1992), Martin Davidson has also pointed to the late 1970s as a turning-point in advertising quality. The world of advertising began to attract the traditional art hierarchy, using talented graphic artists on the one hand and providing them with their raw material on the other. He identifies the Benson and Hedges ads made by Collett Dickenson Pearce as especially significant. One distinctive feature about them was the sophisticated way in which they used high art, not just quoting from it but 'playing' with it, flaunting their cleverness: 'beautifully composed, art-directed and photographed, they were the first ads to be so clever with art, to appear to make such demands on the onlooker' (Davidson 1992, p. 135).

Although Davidson is more sceptical than Price of the value of certain products, he is also prepared to claim much more for advertising as a cultural phenomenon. Rather than seeing advertising in the traditional manner as part of a conspiracy with consumption against culture, he sees it as forming a bridge between them, linking what he calls the consumptive and the 'romantic' poles of life. The advertisement, like art generally, cannot be defended or attacked on grounds of social responsibility, truthfulness or authenticity. This is to miss the point; both are born 'not of utility and rationality, but from a principle of creativity in excess of physical need' (Davidson 1992, p. 120). Like all forms of artistic expression, advertisements are part of a process of individual and social self-fashioning, 'in which they are directly constitutive of our understanding of ourselves and others' (Mary Douglas 1982, p. 124). One of the reasons why postmodernism has been so accommodating to advertising is that both are interested in the process of self-construction. The underlying deceitfulness of advertising which worried critics so much in the past no longer seems to be a problem, or at least not a problem in the same way. We have come to be sceptical of the truth-telling, illuminative, function of art in general. We do not expect the 'you' which any art work constructs for us as we read or look at it to be more than a temporary fiction. We are less worried about advertisements manipulating identity because we have come to see this as characteristic of all 'writing'. The 'you' which one ad creates for us will be balanced and countered by other versions of our self created in other texts. At least advertising makes plain its constructedness and fictionality.

The new art-form which seems to epitomise those features of the postmodern I have been describing is the rock music video. It depends on the existence not just of a new technology but one which has the possibility for far greater participation than other forms of electronic media. It is closely linked to advertising, indeed its *raison d'être* is commercial—to stimulate sales of the records. Moreover, the circumstances of production—the 'reliance on freelance crews, the omission of production credits and the financial tie-in to the record companies'—all duplicate, in the words of Ann Kaplan, 'the production situation of ads' (Kaplan 1987, p. 13). The television channel in America most associated with rock music video, MTV, looks like one continuous advertisement and is totally focused on consumption.

For critics like Kaplan, the association of rock music video with postmodernism is more than a connection with the commercial world and advertising. Clearly not all advertisements share the same stylistic features even though they may share the same kinds of production situation. In the rock music video, Kaplan detects an avant-gardism, even the beginnings of the emergence of an anti-aesthetic. The kinds of things she identifies are widely associated with postmodern style. Although the videos often tell stories of a kind, there is an abandonment of traditional narrative devices, especially the traditional features of Hollywood realism, although Hollywood is almost constantly invoked generically. Characters are flat and two-dimensional. The narrative is decentred with elements of the text undercutting each other. There is a similar questioning of the nature of the image of the traditional 'illusionist' text; no representation is stable or allowed to remain fixed or unchallenged. A related aspect of the videos' abandonment of realism is their self-reflexivity: 'we may see the video we are watching being played on a TV monitor within the frame' (Kaplan 1987, p. 34). There is a wide use of pastiche—the juxtaposition of different styles without a sense of some fixed point of reference from which they are viewed—which Jameson sees as one of the hallmarks of the postmodern. In all, MTV manages to be both genuinely popular and avant-garde at the same time. And yet its avant-gardism is of a very different kind from that of the 1920s as described by Bürger or Huyssen. The challenge to traditional style is not accompanied by any corresponding sense of challenge to the dominant culture understood in broader terms. Socially conscious video is represented only in the British rock video, where there seems to be a longer continuous tradition of rock counter-culture. Even there, this was a brief affair of the early 1980s. From 1985, according to Kaplan, 'social themes exist *merely* as representations and lack any political referents any more' (Kaplan 1987, p. 68). It is not too difficult to see the influence of Baudrillard in Kaplan's analysis of the music video.

The features of this view of the postmodern—its effacement of traditional boundaries between experimental art and mass culture, the symbiotic relationship between art, business and advertising, the emergence of an anti-aesthetic to modernism—have not been universally accepted, however. Forty years ago, Adorno warned of the dangers of accepting too complacently the notion of a reconciliation in the products of the culture industry between high art and popular art, to the mutual detriment of both, with popular art especially forgoing its rebellious role as social alternative. Other critics have pointed to the falseness of the characterisation of much of modernist art. Many of the features of the postmodern, especially those which emphasise its fragmentariness, its self-relexiveness and its abandonment of traditional narrative are really features of modernism itself; in some cases they are not even peripheral but central manifestations of it.

Objections have been made as well to the conclusions drawn from the analysis of some of the most frequently cited texts. Simon Frith has consistently emphasised the premium that the rock bands themselves place on unfashionably modernist criteria like originality and self-expression. Even the lowliest performers—the short apprenticeship system of the rock world, in contrast to the long apprenticeship tradition of classical music, propels many bands onto the public stage before they are very accomplished—believe they have something important to say. Their aim is to be popular but this means first and foremost 'occupying a particular place in the community rather than just accumulating large record sales' (Frith 1992, p. 176). Far from complacent acceptance of their role within a commercial culture many see themselves locked in a struggle with the formulae production of the charts. Kaplan's reading of the postmodern music video, in particular, has been criticised on several counts. According to Andrew Goodwin, few postmodern analyses of music video pay enough attention to the music. That 'fragmentation' which seems so marked a feature of the visual discourse of the video is at odds with the 'regimes of repetition and tonality that are highly ordered and predictable' (Goodwin 1993, p. 47) in the music itself. The careful correlation and interdependence of sound and music is fundamentally incompatible with the notion of 'blank pastiche' that stems from

Jameson's description of the postmodern style. Even within MTV itself, the postmodern description fits only a relatively short period of its output, the initial phase up to about 1983. It is only in that period that the continuous flow structure had the effect of blurring the categories of 'art-rock' and pop. After 1983, the station abandoned continuous flow programming, using discrete program slots and favouring performance rather than 'narrative fiction' video clips.

Postmodernism as 'double-coding'

Another, and, in my view, better way of analysing the coalescence of high culture and popular culture within the framework of postmodernism has been developed by the architectural historian, Charles Jencks. He has criticised Jameson's use of the term 'postmodernism' as an umbrella to cover all sorts of different reactions to high modernism, and he has queried the meaning and context of some of the features commonly ascribed to it, such as pastiche, schizophrenia and the levelling of distinctions between high and mass culture. In architecture especially, many of the features associated with postmodernism are, for Jencks, really features of a late modernism, a kind of modernism carried to extremes. This is where he would place much of the technocentric side of postmodernism. The essence of the postmodern for Jencks is its hybrid style and the 'double code' of its architectural language. Whereas for theorists like Jameson the postmodern collapses and obliterates the difference between high art and mass art in the creation of a new culture, for Jencks modernism (as he defines it) is alive and well in the postmodern, but it is there with something else. Postmodernism is not against modernism per se and modernist features can be incorporated within it. It is modernism *plus* something else: 'the Post-Modern building is . . . one which speaks on at least two levels at once: to architects and a concerned minority . . . and to the public at large, who care about other issues' (Jencks 1978, p. 6).

Although, in theory, any style can be part of the hybrid, it is first and foremost an amalgam of high and popular discourses. It grew out of a perception amongst modernist architects themselves in the 1960s that their work had lost contact with the mass of people whom architects were supposed to be working for, a growing sense of an impasse of incommunicability. While modernist architects thought they were using a universal language—the international style—in reality it was a style of no one, communicating with nobody. The ubiquitous glass and steel box defiled the cityscape. The blocks of flats put up by governments throughout the world to solve one set of social problems, with their clean lines and geometrical shape, their curtain walls inspired by Mies van der Rohe, seemed to usher in another set of problems, even harder to deal with. Although there was still an obvious need for architects to work with their peers, to use the new technologies, the clarity of vision and rationalist aesthetic of modernist building, many others—the real postmodernists in Jencks's sense—sought out a more comprehensible language as well to add to this. The élitism of modernist architecture was transcended, not by dropping it, but 'rather by extending the language of architecture . . . into the vernacular, towards tradition and the commercial slang of the street' (Jencks 1978, p. 8). This conscious populism included, amongst much else: the traditions of social realism, the conservation of old buildings, an eclectic use of popular styles, a mixture of conventional and abstract form, a variable mixed aesthetic depending on context, a critique of the dominant modernist aesthetic of functionalism in building, and a critique of the alliance between modernist architecture and big business. The result is a popular style of building which is pluralist, both élitist and participative, piecemeal, with a strong sense of the history of building and art in general as well as the immediate social context of the project. This pluralist coding is saved from pastiche by 'participatory design', by architects asking their clients what they actually want, with the designer subjected to codes not necessarily his or her own, which must be respected and negotiated with.[2]

Populism

Jencks's work reveals how important the need to take seriously the people and their culture—what they actually like and do as opposed to a mythology about them—has become in the study of culture in the last forty years. One of the first instances of the term 'postmodern' uncovered by Margaret A. Rose in her book, *The Post-Modern and the Post-Industrial* (1991), and perhaps the first application to the visual arts in the twentieth century, is by the Australian art historian Bernard Smith, in the conclusion to his *Place, Taste and Tradition*

(1945). Smith uses the term to characterise the work of Australian artists such as Noel Counihan, Josl Bergner and Victor O'Connor, moving away from the intellectualist stance of abstraction in modern art towards a more widely comprehensible social and political realism.

The onset of this populism has much to do with the increasing global prominence of America in the aftermath of the Second World War. The war forced an awareness of America and its culture upon people everywhere. Between 1974 and 1980 more Americans visited Europe than Europeans migrated to America in the whole period 1820 to 1970.[3] The profound impact of this on Australia has been well documented. In Britain, where rationing continued into the early 1950s, the manifestations of American popular culture—its films, music and television, its consumerism—offered a vision of a glamourous world, very different from the daily lives of the British working class. While the line of anxiety about the influence of America which runs from Arnold to Leavis continues—one of the themes which links the studies done of English popular culture by Orwell in the 1930s and Hoggart in the late 1950s, for example, is a dislike of the 'Americanisation' of working-class life—the balance seems to have begun to shift irrevocably in the other direction in the later 1950s and 1960s. The gradual and grudging acceptance of American influence in the reconstructed world after the war cannot be separated from an acceptance of mass culture, so closely are the two intertwined.

In America itself there were notable changes as well, towards the development of a new counter-aesthetic of 'pop', although one should still bear in mind the survival of a powerful mass culture critique in America as well as in Europe. Andrew Ross has seen the shift in the early 1950s of left-liberal intellectuals away from the mass culture critique of the 1930s and 1940s as part of a more general political alignment towards the centre, accompanied by an affirmation of the values of 'free' American culture—and this will mean, in certain circumstances, mass culture as well—against the patent corruption of values of the Stalinism of the old left. Many American intellectuals began to worry (with good reason) about the possibility for taking an autonomous intellectual standpoint in communist countries. Lionel Trilling is, perhaps, one of the most conspicuous cases of this in America. There are plenty of examples of this drift towards the political centre and right in Australia as well, for example the careers of John Anderson and James McAuley. While never a Marxist in any orthodox sense, by the 1950s Anderson had compromised on the pluralism which had been the bedrock of his intellectual life in favour of attacking communism in the 'national interest'. He now found it possible to lessen his opposition to the influence of the Catholic church, to attack the anti-conscription committee, even to support Prime Minister Chifley's sending in the troops to break up the miners' strike. Freedom came to be identified with the democratic West, that is, America. McAuley, who had been influenced by Anderson in the 1930s, was closely associated in the 1950s with the Australian Association for Cultural Freedom, part of the worldwide Congress for Cultural Freedom, based in Paris although funded, ultimately, by the CIA. His foundation of *Quadrant*, a kind of antipodean *Encounter*, in 1956 was part of this conservative challenge to the prevailing leftism of pre-war intellectual circles. The ascendancy of American cultural influence in Australia continued throughout the 1950s and early 1960s and was not really challenged until the battles over Australian involvement in the Vietnam war and the development of other movements of cultural and social liberation.

In 1952, *Partisan Review*, a leading journal in American liberal circles, convened a symposium on the subject 'Our Country and Our Culture'. As part of the symposium, David Riesman made the important point that popular culture is not a monolith and that it can be 'used' in different ways by different groups. This challenge to the notion of the passivity of the audience of popular culture has subsequently become important.

The aesthetic of 'pop' and its art gathered strength throughout the 1950s and 1960s in America and subsequently became influential elsewhere. Roy Lichtenstein's paintings used commercial art, comic strips especially, as subject matter. His exhibition at the Tate Gallery in London in the early 1960s caused a furore. Andy Warhol's work at his 'Factory' in New York were not just paintings of everyday objects like soup tins, in many cases they were not even paintings at all. 'Marilyn Monroe' (1962), a subject drawn it goes without saying from the world of mass culture, was not a portrait but derived from a photograph, a reproduction of a reproduction. One of Benjamin's points is the possibility for endless replication of the new art forms. The art of Pop is not a religion but something profane and concrete, suitable for mass consumption. Pop problematises the nature of taste itself: what is valuable is not what is original but what is replicated, not what is timeless but what is by its nature ephemeral and obsolescent.

In American critical writing of the period, Leslie Fiedler began to attack 'middle-brow' culture, asserting that the American fear of the vulgar was as strong as its fear of excellence. In his essay, 'Death of avant-garde literature' (1964), he launched an attack, not so much on the avant-garde, as against the aesthetics of high modernism, with the intention of validating popular culture. This line of thought has continued strongly, in later work associating the obsession with standards of literary critics with the 'cultural insecurity of the rich merchants and the nascent industrialists' of the nineteenth century (Fiedler 1975, p. 33). He has seen the need to differentiate high and low art as a manifestation of a puritan unease with the animal side of our nature, with 'the impulsive or irrational aspects' of the psyche (Fiedler 1975, pp. 38–9), with an attempt to repress the essentially dionysiac, disruptive side of the power of art. What literature does is to release us, albeit temporarily, from the shackles of reason, the boundaries of the ego and the burden of consciousness. Literary experience is analogous to dreaming or even 'tripping out', but somehow even better, compatible with waking awareness in ways that they are not. He urges the downgrading of ethics and aesthetics in literary study in favour of what he calls *ekstasis*, a term he finds in Longinus's *On the Sublime*. This means less of theme, structure, style, ideology and significance—the prime concerns of modernist criticism—and more of 'myth, fable, archetype, fantasy, magic', in short more 'wonder' (Fiedler 1975, p. 41). Susan Sontag likewise calls for an 'erotics' of the text, a study of how art makes its impact and gives its pleasure rather than how it means. Her 'Notes on camp' (1964) is an important text of the period, describing an aesthetic which is very much part of modern experience and yet almost totally unstudied. She sees camp taste as a related phenomenon to pop art but less serious and detached. Pop art has a kind of committed posture that camp lacks. The whole point of camp is 'to dethrone the serious . . . [It] is playful, anti-serious. More precisely, Camp involves a new, more complex relation to "the serious". One can be serious about the frivolous, frivolous about the serious' (Sontag 1986, p. 288). As such it is a radical departure from the good–bad axis which is the basis of conventional aesthetics. Value is detached from moral seriousness. Camp is not the first to do this, of course; there is a long line of

'Art for art's sake' stretching back through the dandy figures of the nineteenth century. But it differs from conventional dilettantism in that it is not offended by vulgarity. The connoisseur of camp is not bored by life or offended by mass taste but glories in it. Most of the great successes of camp would have appalled the dilettantes of the past: 'Camp is the modern dandyism. Camp is the answer to the problem: how to be a dandy in the age of mass culture' (Sontag 1986, p. 288). In 'Against interpretation' (1964), in the same collection, she defends what she has termed the 'transparency' of the texts of popular art, their immediacy of impact and indeed their ephemerality, their very lack of stylistic complexity, moral seriousness and depth.

Sociologies of 'everyday life' and the search for a counter-aesthetic

The work of the French sociologists Pierre Bourdieu and Michel de Certeau, which has been influential in changing the ways mass culture is conceptualised and criticised in the English-speaking world in the 1980s, needs to be set alongside this American counter-cultural practice and theory. They have emphasised the active nature of the consumption of mass culture—how people find ways to resist and fight back even in the very process of consuming it—rather than the passive soaking up—which is one of the basic tenets of modernist cultural criticism. A related, though some might say less acknowledged, area of study derives from Mikhail Bakhtin's work on carnival, originally written in the 1930s but not published in Russian until 1965, and not available in English translation until a few years later. Bakhtin likewise stresses the resistant nature of popular culture, its disruptive presence in the midst of the establishment. In the last ten years, particularly strongly in Australia, one can discern, under the influence of these writers, a new aggressive style of writing about popular culture. For Australian writers like John Docker, John Fiske, John Hartley and others the distinctive claim to quality in popular art is what it rejects in terms of conventional, high cultural aesthetics. A kind of circle has been completed. Whereas the discipline of English established itself in the earlier part of the twentieth century through a defensiveness of high culture and the effective exclusion of popular art, in the 1980s the study of popular culture has become a vital part of what we call the 'New Humanities'. Its academic respectability, its seizure of the high ground, can be seen expressed in the title of Colin MacCabe's book, *High Theory/Low Culture*, published in 1986. If anything needs defending now, it is that very high culture whose position in the university had once seemed so impregnable.

The heart of Bourdieu's work is a criticism of the Kantian aesthetics which has been the foundation of the criticism of art and literature in all manner of different guises for a long time, for instance, in the doctrine of 'Art for art's sake' at the end of the nineteenth century or in American New Criticism's purificatory appreciation of the poem as verbal icon in the mid-twentieth century. Sometimes in reading Kant one seems to see a vista of two hundred years of literary criticism opening up. It is hard to imagine an aesthetics of any branch of art in the last two hundred years that does not derive from it in some way. As I said in chapter 1, Kant's understanding of the nature of the artist, his emphasis on originality and genius, his sense of the appreciation of form as the basis of aesthetic pleasure, his differentiation of the 'consumption' of art from other kinds of pleasures, are all fundamental to the way in which high art and the artist have been conceived.

Bourdieu's most penetrating criticism of this line of argument is advanced in his book, *Distinction*, which describes and analyses the nature of the aesthetic judgements of different sections of society. Bourdieu finds that the type of discrimination associated with the tradition of Kantian aesthetics is encountered only in a small social group, a group which corresponds to a marked degree with the upper social class. This, of itself, is not new. It is fully in accord with a great deal of modernist analysis of culture. In the 1920s Clive Bell (1928) had connected the survival of civilisation to a small group of sensibility, differentiated by its ability to distinguish 'pure form' and indifferent to the emotional or factual side of art. Artistic taste is a powerful marker of class: 'Nothing more rigorously distinguishes the different classes than the disposition objectively demanded by the legitimate consumption of legitimate works, the aptitude for taking a specifically aesthetic point of view' (Bourdieu 1980, p. 243). This kind of discrimination is not, however, socially neutral, natural, and so in theory available to all, but is acquired in very specific circumstances. A taste for art and the ability to talk about it is a kind of 'capital', passed down like money or property through families and certain social institutions. The 'pure' Kantian aesthetic and, with it the ability to respond to great art, is learned—albeit sometimes in an indirect, even unconscious way—in the school and in the family. Working people do not naturally dislike high art nor are they born with rough powers of judgement; rather, they have not been educated, in the narrow way of the school or the broad way of the home and social group, to appreciate it. In particular, they have not been educated or socialised to appreciate it in the 'right' ways.

How then do the people make aesthetic judgements; what is the nature of this popular aesthetic and, by implication, what is the nature of this popular art which is admired? Bourdieu finds that it is not so much a dilution or misprision of Kantian aesthetics as its antithesis. Indeed, it is not aesthetic judgement at all in Kant's terms. Fundamental to the popular aesthetic is the abolition of most of the distinctions Kant makes. There is no distinction between the realms of art and life. There is no distinction between the 'taste of sense' and the 'taste of reflection'. The pleasure art confers is not qualitatively different from other pleasures. Popular aesthetic is based rather on the integration of aesthetic consumption into the world of ordinary consumption.

Bourdieu's research was based upon a series of questions asked of people from different sections of society about what works of art they knew, which they liked, what kinds of objects they thought beautiful, etc. He found that working people were the least likely to value art for the sake of form alone—a central tenet of Kant's aesthetics. An extreme manifestation of this was a hostility to formal experimentation. Rather, working people stressed the connection between art and life; they demanded a clear notion of function in art (even if only as sign) and constantly made reference in their judgements both to moral categories and to what is 'agreeable'. The aesthetic distance, essential to the Kantian aesthetic, was always broken; appreciation was based on the object's 'informative, tangible or moral interest' (Bourdieu 1980, p. 245) and there was a deep-rooted demand for participation in experiencing the art object. One illustration of this is that working people were the least likely to see the beauty of form in an ordinary or common object or in a representation of one. Only a small group of people, those with the most cultural capital through social class or education, were willing to concede that it was possible to have a beautiful representation of an ugly thing. Working people would recognise the beauty in a photograph of a beautiful person or, more subtly, the beautiful way in which the beautiful person had been photographed, but they were unlikely to allow for the possibility of a beautiful photograph of, say, a cabbage. A work of art is worthwhile if the thing represented is worthy of being represented.

Bourdieu's popular aesthetic reverses many of the traditional categories of value in the appreciation of high art. Instead, it opens up the possibility for appreciation and validation of different things in art and for different kinds of art. Put simply, Bourdieu's work enables us to see why certain things in art have been valued—for instance he links the obsession with aesthetic distance to a bourgeois life-style characterised by lack of urgency, the daily squandering of time, money and ease on what are, strictly speaking, unnecessary things—and to find ways of valuing elements which have formerly been put beyond the pale.

The search for a counter-aesthetic in popular art has been taken up by many other writers, whether influenced directly by Bourdieu or not. Laura Mulvey (1986, p. 84) has drawn attention to the long history of melodrama, for example, as an illustration of the operation of a kind of anti-aesthetic in Kantian terms. In the nineteenth century, political instruments such as the *Licensing Acts* narrowly restricted the operation of drama. The popular, illegitimate theatre defined itself in opposition to the qualities that characterised high cultural production. Whereas high art in the theatre was marked by a mastery over language and music, popular theatrical forms like melodrama developed techniques which displaced in particular the power of the word. Its discourse relied to a marked degree on a language of visual signs, movement and gesture. The cinema occupies an interesting role in this tradition as well, born mute and having to develop for the first thirty years of its life a mode of discourse which was non-verbal.

This view of popular culture as counter-aesthetic has become one of the strongest features in the criticism of the 1980s. It is not based on Bourdieu alone, but also on the carnival theory of Bakhtin, and the theory of 'everyday life' of Michel de Certeau. The work of Jean Baudrillard, which has pulled much of the modernist view of culture inside out by praising rather than condemning the 'spectacle' of mass culture, finding a kind of revolutionary quality in consumption and in the refusal of meaning and thought in favour of delight and pleasure, seeing in fact a kind of resistance in what he admits to be the very passivity of mass culture, has also been of great significance.[4]

In nearly all criticism of this kind, Bakhtin is a kind of grey eminence, as, indeed, he is in so much of the 'new' literary and cultural theory of the last twenty-five years. At the base of his work is a theory of language as dialogic. Language use is inherently participatory and dialectical. Every statement is an invitation to a response. From a broader point of view, all texts contain manifestations of their opposites, their other. Originally, Bakhtin saw this feature as characteristic of the novel in particular, although his later work sees this dialogic structure as characteristic of the literary text in general. The work on carnival for which he is most famous is an extension of this in social terms; just as the literary text is a conflict between its dominant discourse and a disruptive other, so society is a tension between the establishment and its culture and the people and theirs.

Bakhtin's central work on this, *Rabelais and His World* (1968), ranges widely through ancient and modern culture, focusing specifically on the Renaissance. According to Bakhtin, in the ancient world every festival demonstrated both sides of the dialogic cultural relationship. The solemn tragedy of the Greek theatre was always followed, completed in a sense, by the farcical satyr play; the drama festival is not complete without the performance of both plays, the one parodying and travestying the truths of the other. It is only with the coming of the state in the Renaissance, so Bakhtin's argument runs, that the two cultures become separated, socially and aesthetically, with one culture coming to be seen as the normal, dominating one, with the other in a kind of secondary and subversive relationship to it. The crucial insight of Bakhtin is that the two cultures cannot extinguish each other—in particular, the dominant culture must allow the dominated culture its moments of rule, even though its rule is the abolition of everything the dominant culture stands for. Bakhtin's main example of this is the carnival of the Middle Ages, a brief, yet necessary and inextinguishable period in which the values of the dominant culture are overturned: when a boy becomes the bishop, when the most junior priests play dice on the altar, when sexual licence triumphs over social puritanism. It is a moment when the people find a space in the dominant culture to interpose their own culture and values.

The key feature of Bakhtin's work for the study of popular culture is his notion of how the people use the dominant culture for their own ends. The work of de Certeau seeks in a similar manner to identify the ways in which the people and their culture are not simply suppressed, or made into unwilling recipients of values and discourses they neither want nor understand, but actively resist and expropriate the dominant culture. His book, *The Practice of Everyday Life*, originally published in French in 1974, is dedicated to 'the ordinary man . . . a common hero' and its first sentence tells us that it is 'part of a continuing investigation of the ways in which users—commonly assumed to be passive and guided by established rules—operate' (de Certeau 1988, p. xi). Amongst the ways they operate is to buck the system in all sorts of small ways, by the *perruque* for example, a job done in the boss's time but for purely personal gain. Consumption, shopping, a particular way of using the streets, are all aspects of this, ways in which the people and their culture do not simply accept what is given them.

Popular culture as counter-aesthetic has been a particular feature in the Australian context in the 1980s; in fact it is in danger of becoming our house style. An early manifestation of it can be seen in Sylvia Lawson's fine study of the career of J. F. Archibald and the *Bulletin, The Archibald Paradox* (1983). Part of her aim was to restore the sense of the magazine as a whole, as a 'complete text', populist, racist and xenophobic, warts and all. Twentieth-century literary scholarship, not to speak of social criticism, has been singularly inept in dealing with the *Bulletin* because it has lost its feeling for this kind of populism, for mischief and vaudeville: the 1960s 'could not afford to acknowledge pleasure, anarchic wit, subversive elegance . . . That was a society wherein popular story-telling, indeed all "entertainment", was defined as something to be checked and controlled' (Lawson, 1983, p. 257). The magazine and its importance in the development of Australian culture could only be handled by stripping this away and treating its literary work in a vacuum.

One of the reasons for the prominence of this school of criticism in Australia is that John Fiske, now one of its leading international figures, although coming originally from the University of Wales and now holding a Chair in America, worked in Australia in the 1980s. In his contribution to the recent Cultural Studies reader, edited by Lawrence Grossberg et al. (1992), entitled significantly 'Cultural

Studies and the Culture of Everyday Life', he sees the key feature of high art as its 'distance', its aloofness from history, from historic necessity, and from bodily pleasure. If this view of high culture is very Bourdieu, his view of popular culture owes much to de Certeau. Its creativity lies in its practical adaptation to circumstances: it is a 'bricolage' (making do)—a concept derived from the French structuralist anthropologist, Claude Levi-Strauss, but used extensively in connection with postmodernism and the study of popular culture. In another essay on quiz shows, Fiske defines popular culture as 'the interface between mass produced culture, the product of the powerful, and everyday life, the practices of the weak' (Fiske 1989, p. 75). Those features which put popular culture beyond the pale aesthetically—the flaunting of the values of consumption, the reliance on luck rather than skill—are the very things which validate it in this view. Consumption is not a sign of passive acceptance of the dominant ideology but a form of 'utterance' in de Certeau's words. The money which flows through these programs is gained through native cunning rather than through the subjection to an alien economic morality and system. The quiz show's foregrounding of luck is a way of defeating the meritocratic myth of capitalist society. In a similar way, in 'Transgressive TV' (1989b), Graeme Turner has described a 'transgressive' or 'stretch' television which works by violating all the norms of quality and standards of taste derived from the traditional study of high art. Popular television flaunts the rules in an anarchic way, mixing genres and discourses; it succeeds by violating all the criteria associated since the time of Kant with high art and culture, through its commitment to pleasure, spectacle, and to immediacy rather than reflection.

Cultural populism and its critics

While the 'school of Fiske' has been influential in Australia (and elsewhere), it has also had its critics, not least in Australia. One of the recent books of this type, *Myths of Oz* (1987), edited by John Fiske, Bob Hodge and Graeme Turner, was badly reviewed on the whole, although it has apparently been a commercial success. Meaghan Morris criticised the populist assumptions and the ubiquitousness of this style of criticism in 'Banality in cultural studies' (1990), an article which has become celebrated. The most thorough critical analysis of this whole trend in the study of culture, although not from a totally hostile standpoint, is by Jim McGuigan in *Cultural Populism* (1993). While he sees a populist sentiment and orientation as in many ways fundamental to the enterprise of Cultural Studies, he has serious misgivings about its uncritical stance in relation to popular culture. It is very easy for it to become a simple inversion of the old modernist mass culture critique of the 1920s and 1930s and to repeat its errors. There seems to be no bad side to popular culture, no violence, sexism or racism. Popular readings of texts are always progressive. On the other hand, high art becomes an easy target, linked unproblematically to a conservative political agenda. In fact, living through the 1980s might have taught us the very opposite. The Conservative government in Britain did not seek validation from the world of high culture, a large section of which, especially that concerned with the arts, was implacably opposed to it, but from the supposedly common sense values of 'ordinary people'. Many of the supporters of Thatcherism in Britain received their daily dose of economic liberalism alongside the bare bosoms on page 3 of the *Sun*. Furthermore, McGuigan sees an analogy between the 'semiotic democracy' of cultural populism—its commitment to the idea of a text's multiple meanings as constructed by the audience who read it—and the consumer sovereignty of free market economics. In a review article which dealt extensively with the book, Simon Frith and Jon Savage attacked the cheerful populism which had overtaken Cultural Studies in the 1980s, its 'theoretical pursuit of the joys of consumption' (Frith and Savage 1993, p. 107). Elsewhere, Frith has debunked the common view in Cultural Studies of pop music as a perfect model of consumption: 'an anxiety-driven search by radical intellectuals and rootless academics for a model of consumption—for the perfect consumer, the subcultural idol, the mod, the punk, the cool commodity fetishist, the organic intellectual of the high street who can *stand in for them*' (Frith 1992, p. 180, author's emphasis).

Similar points have been made in the Australian context by Adrian Martin (1993). Not only does he criticise what he terms the 'agonistic' view of high culture and popular culture as presented by writers like Fiske and Docker, but he points to its reductive and anti-intellectual nature. It can become hard to criticise popular culture at all. Quiz shows on television are somehow good because they are bad: their gross materialism and consumption is an antidote to the 'spiritual' values of the middle class, their tacky sets and raucous style are an assault on bourgeois literary criteria like skill, order and coherence. Their shameless derivativeness is a rejection of modernism's obsession with the text's originality. Almost anything, no matter how trashy, can be defended in this way as offering potential for a 'resistant reading'. Not only is there a danger of praising popular texts for *not* being serious or intellectually challenging, but, from the opposite point of view, works which *are* serious or intellectually challenging can end up in the enemy camp, on the bad side of the cultural divide.

The last of Sontag's 'Notes on camp', the fifty-eighth, the 'ultimate' camp statement, is that 'it's good because it's awful' (Sontag 1986, p. 292). She immediately adds that one should only say that under certain conditions—it is not always true. This is excellent advice. Camp and other kinds of populism work best as aesthetics on the margins. To adopt them as a universal aesthetic can become a particularly dangerous and intellectually ruinous form of treason of the clerks.

4

ÉLITISM AND POPULISM IN THE CONSTRUCTION OF AUSTRALIAN CULTURAL IDENTITY

The Great Dividing Range

When, in September 1992, John Singleton and Phillip Adams met on Channel Nine's *A Current Affair* to discuss the regulation of advertising on television, the argument quickly found the bottom line. According to Singleton, Adams's support for regulation revealed him to be something other at heart than a 'real fair dinkum Aussie'. It was not hard to discover what this real Australianness might consist of:

> You don't drink, you don't smoke, you don't go the football, you don't go to races. You don't live in the real world. You live in a government-tax-bludging society. You are a million words in search of an editor. You are a commissioner for the future style of person. You are not a real fair dinkum Aussie. (Bogle 1992, p. 23)

Although all societies have grappled with the nature of their identity, the centrality of this debate in Australian life and the passion with which it has been pursued is striking. Richard White has called it a 'national obsession' (White 1981, p. x). Doubtless, this is a reflex of the fact that white Australia's history is a creation of the last two hundred years, not just an age of nationalism in almost every country with a European connection, but also an age in which the scientific study of phenomena and thus of an interest in classification and typology generally was born. Nevertheless, there is something distinctively Australian about the form our national self-analysis has taken and seems doomed to continue to take. When the American Senate set about trying to define un-American activities in the 1950s, it did not automatically assume that one's patriotism was somehow a function of one's attitude to art, that a person who didn't go to the football but who wrote books could not simultaneously be a patriotic American. Discussions of Australian identity, however, have almost always held to this particular polarity, as if high culture and

'Australianness' were somehow intrinsically at odds with each other. Deborah Bogle's article in the *Weekend Australian*, saw the conflict between Singleton and Adams in terms of a 'great divide', 'the plain-speaking ocker versus the intellectual humanist': on one hand, Singleton, 'abrasive, a knockabout, beer-drinking bloke who loves pubs, restaurants, the races and the footy'; on the other, Adams, 'a rare drinker who shuns social functions, speaks in mellifluous and considered tones and prefers reclusive weekends in the country and intimate weeknight dinners with a friend' (Bogle 1992, p. 23). Furthermore, a sense of the polarity of Australian culture in these terms has united cultural critics as different in every way as G. A. Wilkes and John Docker, although they have tended to put themselves on different sides of the divide. Wilkes's (1981) image of the conflict has been to see the model of Australian cultural development in an opposition of genteel and robust, refined and crude, what he calls in the title of his book, the antithesis of stockyard and croquet lawn. Docker's (1974, 1984) way of understanding the conflict has been to see it in terms of a struggle between a school of radical nationalism and what he calls the 'metaphysical ascendency', a division reinforced (in complex ways) by the different intellectual traditions of Australia's two largest cities, Melbourne and Sydney. The hostile reception in some quarters to the publication of Leonie Kramer's *Oxford History of Australian Literature* (1981), which emphasised the Brennan (high cultural) rather than the Lawson (popular) tradition in Australian literature, was but one recent instance of the persistence of this kind of thinking.

The achievements of colonial culture

While these writers are undoubtedly right about the presence in Australian culture of this antithesis, the battle has hardly been an equal one. Until quite recently, the late 1950s and early 1960s, the democratic–populist paradigm of national identity was not seriously or widely challenged, and in some respects—for example the sense of urgency which has accompanied the imperative in Australian politics in the last five years for us to become a 'clever' rather than a 'lucky' country—it is still perceived to be deeply ingrained in the national consciousness. Docker, on the other hand, has consistently argued since the mid-1970s that in more recent times it has been the populist paradigm that has needed re-emphasising. Yet, despite the fact that, as Tim Rowse (1978) points out, the history of white Australia falls wholly within the period of the rise of European liberalism, with no feudal or peasant inheritance in Australia to resist it, the origins of European settlement did not, however, inevitably lead towards this populist social model. There were talented people among the early governors of New South Wales. At least some of the early settlers in the colony dared to dream of a future of high cultural greatness for Australia, affirming its cultural superiority over the nations of the old world, not the opposite picture which is so familiar a part of colonial and postcolonial experience: 'I beheld a second Rome, rising from a coalition of banditti . . . looking down with proud superiority upon the barbarous nations of the northern hemisphere'.[1]

In some ways this visionary strain, imagining the future of Australia as a new culture rising above the ashes of the old world, has had a long history. It survived through the nineteenth century, in notions of Australia as the working man's paradise, and into our own time as Australia the model of the multicultural society of the future. It is a marked feature of political polemic; politicians like to vilify their opponents as people without 'vision'. In the recent argument about the demolition of the Cahill Expressway in Sydney, Paul Keating presented himself as a man with a vision for the city, a faculty which the State Premier supposedly lacked. In the early days of settlement, this visionary tendency was soon challenged, however. While the picture of Australia as botanical marvel survived, reproduced in expensive folios for scholars and gentlemen connoisseurs, the alternative picture from the other end of the cultural spectrum, of colonial hell on earth, graphically realised in inexpensive chapbooks, quickly challenged it, in the popular mind especially. In the vigorous debate in the last thirty years about the nature of colonial Australian culture, the traditional view is that high cultural value systems were dislodged very quickly. Cultural historians of the colonial period like Geoffrey Serle have pointed to the early erosion of 'tory' consciousness, especially during the explosive growth of the squatter class in the 1830s and 1840s. There was little of the patronage of the arts traditionally associated with the aristocracy, nor were the churches a source of major cultural stimulus. What intellectual pretensions there were among the squattocracy were widely ridiculed as posturings by the diggers of the Gold Rush in the 1850s.[2]

The distinctiveness and strength of the culture of Australia thus developed most strongly in popular forms.

There is another school of thought, however, associated with literary critics like Wilkes and Kramer and with historians like Manning Clark. One of the key essays here is Clark's (1980) 'Rewriting Australian history', published in 1956, although first given two years previously as a lecture. Clark urged much more caution in dealing with the whole tradition of Australian history in terms of its progressive social democracy, on the one hand, and its gross materialism and cultural barbarism, on the other—a tradition that has a great deal to do with the views of itinerant British pundits. This way of writing Australia's history has not only led to much sentimentality about the convict heritage, to a view of Australian history as somehow beginning at Eureka in 1854, and to illusions about the democratic temper of the 1890s, but also to a gross undervaluation of the real achievements of colonial culture before 1850. When Clark published the first volume of his own *History of Australia* in 1962, the first three chapters described the culture of Europeans in the south Pacific in terms of the intellectual traditions and ideologies they brought with them. Sometimes the other side of politicians's vision of the future is an extraordinary blindness to the achievements of the past. In the debate about the republic in our own time, it has been commonly asserted that Australia's constitution was drafted in Whitehall by the Foreign Office. It is a strange kind of nationalism that cannot see the federation of the six colonies into a self-governing entity and the drafting of the federal constitution as one of the great triumphs of Australian history. Likewise, this period of the culture of the squatters, the period of bourgeois civilisation in Australia, should not be so lightly dismissed. It produced many of our most important social institutions: churches, schools, libraries, universities, parliamentary government. There were, moreover, many idealist reformers in the population, like John Dunmore Lang and Caroline Chisholm, who pursued causes such as an end to transportation and criminal law reform, temperance, savings banks and education. The case of adult education is a good corrective to the traditional view of colonial culture. The Mechanics' Institutes, founded in Edinburgh in 1821 and in London in 1823 for the education of working men, quickly found a home in Australia. There were institutes providing libraries, instruction classes, debates, tuition in essay writing, etc., in

Hobart by 1827, in Sydney in 1833, in Newcastle in 1835, and in Melbourne in 1839. The first Principal of Sydney University, John Woolley, was a powerful advocate of the university's extension work in this direction. Whereas 36.9 per cent of the population of rural Australia was illiterate in 1851, by 1911 the rate had been dramatically reduced to less than 1 per cent.

In a similar manner, since the late 1950s Wilkes has stressed the importance of literary traditions in the nineteenth century other than the democratic–populist and nationalist, traditions more aligned to the high cultural heritage of English literature, still often nationalist in feeling, but lacking the sense that Australian identity had to be won at the price of rejecting cultural ties with Europe. Colonial poets like Henry Kendall and Charles Harpur (the son of a convict), for example, wrote about the distinctiveness of Australian experience, especially the experience of the Australian bush, but in a way which was recognisably part of the wider culture of Romanticism. In other words, they adapted the great literature of contemporary Europe to local conditions.

One of the most interesting aspects of Wilkes's work is that he shows us a society at work in which it was not necessary to choose between the 'national' culture and some other culture constructed as alien. The picture Wilkes provides of mid-century reading culture, for example, is far removed from the intellectual wilderness or narrow national populism often imagined. Booksellers's catalogues, even from as early a date as the 1820s, show not just how many titles were offered for sale—4000 in 1826 for example—but more importantly how quickly novels and poetry published overseas arrived in Australia, often serialised in local magazines. Dickens's *Pickwick Papers*, first published in England in 1837, was serialised in the Sydney *Gazette* in 1838, and a local edition was published in Launceston in the same year. In 1853, there were five bookshops in Sydney, the largest advertising well over 200 000 volumes in the 1840s. The books offered for sale catered to a rapidly expanding reading public, comprised of professional people, civil servants, military officers and, increasingly, wealthy emancipists. Circulating libraries grew up in tandem with this expanding reading public.

In particular, Wilkes argues against a notion of two audiences: a high cultural one reading English novelists like Trollope or George Eliot and a popular one reading Australian writers like Henry Lawson.

The reality is a much more mixed and cosmopolitan literary culture than is often realised. The reading public sought Australian literature from at least the 1840s and it remained eager for both local and overseas writers throughout the nineteenth century: '[readers] were able to read [George Eliot's] *Middlemarch* and Trollope's *The Eustace Diamonds* as serials in the *Australasian* in 1871, overlapping with the serialisation of [Marcus Clarke's] *His Natural Life* in the *Australian Journal*' (Wilkes 1981, p. 68).

'Currency' cultural values

At the other end of the social scale, there is no doubt that the working class in the colonial period was disproportionately strong. The vast majority of the population of Australia in the 1830s and 1840s, both convict and immigrant, was unskilled or semi-skilled. The convict element in the population was not just strong numerically but, even according to reformers like Dunmore Lang, dominated the tone of the whole of colonial society. Far from the convicts taking on the moral and social values of the free settlers, it was widely feared that the free settlers would regress to the level of the convicts. Despite the attempts of some historians, notably Russel Ward, to root the collectivist, democratic strains in Australian culture and history in what they see as the closely bonded and self-reliant world of convict society, more recent studies of convict society by historians like M. B. and C. B. Schedvin have painted a different and less romantic picture of convict life. There is no real evidence that convicts formed close personal links; in many ways quite the opposite was true. Amongst other features of convict society, the Schedvins list: restlessness, unwillingness to accept the personal self-discipline necessary for work, reliance on externally provided support, anti-authoritarianism, aggression, wariness of the opposite sex, fantasies of independence unaided by any sense of personal responsibility. Their culture is described as a 'defensive arrangement . . . [stemming] from a profound feeling of inferiority' (M. B. and C. B. Schedvin 1992, p. 108). Within this convict culture, Irish influence was strong; there were few Welsh or Scottish convicts. In 1840, there were three times as many people of Irish descent living in New South Wales as in England and Wales. Even amongst free settlers, more than half were Irish. Most were extremely poor working people.

In many cases, on the other hand, it is clear that the development of institutions of high culture was also conspicuously assisted by the migration of free settlers. Geoffrey Serle uses the example of Sir Redmond Barry, also an Irish migrant, albeit from a very different stratum of society. Famous as the judge who sentenced Ned Kelly to death, he is perhaps better remembered as the moving force behind the development of many of Melbourne's fine public institutions, in particular the splendid public library which in the nineteenth century was justly famed throughout the world. But, on the whole, the number of free settlers who might have brought high culture to the colonies was not only small but dwindling in number and power throughout the nineteenth century. In 1828, convicts, ex-convicts and native-born outnumbered free settlers and officials by seven to one. This was changed temporarily by the discovery of gold in 1851 so that in the census of that year there were only twice as many convicts, emancipists, and native-born Australians as free settlers. By the census of 1861, however, nearly 50 per cent of the population was native-born and by 1901 more than 80 per cent of it was. The culture of this society was patriotic, nationalistic, and anti-British. As Wilkes points out, the culture of the gentry, such as it was, came quickly to seem un-Australian; the middle-class Englishman in particular, ill at ease in the bush, was a particular object of contempt.[3]

The values of the local, largely native-born population, the 'currency' values, were formed in conscious opposition to the perceived values of a higher social class: they stress the practical rather than the reflective, anti-authoritarianism, a contempt for 'new chums', larrikinism. Action is inevitably the prerequisite for success. What is surprising is how quickly and definitively this national type emerged, long before the mass migration of the Gold Rush days. In 1819, the report of Commissioner J. T. Bigge noted how strikingly the native-born differed physically from their parents: tall, slender, fair, less likely to tire than Europeans, active though 'awkward', quick and irascible though not vindictive. The stereotype can also be found in the writing of another early visitor, Peter Cunningham, in *Two Years in New South Wales* (1827). He identifies the open, manly—it is of course very much a male stereotype—simplicity of character of the native-born; they are (again) usually tall and slender in build, with fair hair and blue eyes; they are passionate about sports, especially swimming; they are patriotic; they do not like authority figures and refuse jobs which require them either to accept authority, such as servant positions, or exercise it over others, such as constables. All this by the 1820s.

It is easy to recognise a powerful mythology of Australian identity being created here. Doubtless, as with most mythologies, there were areas of truth in the portrait, but we should recognise the mythological factor at work as well and ask ourselves what principles of exclusion and inclusion were at work in its composition. To start with, Cunningham himself was an outsider, and it is worth remembering that many of the most powerful elements of the myth-making of Australian identity have been constructions from without. The first identification of the bushman as *the* national type in 1893 was by another Englishman, Francis Adams. As well, both Wilkes and Serle have warned how the populist currency model of Australian identity needs to be seen in perspective and balanced with less common or obvious ones. The patriotism of the native born was not necessarily incompatible with a respect for British customs and institutions. William Charles Wentworth, for example, used his knowledge of constitutional law gained from experience at the English bar as a basis for his support for self-government in New South Wales; he saw the rights of the native born co-existing with loyalty to the crown. His conception of the colony was as an extension rather than a rejection of *true* British values, as a kind of new and purified Britannia in the Antipodes.[4]

In addition to mistaking a part of the culture for the whole, we should be aware of the 'constructedness' of the currency myth of Australian identity and its social and historical context. Donald Denoon has emphasised the connections between the currency myth of Australian identity and populist myths of national character in many other countries at the same time. Australia was only one of several 'frontier societies' formed in the eighteenth and nineteenth centuries and they all share certain characteristics. The frontier is populated by 'restless spirits who chafed at restrictions' (Denoon 1983, p. 34), driven there by the expansion of pastoral capitalism. It is a place of individualism, of hostility to people beyond the frontier whose dispossession is the source of the frontiersman's economic strength. Denoon's study of the frontier societies of nineteenth-century Australia, New Zealand, South Africa, Argentina and Brazil leads him to the conclusion that 'Tolstoy's summary of Cossack values might apply equally to Martin Fierro, to Jonker Afrikander of Namibia, and to Adam Kok I of Griqualand' (Denoon 1983, p. 35). A sense of cultural inferiority is clearly one of the most important of these common frontier attributes, coupled with the opposite image of the old world as culturally intimidating. America was clearly the model of this new society and many aspects of what we like to think of as the specifically Australian 'currency' value system can also be identified as characteristics of the democratic society of America. Alexis de Tocqueville's vastly influential study of *Democracy in America* (1946, originally published in 1835, 1840) lamented the absence of that aristocracy, which he thought was alone the conduit for the survival of great art in a society, and traced the inevitable decline of standards, the preference for the practical rather than the beautiful. In the opinion of Keith Hancock's *Australia* (1930), a book which, in its local context, was every bit as influential, Tocqueville's views were just as true of Australia, while in the opinion of Kenneth Dempsey (1992), Tocqueville's analysis was much more appropriate to Australia. This connection between the new societies did not go unnoticed at the time. Tocqueville's views were present in the minds of members of the British government at the time when self-government was gradually being extended to the Australian colonies. Richard White (1981, p. 54) notes that Wentworth's speech on the New South Wales Constitution Bill contains large quotations from Tocqueville, and he hoped for a conservative British constitution rather than a 'Yankee' one which might lead inevitably to republicanism.

Despite the hopes of people like Wentworth that American democratic influence on the constitution and the culture generally would not eventuate, it is hard not to recognise the close correspondence between the currency stereotype and American cultural types. Ward points to Fenimore Cooper's novels, in which the character of Deerslayer shares many of the same attributes. The currency lad evokes the common features of the myths of the noble frontiersman in other countries in the nineteenth century: respect for action and the practical, an indifference if not outright hostility to thought and learning, an overwhelming preference for the remoteness and solitude of the countryside to the crowds and culture of the towns. Nor is the frontiersman the only widely spread and trans-national myth comparable to that of the native-born Australian currency lad. White goes on to ask whether the features of the currency lad are not the features of the younger generation throughout the ages and in many different cultures: athletic, in possession of unaffected and untutored natural grace and beauty, disrespectful of authority and tradition, possessed of great self-reliance. These manifestations of the cult of youth and, in slightly narrower focus, what White calls the 'coming man', are extolled in the popular literature of many societies in the nineteenth century. They are not exclusive to Australia but can be found throughout the work of writers like Fenimore Cooper, Kipling, and John Buchan.

The populist myth of the bushman

The most enduring myth of the Australian national character consolidated in the latter part of the nineteenth century around the populist figure of the 'bushman', a clear descendant of the currency lad. The currency 'lass' has—rather pointedly—little to contribute to this particular myth. Indeed, it has been argued that the myth is not just constructed in the absence of women but in terms of their deliberate rejection. The bush ethos, and the urban bohemian culture of the *Bulletin* which propagated it, extolled a kind of solitariness, the 'lone hand' or purely masculine camaraderie, with pleasure taken in hard drinking and gambling, that was the very antithesis of the idealisation of home life and domesticity characteristic of nineteenth-century Evangelicalism. It was particularly opposed to the Temperance movement in which women were a vital force.[5]

It was Francis Adams who first identified the bushman as the national type of the Australian in his book *The Australians* (1893), and a full scholarly treatment of the myth from its origins to its decline was provided by the historian Russel Ward in *The Australian Legend*, first published in 1958. Ward's thesis, to quote the foreword to the second edition, is:

> that a specifically Australian outlook grew up first and most clearly among the bush workers in the Australian pastoral industry, and that this group has had an influence, completely disproportionate to its numerical and economic strength, on the attitudes of the whole Australian community. (Ward 1965, p. v)

It is hard to exaggerate the importance in Australian cultural history of these ideas and of this book in particular. Even the most recent studies of the question of Australian identity, such as the second edition of John Carroll's book, *Intruders in the Bush* (1992), still use it as a primary text from which their own differing interpretations take off.

Ward does not dispute the picture of colonial society that is often painted and which I have been describing here—indeed some of the facts and figures that I have used originate in his book—although he does sometimes put a different kind of social or moral inflection on it. He, too, points to the disproportionate strength of unskilled, working-class people in the population, the convict basis, the strong Irish influence, and the currency system of values. He sees colonial culture as a fluid society, one which debased and vulgarised the rich but which, on the other hand, had the tendency to augment the integrity and self-reliance, although not to polish the manners, of working people. Although the culture reinforced the viciousness and brutality of its convict origins, it also fostered physical endurance, resourcefulness, an anti-authoritarian cast of mind and collectivist social outlook.

The myth of the bush developed after the early colonial period was over, and, most importantly for Ward, away from the cities, in the different world across the Great Dividing Range. It was a convict culture transmuted by the harsh conditions of the Australian interior. Despite the many similarities between the cultures of America and Australia as 'new societies', there were important social and economic differences as well in the way the countries were settled. In America, land was sold cheaply or simply given away. This, together with an ethic of individualism, created a society of small-holders. The different conditions of Australia, together with a determination to keep the price of land high, created instead large single properties employing many casual hands. It was the lot of the overwhelming majority of workers on the land to work for someone else, in an essentially impermanent way although often for relatively high wages. For Ward, these conditions are the origin of that semi-nomadic rural working class, almost exclusively male in composition—there were few women in the outback and in many cases married life would have been impossible in the barrack-style accommodation provided for the shearers—which is the basis of the bushman myth. The dangers, loneliness, and sheer hardness of life made the practice of 'mateship' not only necessary for survival, but, in the absence of marriageable women, education, and religion—in short, what we think of as 'culture'—provided the only vehicle for what Eleanor Hodges has called 'emotional release, altruism, and commitment' (Hodges 1992, p. 7).

The decline in the numbers of real-life bushmen of Ward's type as the century wore on was accompanied by an increase in myth-making about them, and the elevation of one particular aspect of the culture of a small section of the people into its most 'typical' status. The pastoral workers, through the strength of the Amalgamated Shearers Union, became in the 1880s and 1890s the backbone of the trade union movement. Their culture thereby became influential on a whole area of Australian life which had little real contact with the bush itself. The most important way, however, in which the populist myth of the bushman as the quintessential Australian was spread was through his discovery by literary men and women in the latter part of the nineteenth century.

While Ward is the first to admit the importance of literary culture in spreading the myth of the bushman, he does not seem quite to see the nature of the paradoxes involved in a process whereby an essentially anti-intellectual outlook was transmitted within what was essentially a culture of intellectuals. Furthermore, the power of the myth was spread by a small and unrepresentative section of the population. Whatever the extent of the real-life bushmen in the outback, the powerful myth of the Australian 'bush' was in many ways the creation of an emergent class of *urban* intellectuals.

Ward himself pointed to one of the most paradoxical cases in Rolf Boldrewood, the *nom de plume* of T. A. Browne. Although Boldrewood reflected the values of the bush workers, he was not himself even remotely of their class. He was not even native born, having come to Australia as a child. His father was an officer of the East India Company and Browne himself lived out the non-literary part of his life as a gentleman squatter, police magistrate and Gold Commissioner. Ward's comment is that 'T. A. Browne, the pillar of morality and respectability, is constantly at the elbow of "Rolf Boldrewood"' (Ward 1965, p. 205). But, in many ways, the paradoxes go much deeper. In his study, 'Sydney and the Bush', Graeme Davison has pointed out the origins of the powerful bush mythologists of the 1880s and 1890s in a city culture. Indeed, the drift of his essay is to reverse the conclusions of Ward. Rather than urban

Australia gradually adopting an outlook forged in the bush, the bush ethos was in fact 'the projection onto the outback of values revered by an alienated urban intelligentsia' (Davison 1992, p. 129). All but a few of the main contributors and most of the occasional correspondents to the *Bulletin*, the principal organ through which stories about the bush, its characters and its ethos were disseminated, were city-dwellers, in particular dwellers in the coastal cities of Sydney and Melbourne. Only Banjo Paterson possessed even a reasonable claim to being a countryman. Even then, he was the product of an old pastoralist family rather than the shearers. He was educated in the city, at Sydney Grammar School and Sydney University, and subsequently practised there as a solicitor. (When Lawson published his second book, it was Paterson who drew up the contract, although not as a fellow author but as a partner in the firm of Street and Paterson.) Moreover, although many of the writers had actually grown up in the country, especially in the declining towns of the goldfields, they subsequently left it for the coastal cities, having had their intellects awakened by country town self-improvement societies. While it is true that almost all the major writers in Australian literary history have been native born, it is surprising how many of the 'second rank' of *Bulletin* writers had come to Australia as children or young adults. Davison sums it up thus: 'rather than bush—or Australian city—origins, the recurrent feature in the biographies of the *Bulletin* writers was their arrival in Sydney or Melbourne as lone, impressionable, ambitious young men' (Davison 1992, p. 111).

Most of the 'rural *émigrés*' (to use Davison's term), who formed the groups of writers who wrote for the *Bulletin*, lived in a world of city boarding-houses. Davison provides two fascinating maps in his essay wherein the connections between the writers, the boarding-houses of the city of Sydney, and what he describes as 'the tidelands of the city: a staging point for immigrants; a haven for the drifter, the outcast, the man or woman with a past; a twilight zone of rootlessness and anomie . . . [a] sleazy urban frontier' (Davison 1992, p. 112) can be traced. Lawson is a typical example of the complex interplay between the mythology of the bush and the daily reality of city life in this strange marginal world of the city, and he shows how sophisticated the cultural mix in the bush writers was and how we should beware of seeing their mythology as a simple oppositional populism to the high cultural world of the town intellectual. Lawson came to live in the city for the first time as an adolescent of sixteen, the son of a bushman of Scandinavian origins, Peter Larsen—this, in itself, is very interesting—and his wife Louisa, a woman who had never settled to the life of a selector's wife in the country. When the marriage broke up and she brought her children to Sydney, Louisa became involved in many of the progressive and radical groups in the city, an 'infant counter-culture' in Davison's words: republican, feminist, socialist, in favour of land reform, and spiritualist, among others.

Although many of the *Bulletin* writers were city-dwelling intellectuals, their writing about the city was on the whole hostile, relentlessly satirical, concerned to reveal its squalor and the sordidness of existence within it. As their sense of the degradation of the city increased, the strength of the bush ideal grew. According to Davison, up to about 1890, a great part of Lawson's work, for example, had consisted of verse and prose about city life and the cause of Australian nationalism. It is only after that year that his interests turned decisively towards the interior of the continent. Similar changes can be observed in other city writers like Paterson. With the depression of the 1890s, with its strikes and riots, Sydney became an increasingly difficult place for a writer actually to live. In 1892, Lawson left the city to journey to the Queensland border, making his one brief—unhappy and unsuccessful—attempt to live in the outback. Even so, he was the exception among *Bulletin* writers in putting the bush ideal to the test of personal experience.

Myths of identity rooted in the life of rural Australia have continued to flourish—what else is the mythology of *Crocodile Dundee*? The four-hour-long television spectacular made to mark the Bicentennial in 1988, 'Celebration of a Nation', 'primarily rejoiced', in the words of Donald Horne, 'in a mindless, larrikin, rural Australia' (Horne 1989, p. 32). Like all enduring myths, the bush myth was able to renew itself periodically and opportunistically with whatever materials lay to hand. John Tulloch has traced its vigorous survival into and through the 1920s, in the early years of the film industry in Australia. One of the things which reinvigorated it was, curiously, the experiences and the mythology of the Australian fighting corps in the First World War. (In a later period, the film *Gallipoli* carried on the myth of an Australian army primarily recruited from the bush—recent research has shown that most of the recruits listed their occupation as 'clerk'.) The Anzacs were supposed to have carried on the traditions of the bush not only in their personal style of behaviour but also in their pioneering a kind of 'bushman' style of fighting as well, emphasising 'fitness, adaptability, respect without servility, a blend of individualism and cooperation' (Tulloch 1981, p. 351). The renewed myth of the bush coalesced in a remarkable way with the attempts of the local film industry to get off the ground. The picture presented of the country was, as one would expect, a partial one. The sexual promiscuity, gambling and stealing which records reveal of country life of the period are seldom mentioned. Tulloch notes in particular the absence of country towns from the films, despite the fact that, historically, these towns had pre-existed the selectors and their culture, having served the squatters since the middle of the nineteenth century in many cases. Their absence, a marked contrast with American films on similar themes at the time, erases an important area of cultural middle ground, and throws the relationship of city and country life into sharper but cruder contrast.

Criticism of populist myths of national identity

Whether the myths about Australian society were exemplified in literature about the pioneers or the bushmen, their view of Australian identity is essentially founded in simple ideas of working life and what is basically a popular culture. This populist view of Australian culture was always susceptible to criticism, particularly of its comprehensiveness and of its details, as I have tried to show in this chapter, but it was first attacked in terms of its fundamentals in the late 1950s and early 1960s, by writers perhaps stirred to action by the success of Ward's study of the bush legend and of works in similar vein, such as Vance Palmer's *Legend of the Nineties* (1954) and Arthur Phillips's *The Australian Tradition* (1958). (Phillips has a lasting place in the cultural history of modern Australia by coining the phrase 'cultural cringe' in 1950 to describe the colonial and dependent mentality of much of Australian history, the assumption that standards are always higher somewhere else and that the local product, especially the local cultural product, will always be inferior.)

Phillips's book was given a searching review by H. P. Heseltine in *Meanjin*, in 1962. He criticised the endlessly reiterated theme of outback values in histories of Australian culture. In particular, he doubted their adequacy as a paradigm or set of norms by which *modern* Australia could be understood, judged and lived in. His own substitute for an image of essential Australian experience was not a political myth, rooted in a particular time and place, but a kind of universal modernist angst. According to Heseltine, the constitutive centre of Australian literature was 'a sense of the horror of sheer existence . . . the terror at the basis of being' (Heseltine 1962, pp. 45, 49). Elsewhere, he offered a revisionist reading of Lawson, dismissing the political side of his work as superficial but seeing in his best writing the expression of profound feelings about the terror of the bush (Heseltine 1960–61). At roughly the same time, Wilkes also argued that the work of the writers of the 1890s in general was overrated:

> the mass of writers are men of minor talent . . . The nationalistic, patriotic, radical tendencies in the writing of the period assure it a place in Australian social history, but its place in Australian literary history must remain in doubt so long as we continue to derive its identity as a period from features such as these. (Wilkes 1962, p. 40)

A year earlier, in a similar fashion, Vincent Buckley had criticised the anti-intellectual traditions of Australian poetry and located the central concern of poetry, not in social relationships, but 'with man at a metaphysical level, reflected in his actual physical surroundings, embodied in his sensuous and spiritual reactions to his world' (Buckley 1957, p. 1).

One of the most influential attacks on the populist theory of Australian culture was delivered in the book of essays edited by Peter Coleman, with the defiant and retaliatory title of *Australian Civilization* (1962). Coleman went on to become an important spokesman for Australian culture from a conservative standpoint. He later became editor of the journal *Quadrant*, founded in 1956, and leader of the parliamentary Liberal party in New South Wales. Several of the contributors to the volume were, and some still are, major figures in the debates about Australian culture: Coleman himself, Vincent Buckley, Manning Clark, Max Harris, Donald Horne, Robert Hughes, Ken Inglis, James McAuley. While not all of the contributors fall as squarely as Coleman himself into the conservative camp, several of them, such as McAuley and Buckley, and the writers they championed like A. D. Hope, are part of an important post-war, conservative, high cultural tradition in Australian letters.

Coleman's introduction called for a re-writing of Australian cultural history which would reject the values—'radical, populist, nationalist, racialist' (Coleman 1962, p. 2)—of the 1890s. The old way of life in Australia had seen democracy and culture as somehow at odds. In the process of writing this revisionist history, some of the most precious icons of this view of Australian culture would have to be torn down. The *Bulletin* was not a saviour of the nation's art but debased and reduced literature to no more than a 'good yarn'; it fomented a naked anti-intellectualism, attacking the universities, for example. Not for the first or the last time, Lawson's chilling line that the 'rich an' educated shall be educated down' is quoted. The collection consciously foregrounds high culture, with essays on 'Liberty', 'Manners and morals', 'Intellectuals', 'The schools', 'Literature and the arts', and 'Painting'. Other essays in the collection attack familiar features of the dominant democratic–populist reading of Australian culture. McAuley, poet and university professor of English, criticises the narrow nationalism inherent in the 'radical' tradition, especially its preoccupation with the whole question of what the real, essential Australia is. This 'myth of true Australianity', found in influential works like Phillips's *Australian Tradition*, is one of the most troublesome inheritances from the dominance of 1890s' views of Australian culture. One of the features of critics in the alternative, conservative view of Australian literary history, on the other hand, is an emphasis on those writers who were in full communion, as it were, with other literary traditions, especially the central traditions of European literature and its classical background. For McAuley, the alternative tradition in Australian literary culture derives from poets such as Christopher Brennan, Associate Professor of German at Sydney University at the turn of the century. The connection with languages and cultures other than English is important to this view. Brennan's inspirations were the French poets of the Symbolist movement, with their origins in 'aristocratic' theories of 'Art for art's sake', rather than democratic populism.

For Coleman, the decisive changes in the nature of Australian society and its culture took place in the 1930s. He speaks of a 'counter-revolution' in culture, poetry and historiography at the time. 'Counter-revolution' sounds a bit like counter reformation and it is hard to resist the impression that some of the writers in the volume saw themselves engaged in a conservative backlash analogous to the Catholic church's response to the Protestant Reformation in the sixteenth and seventeenth centuries. Both Buckley and McAuley were, of course, prominent Catholic laymen, and even Manning Clark, who was not a Catholic but an Anglican, provides an essay re-assessing the religious aspects of Australian culture entitled simply 'Faith'. Ward points out in his book, by contrast, how hostile to religion the bushmen and their culture were. The dominant writers in this counter-revolution, which gave Australians a new sense of their cultural identity, are writers who began to come into prominence in the 1930s and 1940s: the poets Buckley, McAuley, Kenneth Slessor, A. D. Hope, and Douglas Stewart, and the novelists Henry Handel Richardson, and Patrick White. For Buckley, these writers are united by what he calls 'vitalism', which takes many forms, but which may include:

> an insistence on the almost metaphysical status of sheer *Will,* a mental energy working beyond moral considerations, beyond Good and Evil. It may be a Bergsonian sort of reliance on the power of an evolving nature, which man must co-operate with. It may be a mental or aesthetic Dionysianism . . . it may be a reliance on the supreme importance of the moment, on joyful self-expression, on impulse and sensation, with an overture played by an orchestra of resuscitated Pagan deities. (Buckley 1959b, pp. 46–7)

It is very striking in this view how important it has become to speak of Australian culture in ways which transcend the limitations of local history, or time and space in general for that matter, which stress the role of the individual imagination and will rather than the experience of the collective, and find ways of contextualising Australian identity which link it with European high culture and philosophy, with Bergson and Nietzsche, and with the wider history and mythology of the classical world, with Dionysus and pagan deities.

Nor did attacks on the democratic–populist conception of Australian identity come only from the political right. The emergent 'new left' of the late 1960s also found much of the *Bulletin* and its culture hard to stomach. The most influential book produced in this line of thought in the period, Humphrey McQueen's *A New Britannia* (1970), argued that almost all aspects of white Australian culture pre-1915 were tainted with racism and nationalism. Because of this right-wing populist legacy, the orthodox channels of Australian radicalism, such as the Labor party, were doomed to ineffectiveness. Another important essay from this direction at this time is R. W. Connell's 'Images of Australia' (1968). Connell criticised the endless repetition of a small group of themes, even the repetition of certain words and phrases, which he traced back to the power of the influence of Hancock's *Australia*. Hancock had established a distinctive pattern of motifs in talking about Australian culture: the shaping of society through the harsh conditions of living on the land and conquering it; the development of sectional conflict, although in a vacuum of ideas—socialism without doctrines; the emergence of a democratic order coupled with Australian nationalism. This nationalism was essentially a working-class phenomenon in opposition to the value systems of an Anglicised upper class. The great weakness in all of this, according to Connell, is that Hancock is 'insensitive to the role of ideas in Australian public life' (Connell 1968, p. 16)—a theme which strongly echoes the viewpoint of Manning Clark, of course. One of the consequences of this stance was that for all the attention paid to life in the bush almost none was paid to the growth of Australian cities and Australia's urban culture. Writing in 1968, Connell could not find 'one competent history of any of Australia's major cities' (Connell 1968, p. 12) in any of the general histories of Australia.

Australian culture, 1930–50

How accurate is Coleman's sense of the 1930s marking an epoch in the history of Australian culture? As I have tried to show in chapter 2, it was certainly a period in which there was much soul-searching about 'culture' all over the western world. If nationalism dominated nineteenth-century speculations about cultural identity—leading to nationalist myths like the bushman in Australia—then the early twentieth century was characterised by speculation about culture in which it was the international rather than the national angle which predominated. The urgent questions of the modern world were not whether one's culture was English, or Australian, or whatever, but whether the modern world supported culture in a traditional sense at all, whether the artistic standards of one's society were locked in an inevitable slide or not. F. R. Leavis had a powerful—sometimes contradictory and always complex—influence on many aspects of

Australian thinking about art and culture in this period and for a long time after. Leavis was a potent influence on Buckley for example, underpinning his concern to form a canon of Australian literature, an alternative to the one which had been handed down from the 1890s.[6] Through his abiding concern with critical evaluation and cultural 'standards', Leavis was a strong influence on other members of the conservative group as well, like Leonie Kramer, Professor of Australian Literature and later Chancellor of the University of Sydney. On the other hand, Hope and McAuley were hostile to his influence, in particular because of the high valuation he placed on the great poets of the modernist movement, like Eliot.

Many of the laments about culture made by Leavis and his circle in England found their counterparts in Australia, and there was often the same kind of hope for an alternative. One of the most influential, as Connell pointed out, was Keith Hancock's cultural history of Australia, called simply *Australia*, and published in 1930. Hancock applied Tocqueville's analysis of the democratic culture of America to Australia, seeing the new federal capital of Canberra itself as a massive symbol of the 'middling standard' that he had castigated as one of the by-products of the democratic system. In the chapter on 'Literature and art', aside from giving some lukewarm praise for a handful of books and authors, his chief culprit is in the field of literary criticism, where 'the "middling standard" is nowhere more apparent. Australia, as always, is merciful to the average' (Hancock 1961, p. 262). This democratic curse of mediocrity can be found even in the language that Australians use. The Australian language is smaller and simpler than the vocabulary of the middle-class Englishman, 'for Australia does not tolerate forms of thought and expression (such as irony) which are perplexing or offensive to the average man' (Hancock 1961, p. 252). On the other hand, Hancock certainly did not see the future as all gloom. He found a 'new wealth' in some areas of the language as well, 'expressive of a vigorous and distinctive life, material for an individual literature' (Hancock 1961, p. 252). The best hope was for a new, strong cultural leadership, a claim echoed many times in other writing in the 1920s and 1930s. It can be seen, for instance, in *Kangaroo* (1923), D. H. Lawrence's novel about Australia.

This was not the first time that the desire for leadership in Australian culture in a more traditional, high cultural, sense was voiced. David Walker (1976) has traced the careers of the circle which congregated around Vance and Nettie Palmer in Melbourne from the time of the First World War, which for many years provided a strong focus for Australian intellectual life. The Palmers in particular were indefatigable writers, critics and, later on, broadcasters on a wide range of aspects of Australian culture, with a particularly strong commitment to Australian literature. The temper of the Palmers's intellectual life, a mixture of literary, left political and nationalist commitment has gone deep into the wider intellectual life of Australia, and can still be traced in the continued existence of journals like *Meanjin*, which they helped to found in 1940. The difference between them and the writers that Coleman is discussing is that they remained committed to a view of Australia rooted in the traditions of the 1890s; one of Vance Palmer's last books, published in 1954, was *The Legend of the Nineties*. The last chapter, 'A lost tradition?', still sees the tradition of democratic writing strongly marked in Australian fiction: 'never, or very rarely, written from the eyrie of a detached observer, well above the crowd, but from some point in the working community' (Palmer 1954, p. 149). It was their hope that an Australian culture could still be built which would be loyal to the values of Furphy and Lawson, working-class and nationalistic, with the bush continuing to be the mainspring of its literature, and yet free of their parochialism. It was a tall order and the delicate balance implied was destined to be broken. In a way, Palmer himself realised this. He rejected the help of the world of the universities as being too conservative and still saw some necessary conflict between fine writing and politics, declaring in a famous statement that it was nationalists, not cultured writers, who were needed at present.

The Palmers and their circle struggled in a time which most critics and historians have seen as one of the most barren in Australia's cultural life. Richard White has traced how the bohemian world of the 1890s did a kind of back-flip into taking a stand *against* European decadence by the 1920s. The bohemians of Australia dissociated themselves in particular from the less socially desirable aspects of the *fin de siècle*, its middle-aged world weariness and its revolutionary politics in particular, adopting instead a spirit that was 'healthily boyish' (White 1981, p. 116). In 1916, the painter Frederick McCubbin actually warned native-born artists against visiting Paris, where they might easily be corrupted by fads and fashions. According to White, by the 1920s many of the painters of the late nineteenth century were portrayed as bulwarks of sanity and normality against the unhealthiness of foreign influences. In the ever-increasing stress on physical health and wholesomeness in the national character, the image of outback Australia constructed by the bohemians of the late nineteenth century was gradually reduced to what White calls wattle, sunshine, and White Australia. Over the period 1890–1930, the national image shifted from the bushman to the less socially threatening one of the 'digger', an essentially white-collar worker with a 'larrikin' streak, to the final indignity of the 'little boy from Manly'. Many of the people who might have formed the cultural avant-garde of Australia left the country, spending long periods overseas, twenty or thirty years in some instances, or, in many cases, not returning at all. The phenomenon of expatriation is one of the most striking in the period. Over one-third of Australian Rhodes scholars never returned to their native land.

On the other hand, cultural historians have generally seen the period between 1930 and 1950 as marking a profound change in Australia's *public* culture. Doubtless, as everywhere else, the Second World War was a powerful catalyst of social progress. From the early 1930s there was a marked expansion in many aspects of public life, especially those which affected the higher end of the socio–cultural spectrum. The founding of the Australian Broadcasting Corporation in 1932 was to exercise an immeasurable influence on the public's attitudes to the arts, especially to music. For many years, the production of classical music in Australia was almost synonymous with the ABC as the ABC was the only employer of symphony orchestras in the country. Other manifestations of a wider and more sophisticated patronage of the arts can be seen, for example, in the establishment of the Contemporary Art Society in 1938, the influential exhibition of modern art sponsored by the *Melbourne Herald* in 1939, and the founding of the literary magazines, *Southerly*, in 1939, and *Meanjin*, in 1940. (Both these magazines continue to flourish, incidentally.) In public life understood in less obviously artistic terms, the Commonwealth Scientific and Industrial Research Organization was also a product of the 1930s and was part of a major expansion of the public service in Australia, not only in terms of absolute numbers but in terms of significance and influence. A similar kind of expansion in the public domain occurred in the universities as well and had a similar effect; a slightly later manifestation of this is the foundation of the Australian National University in 1946. Indeed, a major contribution of the universities to the wider national life was felt for the first time in this period. When H. C. ('Nugget') Coombs joined the Treasury in the 1930s, he was only the second university trained economist to be employed in that branch of the public service. By the 1940s, however, there was for the first time a powerful intelligentsia involved in government decision making. Even dissident intellectuals became more prominent in public life in the period; they had become, paradoxically, both more central to and more critical of public policy than ever before.

Richard White sees the new sophistication of public life as linked, interestingly, to a new industrialism. This is a significant local inflexion of the widespread hostility of high culture to industrialism elsewhere, in England and Germany, for example. White points to joint schemes mooted between art and industry in this period. The *Australia National Journal,* founded in 1939, edited by Sydney Ure Smith and backed by Charles Lloyd Jones, the retailer, aimed 'to give expression to our progress in Art, Architecture and Industry'. The editor hoped that Australia's isolation would end and that the journal 'should quickly become a vehicle for all forms of expression in the Arts and Industry . . . and form a practical link between them' (White 1981, pp. 148–9). One aspect of this sophisticated industrialism during this period was the sustained attempt to move the national self-image of Australia and Australians away from the relatively simple picture of rural Australia to that of a more sophisticated urban culture. This was in many ways more than wishful thinking. The percentage of Australia's workforce engaged in primary production continued to fall throughout the 1930s and 1940s, again doubtless partly due to the coming of the war. The shift from country can also be seen in the transformations of Australia's cultural icons and myths. White associates this period with the growth of the cult of the Bondi lifesaver. While this is a development of the digger and still a myth centred on physical prowess and 'health'—it is hardly a sophisticated image—it is obviously a strong city image as well. It locates the 'real' Australia away from the bush, in the coastal city, and not just in any coastal town but in the metropolis of Sydney. It was the first time, perhaps, that the essentially urban nature of the Australian population and its aspirations had been so freely admitted.

The 'great Australian stupor'

The period since the end of the Second World War has been marked by similar oscillations between populist and more sophisticated, élitist conceptions of what the distinctive nature of Australian culture is. The socially progressive years of the war were ended by the long period of conservative government, many of them under R. G. Menzies—a period encapsulated in Ronald Conway's (1971) famous phrase as the 'great Australian stupor'. Whatever the material advantages of life in the period, few people who grew up in Australia in the 1950s and early 1960s remember it as an exciting place to be for intellectuals. (I suspect that this scenario was not unique and that similar points could be made about growing up in that period elsewhere too.) In another memorable phrase, the novelist Patrick White, who returned to Australia in 1948 after a long period of living in Europe, referred to 'the Great Australian Emptiness', (White 1958, p. 38) where the mind is the least important of possessions, and where what little intellectual life there is is run by journalists and schoolteachers. In the 1950s, Australia became part of the international cold war propaganda which linked materialism and a conservative outlook with the preservation of democracy.

Yet attacks on this gross materialism, hedonism and philistinism of Australian society are one of the most prominent themes of writing about Australia in the 1950s and 1960s and came from both the left and the right. On the left, the 'Godzone' debate in journals like *Meanjin* in the mid-1960s vilified Australians as willing, not just passive, victims, in this grotesque materialism, betraying the Australian sense of identity which intellectuals had defended. From the right, one of the most influential commentaries was *Australian Accent* by John Douglas Pringle, published in 1958. Pringle indeed lamented the anti-intellectual nature of Australian life, but, on the other hand, he also saw possibilities for a new Australian culture in writers like McAuley, Stewart and Hope. His chapter on poetry is subtitled, interestingly in the light of Coleman's slightly later book, 'the counter-revolution'. What intrigued Pringle is that this new Australian literature of quality should have turned its back so deliberately on Australia itself and its literary traditions, as if quality, almost by definition, could not be found in local models, and that nationalism and artistic excellence were doomed to fight on opposite sides.

The most important commentary on the post-war period, though, was Donald Horne's *The Lucky Country*, published in 1964. The twin themes of the book are Australia's material prosperity and the meagreness of its intellectual achievements. As is well realised by people who have actually read the book, its title is ironic: fully thirty years ago, Horne was in no doubt that national prosperity in the future would be linked to intellectual rather than material resources and that Australia's luck in one department could well be its ruin in another. For Horne, the fundamental mark of distinction for Australia is that it is 'deeply populist' (Horne 1971, p. 47)—its dominant ideologies are egalitarianism, fraternalism, gregariousness. Moreover, these are no longer the traits of an oppositional working class. Like many other commentators of the period, Horne sees Australia as a triumph of *embourgeoisement*: the populism of Australian society is no longer expressed in class conflict or radical nationalism but in suburbanism. The other side of this, of course, is the poverty of Australia's 'culture'—in this respect Horne is squarely in the tradition of modernist thought. Cleverness is considered un-Australian; everyday life is dull; such élites as exist are second-rate, and over everything there is a 'triumphant mediocrity' (Horne 1971, p. 22). Even in those areas of conscious high culture, the tone is often banal. ABC concerts show a preference for the middle-brow; there is a diffidence about quality—the majority want to consume culture, to enjoy it—so that there is a kind of 'give-it-a-go flavour' in Australian art. Criticism is poor and cliquish, full of knocking and backbiting. Australian schools are poor: in some secondary schools as many as 50 per cent of the teachers do not have degrees. Whereas before 1939, our universities were 'high provincial standard' (Horne 1971, p. 205), faithful if rather dull copies of English and Scottish red-brick, now they have become degree-shops. Staff–student ratios are far too high. Few non-scientist academics are distinguished, and the prevailing tone is one of 'isolation and self-pity' (Horne 1971, p. 208). Australia has never had a cultivated leisure class and lacks one now. There are no periodicals or quality press, so that people get away with expressing things that would not be tolerated in more sophisticated societies; politicians go unsatirised. Intellectuals, in the sense of creative thinkers who are publicly influential, simply do not exist in Australia [what did Horne think of his own role, one wonders] making 'Australia one of the oddest countries in the world' (Horne 1971, p. 213).

Recently, however, a more balanced picture of the era has begun to emerge. Something of the change can be gauged from the way articles about Australia in the 1950s have been appearing in magazines and colour supplements, always good indices of changes in fashion. On 18 September 1993, the *Australian*'s entire weekend magazine was given over to a retrospective on the 1950s, in which the suburban material prosperity of the period seemed now innocently charming— certainly as compared with the Roman excesses of the 1980s—rather than the end of culture as we know it. Looked at from the perspective of the early 1990s, after several years of deep recession and high unemployment, the economic well-being of the period is less lightly dismissed. Much of the hostility to the period is a function of Labor party mythology, a feeling that Labor was unfairly robbed of govern- ment in the middle of the decade. The morning after Paul Keating won (against all expectations) a fifth term for Labor in 1993, after the traditional speeches of reconciliation given the night before, he spoke on television of the pleasure it gave him to have driven a dagger into the heart of Menzies-style liberalism. Nevertheless, the real social achievements and changes of the 1950s—not the least of which was presiding over a program of mass migration which totally transformed the nature of Australian society and culture—make the social changes of the 1980s, though admittedly under very different economic circumstances, seem rather insubstantial.

There is a great need to hold a more circumspect view of the culture of the period as well. Wilkes, for example, has stressed the high cultural achievements of the period, such as the Elizabethan Theatre Trust, which was founded in 1954 following the historic visit to Australia of Queen Elizabeth and Prince Philip—the first visit to Australia by a reigning monarch. The Trust was established to improve the standards of the performing arts in Australia, although it was soon criticised for raising these standards at the expense of importing too many overseas stars and of betraying its artistic mission by pandering to the box office. Wilkes has also drawn attention to the differences between the views of writers and social critics. While the social critics continued to assail the cultural emptiness and materialism of Australia, creative writers worked to identify a strain of idealism in Australian life. In some ways this is a development of the Buckley thesis about the importance of vitalism in Australian literature. One might add that the very strength of the criticism of national life and culture is a testimony to the presence, albeit in a minority, of a vigorous intellectual climate. The other side of the vilification of what Australia has become is an idealism of what it might be. McAuley's work in the period often plays off this contrast. While one would not want to agree with all that was produced by the conservative intellectual tradition in the period, it is still an impressive body of work. When one looks back at the period it is surprising how long the list of high cultural achievement is: the beginning of Clark's history of Australia; the work of poets in the Brennan tradition like Buckley, Hope, Slessor and McAuley; the internationally recognised work of artists like Nolan and Boyd. We may not have had a film industry, but we had the novels of Patrick White.

Whitlam and after

The election of the Labor government of Gough Whitlam in 1972 has been widely perceived as a watershed in many aspects of Australian culture, in the arts not least of them. It was the first time that any political party in Australia had provided an arts policy for a general election. Many new initiatives in the arts and culture became associated with this government and other Labor governments of the period, like Don Dunstan's in South Australia, and, slightly later on, Neville Wran's in New South Wales. One of the first was the establishment of the Australia Council, the major government funding body for the arts, in December 1972, although it was based upon authorities set in place by prior conservative governments. The most distinctive features of the Council were its independence from political interference—a complaint often levelled against arts funding bodies which existed previously—and the sheer expansion of its budget. The Labor government effectively doubled the amount spent on the arts, from $7.5 million at the time of its election to around $14 million at the establishment of the Australia Council. Arts funding has never regained the level of those heady days and was severely cut back during the terms of the Fraser coalition government: the Council's 1993 budget of $53 million—slightly less than the City of Berlin's annual expenditure on its philharmonic orchestra—is nowhere near the 1972 funding level in real terms.[7] Not surprisingly the Whitlam government was widely supported by artists and intellectuals. When it was threatened in 1974, Australia's recent Nobel Laureate in Literature, Patrick White, spoke at public meetings in support of it. Whitlam himself took on the Arts portfolio and his own scholarly bearing, a QC well read in classical history among many other things, seemed to epitomise the new sense of direction. Perhaps the most important underlying change was the re-association of nationalism, left politics and high art. For the first time a revived Australian nationalism became possible within the framework of high culture, rather than in opposition to it.

One would still be wise, however, to avoid simple antinomies between high culture and populism in views of the national self-image since the 1970s. At times these two views of Australian culture seem opposites only in the sense of being two sides of the same coin. The Whitlam years saw as well the birth of the latest manifestation of the image of Australian philistinism in the figure of the 'ocker', even more dedicated to the overthrow of sophisticated values than any of his many predecessors. Something of the contradictory nature of this can be seen in the fate of the film industry. The changed cultural temper of the 1970s was nowhere more visible, surely, than in the restored Australian film industry. The new wave of Australian film did not just give us 'quality' products—romantic images of our national past like *Picnic at Hanging Rock*, whose pictures were closely linked to the already legitimated art of the Heidelberg School, or searching, critical looks at our history like *The Chant of Jimmy Blacksmith*—it also positively celebrated the very philistinism it was supposed to be destroying. One of the very earliest of the successes of this new wave, and certainly the first to be a major success overseas, was *The Adventures of Barry Mackenzie*. It was an odd film to inaugurate an intellectual renaissance, glorifying as it did all the coarsest features of Australian populism: boozing, womanising, xenophobia, contempt for artists and intellectuals in particular. The production of the film was made possible through the heroic efforts of Barry Jones and Phillip Adams especially, two warriors in the cause of Australian culture if there ever were ones. Yet, most paradoxical of all, Whitlam himself conspired with this ockerism, actually appearing *in propria persona* in the sequel, *Barry Mackenzie Holds His Own*.

The story of Barry Mackenzie illustrates the close and sometimes contradictory connection between high art and popular culture that has always been a peculiar feature of Australian life. In some ways, this could be claimed to be the most distinctive aspect of our national culture. Much of our popular culture has been the creation of our intellectuals. This has been the case from the myths of the bush created amongst a radical city intelligentsia in the 1890s to the satirical masterpieces of Barry Humphries in our own time. The creator of the character on which the film of Barry Mackenzie was based, Humphries is a striking witness of this. It is extraordinary that the person who has done more to expose the worst excesses of Australian philistinism to the rest of the world should be himself a kind of antipodean Oscar Wilde: aesthete and dandy, practitioner of the arts—painter and poet, but also scholar and collector—expert on the art, literature and culture of modernism.

In the late 1980s and 1990s, this paradoxical nature of Australian culture continues to assert itself. Reports of the death of populism are greatly exaggerated. As late as 1988, in the very year of Australia's Bicentennary celebrations, it was widely believed that the next federal prime minister might be the Premier of Queensland, Sir Joh Bjelke-Petersen, a man seen by television interviewer Richard Carleton, 'as unable to put three words of the English language together without making a mistake'. The so-called 'white shoe brigade' which backed the 'Joh for PM' campaign so vigorously, provided visible proof that Australian populism was still alive and kicking. On the other hand, the campaign collapsed like a balloon once it crossed the Queensland border. Likewise, the depiction of the boozing, brawling, Donaher family in their opulent waterside house in *Sylvania Waters*—like something straight out of *The Lucky Country* thirty years ago—caused as much consternation amongst middle-class Australian viewers as it did amongst the watchers of the BBC for whom the series was originally made.

Although there is plenty of old-fashioned populism to be had in the beer ads that punctuate the one-day cricket as it is televised on Channel 9, there have been new and subtler forms of it as well, as it has learned to move with the times and take on new forms in a changing world. Noel King and Tim Rowse have traced a particularly interesting manifestation of it in the 'humanity ads' which are now so common on our television screens. These are the advertisements which begin with a narrative or voice-over, coming from the voices of 'ordinary Australians', depicting plain virtues and offering home-spun social commentary. Only towards the end of the clip does it become apparent that it is an advertisement at all and the name of the product is revealed. There is very little said about the product being advertised: 'the ad is calculated not to *describe* a good but to *identify* a product, a sentiment or a service with an imagined community' (King and Rowse 1990, p. 39). It is often hard to differentiate these kinds of ads from genuine community messages, such as those issued by the 'I am Australian' group, which follow a similar format and end telling the astonished viewer that 'I am—you are—we are . . . Australian'. King and Rowse see the historical context of these ads stretching back to the 1940s in the sense of fraternalism that is so strong a part of Australian tradition, especially on the left. But the distinctive feature of this populism is its lack of an aggressive edge, the absence of an 'other' at the expense of whose exclusion this sense of fraternalism is gained. This was the distinctive feature of the populism of the past: the mateship of the shearers was built on the exclusion of Aborigines, women and the Chinese. In contrast this seems a populism of Australia in a multicultural era. Its distinctiveness is its inclusiveness. It is a 'non-antagonistic mobilisation of a sense of community' (King and Rowse 1990, p. 39). The only qualification for membership is that you are ordinary and unpretentious. Perhaps here though, despite what King and Rowse say, there is an other being constructed for exclusion—what of those who don't warm to this kind of propaganda, who don't see preten-tiousness as invariably a moral and social weakness? For all its triteness, the 'I am Australian' campaign seems to imply that there are some people inhabiting this country who are *not* Australians, that there is something more to being an Australian—what and defined by whom?—than living here and paying one's taxes.

Since the Dawkins' reforms in higher education in the late 1980s, it has become commonplace to speak of Australia's need to become a clever country, and yet Dr Hewson's doctorate continued to be useful as a stick to beat him with. It seemed to epitomise his widely perceived lack of the moral and social values of ordinary Australians. I wonder what John Singleton thinks of *him*. When the Prime Minister wanted to really get at him, he created even more damage with his erstwhile title of 'professor'. Bob Hawke, on the other hand, had been a Rhodes scholar at Oxford (like one or two of the other members of his government), the possessor like Hewson of a post-graduate degree, yet his public image was if anything even more 'ocker' than that of many less academically honoured prime ministers of the past—think of how he compares with Fraser or Menzies. It has been left to his successor as prime minister to ally himself with the high culture lobby.

Paul Keating is a good place to end, because he illustrates the complex nature of the populism of both the past and the present. He must be one of the least educated in conventional terms in his party and yet, curiously, his image contains quite a lot of the dour intellectual. He is a skilled player of hard ball in the House and in the party room and yet he has almost nothing of the populist campaigner about him. He has made no secret of his distaste for the 'vaudeville' of politics, 'trailing round shopping centres, tripping over television leads' as he said memorably of the former prime minister. Unlike his predecessor he has little interest in sport, while much is made of his knowledge of antique clocks and his liking for classical music. In a strange way he has made a kind of larrikinism—a refusal to do what was expected—out of *not* being a boozer, womaniser, sports fanatic or whatever. Annita Keating complements this picture in interesting ways as well. She is an odd piece in the multicultural picture of contemporary Australia. Her 'foreignness', especially her strong accent, is a decided asset here, but it is not her 'ordinariness' exactly, after the manner of the humanity ad, which is made use of. At the 2000 Olympics selection in Monte Carlo in 1993, her accent and the sentence she spoke in three *European* languages were a valuable counterpoint to the conventional populism, slouch hats and beaches which seemed to dominate much of the rest of the presen-tation. Her Europeanness is very much part of the Keatings' myth of a new cultured Australia. When she launched Children's Book Week on Television and Cinema in August 1993, she made no secret of her own distaste for television. Her own four children were seldom allowed to watch it—'they're simply too busy with things such as piano practice, ballet and choir', she said. She saw the main value of 'quality' films and television (somewhat paradoxically) in encouraging children to read—and presumably watch television a lot less.[8]

It is widely recognised that the support of the arts community played a significant role in the surprise re-election of the Labor government in 1993. The warm reception the Prime Minister got when he launched Labor's arts policy himself at the State Theatre in Sydney has been seen as a turning-point in the fortunes of Labor's whole campaign. In the Budget which followed the win, the arts community was treated favourably at a time of some financial restraint. Another part of this new prominence for the arts was the development of a new Cultural Policy, first scheduled to appear in early 1994, but delayed until October 1994.

Part of the problem formulating cultural policy seems to be with the ministerial portfolio itself. Ministries of 'Culture' are quite common in Europe, but the English-speaking world has shown a marked aversion to them, preferring the more readily definable, but also more limited, portfolio for the 'Arts'. In this, Australia is no different. Added to this, the portfolio is held usually by a very junior minister, on his or her way to something more interesting like Finance or Employment, or, at the other extreme, by the Prime Minister. It is surprising how many prime ministers and state premiers, especially Labor ones, have liked the idea of combining the Arts portfolio with their other duties. After the 1993 election, the leader of the Opposition took over the shadow Arts portfolio himself as well. While this ensures the Arts get a 'profile', it can hardly ensure that cultural policy gets much real attention from an already seriously overworked chief executive. The situation is a curious vestige of a nineteenth-century idea that the arts are something in which a gentleman takes interest in his spare time, like Gladstone producing translations of Homer. Much the same situation has operated with this government's cultural policy: there is no doubt that the Prime Minister is a strong and genuine supporter of the arts, but the ministry seems doomed to be passed around like a hot potato, or perhaps a cold potato is the more apt simile. Nobody in it ever seems to actually know anything about art or culture, although they always seem very keen—they talk a lot about the 'learning curve' on which they are embarked. Arts ministers come and go with a predictable regularity. The minister appointed after the 1993 election, Senator McMullan, from whom much was expected in terms of policy, lasted only a few months; following a cabinet reshuffle, he went on to higher things at the ministry of Trade. What had been a separate Arts portfolio was once again combined with Communications and Tourism; McMullan was replaced by a very young new minister, Michael Lee, tipped for future high office by the Prime Minister himself, although again on his own admission knowing almost nothing about the field.

The policy, entitled *Creative Nation*, was finally released in October 1994 with much fanfare. By way of build-up, in announcing the recipients of the Senior Creative Fellowships (almost universally known as 'the Keatings') the day before, the Prime Minister said that the awards were unashamedly about excellence. He encapsulated the philosophy behind them as: 'if you're good, you're in it; if you're not, you're out'.

On the whole, however, the policy clearly aimed to strike a balance in pursuing what it described as the 'twin goals of democracy and excellence' (*Creative Nation*, p. 5). The epigraph to the preamble, prepared by the Cultural Policy Advisory Panel, established in July 1992 before the 1993 election, states that 'Democracy is the key to cultural value' (*Creative Nation*, p. 1). Both the preamble and the introduction are a mixture of Raymond Williams and Matthew Arnold: Australian culture is 'our entire mode of life' (*Creative Nation*, p.1); 'it at once assures us of who we are and inspires us with intimations of the heights we might reach' (*Creative Nation*, p. 5). The other side to this discourse is, however, always present, in terms familiar from the modernist critique of the 1930s: 'what is distinctively Australian about our culture is under assault from homogenised international mass culture' (*Creative Nation*, p. 1).

The document oscillates (sometimes markedly) between these views of Australia's cultural future. Despite the Arnoldian professions of the introduction, within a few pages of the beginning, the policy is clearly focused on 'Art'. One of the main initiatives of the policy is to establish a new board of the Australia Council, the Major Organisations Board, to recognise the 'special requirements of major performing arts organisations' (*Creative Nation*, p. 16). (There has already been some criticism from smaller organisations about the imbalance in funding this is likely to create.) The policy proposes the establishment of a National Institute for Indigenous Performing Arts to have the same status as the National Institute for Dramatic Art, the Australian Ballet School and the Australian Film, Television and Radio School—and the establishment of a National Academy of Music, to focus on 'fine music, including contemporary and Australian works' (*Creative Nation*, p. 25). Perhaps the most overtly élitist move is the transfer of the Sydney Symphony Orchestra from the ABC to local control and the injection of significant funds 'for developing it to world standard' (*Creative Nation*, p. 26). The previous managerial arrangement is criticised for being 'concerned with equalising standards, [which] . . . while democratic in spirit . . . can have a flattening effect on quality, style and enthusiasm. It is time for the Sydney orchestra to be given the opportunity and freedom to excel' (*Creative Nation*, p. 27).

It was widely rumoured that this kind of cultural élitism, especially the musical emphasis, displayed the Prime Minister's personal stamp, but the document is interesting in that it appears to reflect other aspects of his personal views as well, in particular the concern for broad cultural vision and a sense of the interconnection between culture, technology and the economy. From the beginning, cultural 'openness' is seen as a kind of parallel to economic deregulation: 'there is much to gain and little to fear from being open to the world. It is as true of the culture as it is of the economy (*Creative Nation*, p. 6). There is a thorough-going optimism about the economic spin-offs of cultural innovation. The last few chapters of the policy bear titles such as 'Investing in our culture', and 'Cultural tourism'. The phrase 'cultural industry' is used throughout the document in a manner which seems unaware of the pejorative connotations that Adorno, its originator, gave to it. The focus of this in *Creative Nation* is on the development of multi-media, in essence the production of CD-ROM titles for personal computers, described in the chapter's subtitle as 'Cultural production in an information age' (*Creative Nation*, p. 55). The policy has a firm sense of the changed role of technology in culture in the 1990s: information technology has 'crossed the technical into the realm of consciousness, the realm of culture' (*Creative Nation*, p. 55).

At the same time, it is not always easy to see exactly what is 'cultural' about the policy of investing in the production of multi-media 'content'. The primary motives seem economic; there is little sense in the document of the 'artistic' potential of multi-media, for example. There is, overall, an unbridged gap between a cultural policy of the high arts, on the one hand, and a policy of social and economic life more broadly defined, on the other. The twin goals of democracy and culture, which the policy identifies in its introduction, are the ones which have been at issue since the beginnings of the European settlement of Australia. *Creative Nation* is a genuine attempt to address both, but it seems too early to speak of a rapprochement between them.

QUALITY AND POPULARITY IN THE AUSTRALIAN MEDIA

The development of the mass media

Modernism's anxiety complex about mass culture developed in an era which saw an unprecedented expansion in the amount and availability of written information and of profound changes in the techniques of its transmission. The world of international capitalism, which in Queen Victoria's reign had England at its heart, relied upon the labours of a whole army of clerks. The number of male white-collar workers increased from 262 000 in 1871 to 918 000 in 1911.[1] By 1911, the clerical profession, including a significant 124 000 women, was the largest and most rapidly expanding occupational group in Britain. The sheer scale of the 'textuality' over which they presided is quite daunting.

This sector of the economy was increasingly affluent. It had more money to spend and, with the drop in the average working week after 1918 from 55 hours to 48, more leisure hours to spend it in. Although it was upwardly mobile socially, this necessarily literate work force was not, however, well-educated. In 1900, 40 per cent of English children still left school before the statutory age of fourteen.[2] In 1926, less than ten per cent of children proceeded from elementary school to secondary school. It was rare for children of poor backgrounds to go to university. Financial aid was limited: in 1921, more than 2000 qualified for the 200 available state scholarships; on the other hand, more than 75 per cent of those attending university went without any form of scholarship at all.

The modern popular daily press, which effectively began in Britain with the publication in 1896 of Lord Northcliffe's *Daily Mail*, was designed to cater for this imperfectly educated yet literate and upwardly mobile readership. Northcliffe directed his journalists to write for 'an audience eager to keep up appearances' (LeMahieu 1988, p. 8). The majority of these journalists, like their readers, were poorly educated: most were recruited from the provinces and few had been educated beyond the age of fourteen. As a result, the papers espoused an anti-intellectualism on the one hand and a marked populism on the other. Much of their style and many of their practices derived from the traditions of nineteenth-century popular culture. The 'news' had a way of becoming the 'human interest' story, written up according to the conventions of nineteenth-century melodrama. These papers created also a pantheon of 'personalities', journalists who wrote regular columns, a practice which had its counterpart in the star system of the movies.

It would be a mistake, however, to fail to acknowledge the inherent social (and even, occasionally, intellectual and aesthetic) progressiveness of the popular press. Northcliffe was obsessed with *modernity*; he was fascinated by speed and technology. The slogan of the *Daily Mail* was the 'Busy Man's Newspaper'. He was convinced also of the coming economic and social power of women; the *Daily Mirror* was originally designed not only to be read by women as the first 'women's paper' but, more astonishingly given the time in which it was first published, to be written entirely by a staff of female journalists. Journalism by and for women began in the popular press. The house style of the popular press, summed up in the word 'tabloid' coined by Northcliffe himself in 1900–the terse prose, the use of bold headlines, the move towards a predominantly graphic style, producing a paper which would not so much be read as 'looked-at'— gradually transformed the quality press as well. Photojournalism, which had been pioneered in the British popular press in the early part of the century, was eventually adopted by the *Times* in 1922 when it published its first picture page. LeMahieu's conclusion is that the *Times* of 1930 looked much more like the *Daily Mail* of 1900 than the *Times* of 1900.

The origins of film, like the popular press, lie deep in nineteenth-century popular culture, in vaudeville and music hall as well as in melodrama. The first film ever to be shown in Australia was presented by Carl Hertz, an American vaudeville entertainer, in Melbourne in May 1896. Ruth Megaw's comment on the very early history of film in Australia is that 'for many years the film continued to be regarded as a form of cheap popular entertainment, similar to the circus, and without the artistic potential of the theatre' (Megaw 1985, p. 25).

The aura of cheapness was tempered fairly quickly, however, by some of the huge and ornate film venues available as early as 1910 in the major cities (the Melba in Melbourne and the Crystal Palace in Sydney). Likewise, film developed in artistic terms. In America, directors such as D. W. Griffith took on vast and impressive subjects. LeMahieu credits Griffith's success as a director with 'his ability to integrate cinematic technique with the dramatic traditions of popular theatre' (LeMahieu 1988, pp. 65–6). His development of rapid and dramatic cutting between scenes, used in a melodramatic way to heighten the emotional impact of his narratives, was later developed in a more consciously artful manner as 'montage' by the great Russian director Sergei Eisenstein. The films of Charlie Chaplin, which made him one of the earliest superstars of the cinema, were also some of the first films to be admired widely by intellectuals. Gradually film acquired an intellectual respectability and a canon of film art to go with it. Film Societies encouraged the showing of art films to complement (and in many cases to resist) the commercial cinema. In 1930, John Grierson organised for the London Film Society the first screening in England of Eisenstein's *Battleship Potemkin* (1926), with his own pioneering documentary *Drifters*, influenced by Eisenstein's work and theory, as the support feature. The journal *Close Up* was founded in 1927 as an organ of avant-garde film criticism and ran until 1933. The British Film Institute's *Sight and Sound* has been going strong since 1932. Film criticism began to appear in the quality press in the 1920s and by 1930 Paul Rotha could speak of a whole *tradition* of aesthetic experience in film (Rotha 1949).

Unfortunately, there is a downside to the kind of thinking about film that Rotha's book represents. As a connoisseurship of fine film developed so there was constructed a paradigm of the art and its industry. On one side was Hollywood, admittedly the producer of many notable films, but with its roots irredeemably in popular culture; on the other side, there was Europe, with an antithetical tradition of film 'art'. For Rotha, Europe is unquestionably the source of the best films. In his quest for a legitimate aesthetic of film, he set himself squarely against American influence, its films, its star system, even the development of sound which he saw as a deflection of the essentially visual nature of the medium. In a similar fashion, Grierson, although he had first become strongly interested in the social potential of film while visiting America on a Rockefeller scholarship in the 1920s, distrusted Hollywood and in many ways his whole career was an attempt to orient film making in the opposite direction.

The dichotomy between 'Europe' and 'Hollywood'—these terms are, of course, only on one level geographical entities—has provided the foundation of much criticism of film, including Australian film. It is often constructed as a battle between film as art-work and film as money-spinner, or, as Susan Dermody and Elizabeth Jacka have put it frequently in the Australian context, between film as culture and film as industry. Although the intellectual loyalties of most critics in this debate are where one would expect them to be, there is an important oppositional strand, represented by the work of writers like David Bordwell (Bordwell, Staiger and Thompson 1985), which has found a more sympathetic way of writing about what has come to be called the 'classic' Hollywood style. An Australian application of this different system of values is found in a recent book by Brian McFarlane and Geoff Mayer, *New Australian Cinema: Sources and Parallels in American and British Film* (1992). For them the key to the success of the Hollywood film classic, in popular, commercial, and (for them at least) aesthetic terms, is an 'unmatched grasp of the conventions of melodrama' (McFarlane and Mayer 1992, p. 4), combined with a powerfully naturalistic *mise-en-scène*. One of the striking things about this style was how early it emerged—by 1917 essentially—and how it has continued to dominate Hollywood's output. In an epigraph to a chapter, they cite a description of a meeting between William and Cecil B. de Mille in 1915 at which the essential parameters of the narrative style were worked out. An accompanying epigraph testifies to the harsh penalties exacted from any director who departed from it.

The classic Hollywood style developed out of nineteenth-century popular literature and theatre, itself derived in turn from eighteenth and nineteenth-century French and British melodrama. There is no place in the aesthetic of melodrama for the 'restraint' so admired in modernist literature or the art film; rather, it valorises emotional heightening and powerful cathartic release. This is the key to its ability to emotionally involve large numbers of people, and thus to its rich popular and commercial potential. According to Peter Brooks, the world of melodrama is a world of moral absolutes; there is a preoccupation with moral redemption, where the 'suborners of morality' (Brooks 1976, p. 30) must be confronted and eventually eliminated. The narrative style foregrounds, above all, continuity and motivation, tight cause and effect, and internal coherence. It is strongly naturalist, although naturalistic detail must always be subject to the overwhelming demands of the narrative; compositional motivation always outweighs generic or psychological consistency: 'all other considerations . . . are subordinated to the main concern of the narrative system, its distinctive form of storytelling' (Brooks 1976, p. 25). There is no attempt at self-reflexivity, at what Russian literary theorists of the time called 'baring the device'. The climax is crucial both for the emotional release of the audience and for the plot to reach a satisfactory and coherent resolution. For Brooks, the final act makes the world 'morally legible' (Brooks 1976, p. 30).

While some intellectuals began to form a grudging accommodation with film, broadcasting was another matter. For the Leavises, the 'wireless' was one of the most pernicious threats to culture and, as late as the mid-1930s, a writer with a strong interest in popular culture like George Orwell viewed it with distaste. It is all the more remarkable, therefore, that the BBC, which began wireless transmission in 1922, should so rapidly have allied itself with a powerfully conservative view of English culture. Within a decade of its origins the British Broadcasting Corporation seemed as venerable and British an institution as the Bank of England, a bulwark against the Americanising influence of mass culture rather than its accomplice.

Part of this is a reflection of the vision of its first Director-General, John Reith, and the genuinely high standards he imposed, and partly it is a result of powerful myth-making indulged in by many in the BBC, including Reith himself. Reith's authoritarian manner and Calvinist origins are well-known. They are easily caricatured and there is a danger of exaggerating his personal influence, especially in the 1930s, but there can be little doubt that they gave him a sense not only of the 'elect' nature (in the Calvinist sense) of society's leaders and institutions and thus of the corresponding high moral seriousness of their work, but also a view of life as a ceaseless 'struggle' between higher impulses and lower. It was natural for him, therefore, to see the value of culture in didactic terms, as a means to self-improvement, and to be suspicious of amusement for its own sake. Reith's preoccupation with authority and control is a function of his belief that the élite could only survive by imposing their will on those who did not know any better. For similar reasons, he was unimpressed with the democratic possibilities of mass communication. Democracy in broadcasting was served by giving the whole public *access* to the means of communication, not popular choice. Reith's views on art and culture are thus classically modernist in the terms I outlined in chapter 2. The novelty is that he applied them in the direction of a medium of mass communication.

At the same time, as LeMahieu has shown, there was a great deal of mythology and, in some cases, outright deception, not to speak of self-deception, in this view of the early years of the BBC. The concern with high standards translated itself, often in farcical circumstances, into an obsession with social respectability. Anecdotes of this are legion, such as the requirement that news-readers wear evening dress, or the prohibition on divorced members of staff reading the 'Epilogue', the short religious program which closed the day's transmission. A legitimate concern with maintaining the highest professional standards in broadcasting through the appointment of the best people for the job often really meant hiring men from the 'right' schools. What LeMahieu in particular debunks is the myth of bourgeois culture the BBC was engaged in constructing. The long hours of classical music, the endless talks, had no basis in what anybody actually wanted to listen to, not even the educated middle class that the BBC most consciously addressed. There was, of course, no commercial pressure on the BBC to cater for a different or broader audience because it held a monopoly on radio broadcasting until the 1960s. Even if Reith had admitted the validity of popular choice as a basis of programming policy, there was no mechanism of audience research to find out what people wanted. It is remarkable, for instance, how willing the BBC was to broadcast music that few would actually go out to listen to. LeMahieu cites the testimony of Percy Scholes who, on one occasion, comprised one of only five people in the concert audience of a performance which was part of a series of contemporary music commissioned for broadcast. Although the BBC often proclaimed that it offered a 'balanced' product, the actual programming details suggest otherwise. Classical music, for instance, was regularly scheduled at the peak time of 8.00–10.30 pm on weekdays, whereas dance music was scheduled after 10.30 pm. In LeMahieu's opinion, '[the BBC] self-consciously invented an idealised version of a fragile, never fully realised, middle-class cultural tradition which it then proclaimed to be the natural and authentic culture of the nation' (LeMahieu, 1988, p. 182).

Although the BBC continued to broadcast music which it knew had a small audience—the Third Programme, for example, begun after the Second World War, attracted less than 1 per cent of the listening audience—attacks on the minority programming of the BBC gathered pace in the 1930s. Alternatives to the BBC came in the availability of popular music, broadcast from foreign stations like Radio Luxembourg. Reith's personal influence necessarily declined as the size of the organisation he headed grew. By the mid-1930s several changes had taken place, mostly in the direction of addressing a more popular audience: broadcasting hours had been extended; more variety and light entertainment were broadcast; and there was a shift away from the financing of classical to popular music. Public chamber concerts had been discontinued, the number of talks had been reduced, and programs of a magazine format had been introduced. The BBC also abandoned its Sabbatarian attitudes towards broadcasting on Sundays and moved to lighten the style of its magazine and program guide, the *Radio Times*. Most significant of all was the surprisingly early appointment of someone with a background in advertising to develop techniques of audience research. By the beginning of the Second World War, according to LeMahieu, the *BBC Handbook* had gone so far as to admit the validity of consumerist principles in broadcasting policy and scheduling.

The early history of the Australian Broadcasting Corporation

The history of the Australian Broadcasting Corporation (originally the Australian Broadcasting Commission), like the history of the BBC, is a rich amalgam of opinion, evidence, and mythology about national culture. The dominant narrative has been that the ABC is engaged in a struggle to save art and 'culture' from the indifference or hostility of commercial broadcasting. A contributory factor in this is the contrast Albert Moran has noted between the flood of books published about the ABC since 1975 and an apparent lack of interest in the history, especially the early history, of commercial broadcasting. Many of these books are reminiscences of a personal nature and they give the impression that the history of the ABC is a series of clashes between 'memorable figures and personalities' (Moran 1992, p. 49). In fact, Moran's conclusion is that there was little difference between the two ABC stations in Sydney, 2FC and 2BL, and that there was much in common between the early ABC and the commercial radio stations. From the beginning, the ABC accepted that it was necessary to locate and build its audience. This is very different from the sense of destiny and sacred mission that seems to characterise much of the early rhetoric of the BBC. An important difference, perhaps the fundamental difference between the two services, was that the ABC never enjoyed a monopoly of the airwaves. Even in the first annual report of the ABC, it was noted that 'the audience is not compellable . . . If good work is to be done it must be done through pleasing listeners. Enlightenment must come through entertainment' (Moran 1992, p. 51).

Even allowing for such fundamental differences as the broadcasting monopoly of the BBC, the ABC saw itself in its early days as in what Moran calls elsewhere a 'filial' relationship with the BBC, although nowhere was it specified that things *had* to be that way: 'it would be difficult to find an ABC *Annual Report* that did not mention the British Corporation' (Moran 1985, p. 45). Another word for 'filial' might be 'colonial', and in the opening broadcast in 1932, the first Chairman of the Commissioners of the ABC, Charles Lloyd Jones, reminded listeners that theirs was a colonial culture. Britain was the obvious model, and not just because Australia was part of the British empire. The Postmaster General, the minister initially responsible for the ABC, told the Australian parliament that the ABC's plan was 'to follow the British system as closely as Australian conditions will permit' (Inglis 1983, p. 19). Even so, from the beginning there were important differences in emphasis between the two services. Whereas the BBC's programming charter defined a need to 'inform, educate and entertain', a formula which was repeated effectively in the opening address on air by the Australian Prime Minister, Joseph Lyons, who spoke of the task of the ABC to 'provide information and entertainment, culture and gaiety' (Inglis 1983, p. 5), the ABC's objectives as set out in its charter were phrased in less culturally specific and value-laden terms as providing 'adequate and comprehensive programs'.

From the earliest days, the ABC's cultural role was hotly discussed and policy was implemented with the aim that it would become an

Australian institution in the same way and with the same social prestige as the BBC had become in Britain. As early as January 1931, Prime Minister Lyons had received a deputation from Melbourne which urged him to see that broadcasting was organised upon an independent basis and that the cultural potential of the service be regarded as a matter of prime importance. The first Commissioners of the ABC were a mixture, but the dominant note was clearly highbrow. The Chairman, in addition to his public role as the man behind the prominent Sydney retailer, David Jones, was a painter and patron of the arts. Another prominent Commissioner was Robert Wallace, the Vice-Chancellor of Sydney University and a former professor of English at Melbourne University. The advertisement for the position of General Manager called for 'a man of culture and artistic taste', but also sensibly added that someone 'possessing business ability and proved administrative capacity; with a wide knowledge of the world and current affairs' (Inglis 1983, p. 22) was being sought. The second Chairman of the Commissioners, W. J. Cleary, though a self-made businessman, was a powerful friend to learning, culture and art. From the beginning, university men and women have continued to be prominent among the Commissioners and board members as well as amongst the staff at large, testimony to an implicit assumption that men and women of liberal and humane cultural values were appropriate to guiding the ABC and that the ABC would espouse these same values. Not everyone has agreed that this is what actually occurred, of course.

The early programming reflected, in its externals if not always in detail, an assumption that its audience would be the sort of people who enjoyed the arts. Broadcasting began at 8.00 pm because that was the time when performances in concert halls and theatres began. A night in front of the wireless was a kind of modest alternative to a night at the opera. One particularly significant aspect of this self-perception of the ABC as a kind of handmaiden to the arts was the decision to establish symphony orchestras in each of the states. Nothing in the Act which established the ABC required it to go in this direction, although it did speak of trying to establish for broadcasting, 'groups of musicians for the rendition of orchestral, choral and band music of high quality' (Inglis 1983, p. 18). At this time there was not one full-time professional symphony orchestra in the whole of Australia. In contrast, the BBC symphony orchestra was but one of several orchestras, including more than one in London itself. In this context, the Chairman of the Commissioners spoke during the opening broadcast of his dream of an Australian national orchestra. Bernard Heinze, one of the prime movers in the development not just of the orchestras but the whole musical programming of the ABC, had studied abroad and was aware of the gulf between local and overseas musicianship. The ABC orchestras would serve not just to raise the artistic standards of the musicians themselves, but also of the listening public. The second Chairman, W. J. Cleary, was, like the first, a passionate supporter of the ABC orchestras, as was the second General Manager, Charles Moses, and in 1942 Cleary (Moran 1992, pp. 59–62) wrote of the decision to establish the orchestras as part of a commitment to developing the musical life of the country, to assisting musicians and not having to rely totally on an imported musical culture.

At first, the Commissioners were not quite so passionate in their enthusiasm for drama, the other branch of the arts which seemed particularly suited for broadcast, although drama production benefitted greatly from the appointment of Frank Clewlow as Federal Controller of Productions. The ABC was, in effect, the only radio station which took drama at all seriously. It not only undertook radio presentations of the classics, for example the production of *all* Shakespeare's plays, albeit in edited form, between 1936 and 1938, but, in great part through the appointment in 1936 of Leslie Rees as a playreader, strove to present plays by Australian writers. Australian drama weeks were organised and by 1937—what seems now a very high proportion—70 per cent of plays produced on ABC radio were written by Australian dramatists. Over the years, some of Australia's best writers were attracted to radio. The catholic nature of Clewlow's taste was of great value to the ABC. During the Second World War, he became responsible for light entertainment as well as drama and described his policy as 'ranging from classical drama to a classical vulgarian like "Mo"' (Inglis 1983, p. 88).

From the beginning, the ABC made extensive use of university staff as presenters of talks. Many of these saw radio as an ideal vehicle for mass education. Walter Murdoch, Professor of English at the University of Western Australia since 1912, was one of the most regular and best loved of these university radio presenters. He had a keen sense of the changing nature of literary culture in the modern world: 'anyone can see that broadcasting will sooner or later take the place of literature for a vast number of people' (Inglis 1983, p. 30). The ABC was also keen to attract university graduates to its permanent staff, like the BBC; but unlike the BBC, it also offered in its early days a kind of parallel career structure for people actually working in universities. For example, Rudi Bronner, a man who had been a university lecturer at Adelaide and Melbourne as well as Freiburg in Germany, was appointed Federal Talks Organiser in the 1930s. The comment of Charles Moses, the General Manager, is revealing of the ambience of the ABC at the time: 'his educational qualifications and gentlemanly demeanour would be valuable in the sphere of Talks' (Inglis 1983, p. 56). Perhaps the best example of this trend in ABC staffing is Clement Semmler, whose career lasted from the 1930s well into the television era of the 1970s, eventually becoming Deputy General Manager. At the time of his original appointment he had to choose between the ABC and the offer of a lectureship in English at the University College at Armidale. Throughout his many years at the ABC he continued to review books for the newspapers and to write literary criticism himself in books and articles. In 1969, he was awarded an Honorary DLitt by the University of New England. The donnish flavour he gave to his work at the ABC was not appreciated by everyone, however. It was the view of later Chairman Madgwick that he would have been better suited as a professor of Australian literature than as an administrator of broadcasting (Inglis 1983, p. 330). In his later years particularly, he attacked what he saw as a relentless drift to populism within the ABC and, although he was not without interests in popular culture himself, as evidenced by his deep interest in jazz, he was hostile to the work of whole sectors of the ABC like the rock music channel Radio 2JJ. On his retirement in 1977, he roundly condemned the anti-intellectualism of the ABC, doubting whether some members of the senior executive had ever read a book in their lives, and dismissed much of television since the mid-1960s as banal, extravagant and stereotyped (Inglis 1983, p. 416).

It would be a mistake though to see what is often referred to as a golden age of Australian radio as unrelievedly highbrow. From the beginning, sport played a large part in the broadcasting policy of the ABC. The view of John Reith was, in fact, that sports broadcasting was 'Australia's most characteristic feature' (Inglis 1983, p. 35). Nor was sport seen as some sort of antithetical discourse to music and drama. The tone for this was set by Moses himself who, although a strong partisan of the ABC's music policy, had started in radio as a sports broadcaster. It was he in fact who did the first 'synthetic' live cricket broadcasts, tapping a teacup with a pencil to mimic the sound of bat on ball. He remained a strong defender of the ABC's broadcasting of sport, believing that it attracted listeners to the ABC, and thus to its more serious programs, who might not otherwise be there.

Nevertheless, there were more straightforward expressions of populism from the early days of the ABC and concern about the audience proportions. As early as 1934, the very first General Manager, Charles Conder, thought that the 'university men' in the ABC were out of touch with ordinary people and clashed with the Commissioners over the amount of air time given to talks. By the late 1930s politicians were worried about the cost of the ABC to the nation. The ABC followed the lead of the BBC in establishing a Listener Research section in 1943, and one of its first reports created alarm at the small size of the ABC's audience. The ABC was widely seen as 'heavy, highbrow, classical, high class, dull, straitlaced, too serious, stiff, stuffy, bit dead, not lively, dry, staid' (Inglis 1983, p. 182). After the war the ABC, like the BBC, made a conscious effort to 'lighten' and popularise its image. Although there was still a heavy recruitment of Englishmen, there was an attempt to change the tone to something warmer, more personal, more Australian. More light music was programmed. Perhaps the most significant change was the abandonment of the founding premise of 'mixed and balanced' programming (in effect highbrow and popular) on both networks. A trend which can be seen from the late 1930s to narrow and specialise the range of programs on each network was completed in 1945–46 by the separation of the networks into two distinct services, one 'serious' and the other 'light'.

The low cultural status of television

The BBC began experimental television transmission in 1930 and started a regular service in 1936, the first anywhere in the world. When the Second World War started, however, the plug was pulled unceremoniously on the new service—in the middle of a Mickey Mouse cartoon, apparently—and it was suspended for the duration of the war. It was during this period that American television surged ahead, defining the new medium in essentially popular and commercial terms.

Television in Australia did not begin until 1956, and, as in radio, a commercial network existed from the beginning in competition with the ABC. One of the reasons that it did not come sooner was a mixture of indifference and hostility on the part of Australian politicians. The prime minister after the war, Ben Chifley, had an essentially populist view of broadcasting; according to Inglis, he was 'bored by ABC programmes and believed that the job of television even more than radio was to deliver entertainment to tired workers' (Inglis 1983, p. 193). The Liberal prime minister who succeeded him and who was in office at the time of the introduction of television, Robert Menzies, despised the medium, as Winston Churchill had done in Britain, and did little to hasten its coming.

This mixture of populism, on the one hand, and indifference and hostility, on the other, has formed the parameters of the public's view of television, in Australia especially. Relatively few intellectuals have been attracted to it unless in a captious spirit as an object of criticism. As John Hartley has satirically observed, departments of television studies, as distinct from film studies, usually have a marginal status in the academy and are not infrequently staffed by a heterogeneous assortment of people, many of whom are openly hostile to the products of the medium. Furthermore, television production has never had the individualist, entrepreneurial nature of film, with the consequence that the networks have been more important than the creative personnel (Hartley 1992). The iconoclastic book by Jonathan Price, praising advertisements as the best thing on television, marked by a much higher degree of artistic professionalism than the programs they are associated with, or the work of John Docker on Australian popular culture for instance, are rare exceptions to this prevailing view. Indeed, in some ways, Price's book reinforces the usual view that television is basically dreadful; the difference is that he contrasts the poor quality of television, not with opera or the Victorian novel, but with the commercials. Those people who cared about the development of a national cinema and lobbied so hard for it in the 1950s and 1960s were not usually interested in the future of Australian television and tended to dismiss it as banal. The working life of Ken G. Hall, who followed up a career as maker of popular films in the

1930s and 1940s with the directorship of Channel 9 in Sydney, is surely the exception which proves the rule.

A common paradigm of the visual media in which film was art and television was popular culture was established early on. Over twenty years ago, in a (significantly titled) report for UNESCO on 'Innovation and Decline in the Treatment of Culture on British Television', Stuart Hall, one of the few intellectuals who was attracted to television, made the point that television seems least comfortable in the domain of high art. He put forward a general rule that the more serious or high cultural in orientation a program is, the less likely it is to be conceived *ex novo* for television, to make use of the technical and cultural practices specific to television. By contrast, for him, the 'purest' spirit of television is expressed at the popular end of its work.[3]

One important manifestation of the peculiarly low cultural status of television is the lack of serious-minded criticism of it in Australia outside specialist publications. In the press, for example, television criticism is handled very differently from other 'arts'; indeed it is usually laid out in the paper in such a way as to exclude it from the domain of the other arts. The arts pages of the *Sydney Morning Herald*, filled with expert reviewing of music (including rock music), theatre and dance, as well as extensive book reviewing at the weekend, almost never review television programs. Whereas there is some arts writing in the *Sydney Morning Herald* every day, usually on the back pages of the main section of the paper, almost all the writing on television is comprehended within its program 'Guide', issued once a week on Mondays, printed on pink paper, thereby (deliberately or not) visually reinforcing the different status of television. Compared with the cultured ambience of the arts pages—Roger Covell, Professor of Music at the University of New South Wales, has been reviewing continuously in the paper since the early 1960s—the pink guide has a very downmarket feel. Line drawings, rather than photographs, predominate visually. There is often a cartoon on the front page, and always a full page of ads on the back page, often for typewriters or computers, but occasionally for discount booze. The tone of writing, both here and in the column on television on Saturday, is humorous, light and gossipy. Clive James seems to have set the pattern for television reviewing in his column in the London *Observer* in the early 1970s, although work in a similar style can be found in John

Carey's reviews in the *Listener* at much the same time. It is not that intelligent people have never reviewed television—indeed, the opposite is often the case—but that these clever reviewers usually give the impression that they are slumming in the medium. Television amuses them, whether it is Miss World or the Wednesday play, and their columns are at heart pieces of comic writing. The *Australian* constructs the relationship of television to the arts in much the same way. While films are reviewed in the arts pages, its stylish 'Arts on Friday' pages rarely include criticism of television. Television, when the subject of any criticism at all, is found in another section, 'TV and Entertainment', usually placed opposite 'Time and Tide', which includes obituaries and other kinds of features.

In a similar vein, while there are good programs on both the ABC and SBS which review books and films, there is a peculiar absence in the medium itself of serious self-reflection. Indeed, as I write this, the promo for virtually the only program that does attempt this, the ABC's 'TVTV', includes a short segment by Edna Everidge bringing out the underlying comedy of 'a television program about a television program'. Apparently even the ABC accepts that the idea of television discussing itself is absurd. In fact, there is a real need for a program to do just this, but 'TVTV' does not seem to me to fit the bill. It goes to air at 6.30 pm, traditionally a 'light' spot, rather than at the more sober hour of 10.00 pm, when 'Review' is scheduled, or as part of the ABC's 'Arts on Sunday'. While the program is not as bad as many of its reviewers make it out to be, it does have a kind of Barnum and Bailey feel to it: the clothes worn by its presenters seem more than usually colourful, their hairdos ever more unlikely. It is fundamentally light and populist, with more than a touch of the fanzine: its original presenter, Simon Townsend, used to end each episode by urging the viewers to remember that television was 'wonderful'. The only other program which attempts something of this kind is 'Media Watch', hosted by Stuart Littlemore, which seems to go to the opposite extreme. Littlemore has a very different television manner, as befits a QC. Its humour is very dry, often turning on amusing typographical errors or lapses of grammar. Again, its tone tends to be amused condescension towards the sillinesses of the media. Its essential focus is not really the 'art' of television at all, but rather television's place in the world of news reporting and current affairs. Its prime concerns seem to be with the content of television, with the construction of news and related issues such as the ethics of reporting.

Attitudes of a similar kind can be seen in the views of television amongst successive Chairmen of the Commissioners of the ABC, especially in the earlier period. At the time of the introduction of television, the Chairman was Richard Boyer, very much a Reithian figure. (The ABC's equivalent of the Reith lectures, delivered annually on BBC radio, are the Boyer lectures.) Boyer's belief in television was in its power to unify and raise Australian culture, in its 'purposeful citizen-making' in the words of biographer, Geoffrey Bolton. Consistently lacking in the minds of the early Chairmen is the sense of the artistic potential of the new medium or even of the genuine pleasure it might bring. Boyer hoped television might be an aid in education, even for a kind of university of the air. Although Richard Downing, appointed in 1972, was a cultured man—in the words of Earle Hackett, another of the Commissioners, he was 'that rare thing, a totally cultivated Australian' (Inglis 1983, p. 339)—he did not even own a television set. Doubtless, that was one of the things which made him seem so cultured. Henry Bland, appointed in 1976, had attended ABC concerts in Melbourne for forty years but confessed that he only watched television on Sunday evenings.

From the very beginning, one of the commonest themes in the discussion of television has been the perceived tension between the popular and minority roles of the ABC. The view of Semmler, for example, consistently expressed, has been that ABC television has been in decline since the mid-1960s, obsessed with ratings like the commercials and with little concern for broadcasting for minorities. Phillip Adams has been another voice castigating the ABC for its populism. In an article along these lines published in 1984, Semmler cites Adams as saying that he has been trying to persuade the ABC to address minorities for twenty years (Semmler 1984). The most recent expression of similar views I have found is an open letter from Adams to the current General Manager, David Hill, in the *Australian* of 7 August 1993. Thirty years is a long time! There is clearly a long evidence of the ABC, like the BBC, worrying about its viewer percentages since the late 1950s and early 1960s. When Talbot Duckmanton became General Manager in 1965, he set out to pursue audiences more energetically, and indeed there is evidence that the ABC's share of the audience did increase in the late 1960s. There was a widely felt need for ABC television to 'brighten up' its image and a department of television presentation was formed within the organisation in 1966.

Many of these worries were brought to a head with the Dix Report, established in 1979 to report by March 1981. The years preceding the report had been some of the most troubled in the ABC's history, marked especially by a dramatic reduction in the ABC's budget. The funding in 1975/76 was the lowest since 1961. Dix himself was a businessman who had for a brief time been an academic. Typically, he had little personal interest in broadcasting; the only program he followed regularly was the music broadcast on FM radio at breakfast time. The report proposed that management should work according to business norms rather than public service ones. (It is possible to detect a similar response in the review of the Australian Film Commission management at much the same time.) In its submission to the reviewing body, the ABC itself suggested corporate underwriting as a means of improving the ABC's financial position and this was accepted, with some provisos, by the report. It was also recommended that the ABC disengage from its responsibility for the state symphony orchestras.

In the event, the Fraser government's implementation was a good deal gentler than the report would have led one to expect. No corporate underwriting was recommended and the orchestras remained an ABC enterprise. It was determined that programming policy should be a mixture of innovation, information, entertainment, and education, balancing mass appeal against the needs of special audiences. Since Dix, there has been an increasing concern with ratings, however, including reports of ugly scenes with the Managing Director, David Hill.[4] Elizabeth Jacka has characterised this period of ABC television thus: 'words like excellence, quality, diversity and innovation feature more prominently and there is less statement of intention to lift community taste or preserve Australian culture from corruption by base popular culture' (Jacka 1991, p. 11).

The construction of the 'arts' on radio and television

As early as 1961, the ABC began to spend more money on television than radio. It was an inevitable decision, of course, because television programs are much more expensive to produce, but thereafter radio was doomed to being a 'poor' medium. Light entertainment resources were moved from radio to television and it seemed clear that ABC radio had little future as a popular medium. Not everyone resented this change and it was the expressed wish of people like Semmler that the radio audience be offered something more serious and challenging. As a first move he proposed reversing the roles of 2FC and 2BL, the former becoming the 'serious' network, with the consequence that the compulsory parliamentary broadcasts interrupted the light network instead. Semmler's belief all along has been that the burden of cultural broadcasting must fall to the ABC: the commercials will simply neglect it, multicultural and public access television have limited capacity, and the ABC is the only network with the potential for national coverage. The ABC is, however, hamstrung, in his view, by the lack of a coherent arts policy, with no separate department for the arts, paralleling the separate departments of sport or religious broadcasting (Semmler 1984).

It is hard to see that there has been much change since Semmler wrote. Radio has its FM classical music service in what is now called ABC Fine Music, but its arts programming is still relatively meagre, despite the ABC's self-advertisement as the 'Arts Network'. The bulk of radio arts programming is done in the 10.00–11.00 am slot each day on Radio National, repeated in the evenings. In early 1994, a change was made to replace the different specialist programs that filled this slot each day—'In the Mix', 'Sightings', 'Book Report', 'Screen', 'Performance'—with a consolidated, magazine-style program, 'Arts Today'. In some ways, it is possible to see this as yet one more capitulation to populism. The previous programs had built up a repertoire of expert opinion and informed discussion, and, to judge from the way the program has been discussed in the press at least, the impulse behind the change was to make arts broadcasting more 'accessible'. The rhetoric which accompanied the new program is composed extensively of words like 'fresh' and 'alive'. In an article in the *Australian* of 11 February 1994, Deborah Bogle quoted its presenter, David Marr, as saying that he wanted the program to be 'vulgar, we want to be unfriendly and as much as possible we want to talk on air as we talk around our own tables'. He suggested 'gossip with authority' as a possible motto for the program. On the other hand, there is a kind of ambivalence in the program's conception of itself: 'vulgarity' and 'unfriendliness' do not sit naturally together, and neither sit with talking around the table. Nor is Marr an obvious choice for a populist figurehead. He has had a long career in the 'quality' side of print journalism and television, such as the ABC's 'Four Corners', and is best known perhaps for his biography of Patrick White. Indeed, in some ways, he is a kind of Semmler figure himself.

ABC television's reporting of the arts (as distinct from its 'coverage' in programs such as 'Esso Night at the Opera') is essentially contained within two programs: 'Review', a half-hour program broadcast on Monday evenings at 10.00 pm, and 'Sunday Afternoon With Peter Ross'. The latter program offers a more traditional view of the arts. Stretching the whole afternoon from 1.00 pm until 5.00 pm (unless it is interrupted by sport), there are usually several separate features, most of them imported, covering a wide range of arts issues. The tone overall is serious, even a little reverential, yet relaxed and expansive—a classic instance of Sunday afternoon art as the substitute religion of the middle class. 'Classical' is not a bad word to characterise the program as a whole; it is not uncommon to find British drama series, usually adaptations of novels and almost always repeats, as the last item of the afternoon; recently, Lord Clark's series 'Civilisation' was re-broadcast to commemorate the twenty-fifth anniversary of the original broadcast. Ross's persona—restrained and dignified, senior and authoritative—colours the program strongly. While it takes its subject seriously, it is not zealous. Ross is accompanied by a guest, whom he interviews, and they sit in easy chairs. There is a regular segment in which he and a writer 'chat' about books.

Ross used to host 'Review', as well, although since the beginning of the new series in 1994, he now does only the occasional item for it. It is hard not to see the new program as a deliberate attempt to exorcise his kind of style and presence. There is no longer a regular host: the only presenter who 'hosts' the show in any way is Nell Schofield. Indeed, there seems a conscious attempt to avoid a central host-figure who would anchor the program to a particular kind of viewpoint. Special 'guest-presenters', people with particular kinds of expertise, often practitioners rather than commentators, are regularly used to present individual items. The new program has a very de-centred feel to it—doubtless this is intentional. Where Ross had regular 'bookchats', book reviewing has vanished in the new series. Whereas 'Sunday Afternoon' is not at all averse to re-running items with words like 'Civilisation' in the title from twenty-five years ago, 'Review' is built around the theme of 'what's on at the moment'. The style is metropolitan and sophisticated—rather consciously 'trendy'. If the design of 'Sunday Afternoon' is minimal—a couple of chairs and a pot-plant so that one will not be too distracted from the 'art'—the designer's role is very conspicuous on 'Review'. At its most extreme, everyone is photographed from a 45° angle or under coloured lights or both, the shots are composed in a riot of multi-media, blazing with colour and design motifs, often with a sound track bearing, as with everything else, a kind of tangential relationship to the subject at issue. It is genuinely hard sometimes to follow the topic under review—doubtless this too is intentional—so obtrusive is the presentation. The program looks as if it has been put together by a team who have gone to art school and taken a series of courses on post-structuralism.

The ABC's polarised style of arts broadcasting makes it clear how much a figure like British television's Melvyn Bragg is lacking, someone with credibility as both creative artist and broadcaster–critic, who does not think it is his role to make himself or the sophisticated style of his presentation the centrepiece of every item. Despite Semmler's misgivings about the ability of SBS to deliver arts broadcasting, in some ways the nearest we have got to this and the most impressive programs have come from this direction in the last five years. Not only does SBS schedule art films extensively, it seems to have the flexibility to program outside the mainstream, both in terms of subject matter and in terms of format and length, for example Peter Brook's *Mahabharata*. Its 'Masterpiece' series screens a lot of imported material on the arts. In 'Eat Carpet', SBS has the only program anywhere on television which deals with experimental visual work. Its book program, its film review program and its new arts program 'Imagine', are, in their combination of knowledge, criticism and unfussiness of presentation, the best on Australian television at present.

Australian television drama

Drama has always been central to the work of television. This was so from the origins of the BBC: its early Programme Organiser, Cecil Madden, worked to the dictum of 'a play a day'. In Australia, drama has likewise consistently dominated screen time. In 1959, it occupied 81 per cent of prime time on Sydney television, according to Albert Moran in *Images and Industry* (1985); in 1979, the figure still stood at 71 per cent.

On the whole, however, television drama has suffered from low status relative to other forms of drama, even radio drama, that has characterised television in general. This view can be found from the beginning, even within the profession itself: Maurice Wiggin commented in 1959 that 'you must forget everything about "fine writing", forget that there ever was such a word as style. This is a department of literature, I suppose, but the word "literary" is an insult to a television playwright' (Brandt 1981, p. 2). The intrinsic ephemerality of the television play—it is shown once, not in a 'run' like a play in the theatre, repeats within a short space of time are unusual (although the use of video cassette recorders may well change our apprehension of this)—seems fundamentally at odds with the idea of the 'timelessness' of great art. Few university departments teach television drama with the same commitment as theatrical drama or, for that matter, film.

Many of the obstacles to television drama establishing itself as a quality product derived from the poor technical quality of early television. Whereas film-based still and moving photography attained great sophistication early on, it was a long time before anything on television actually 'looked' good. The image quality on 405 line receivers was very low definition; the bulky, unmanoeuverable cameras could only be used in the studio. Most important of all, there was no way of editing the image; all plays went to air live and even the most basic techniques of film editing, like montage, were impossible. In time, some of these deficiencies were overcome—videotape was first used in 1958, allowing proper editing; BBC2 began transmission with the higher definition 625 line picture; several directors in the 1960s began to use film for plays; and colour transmission began in England between 1967 and 1969, and in Australia in 1974—but television drama has found it hard to transcend this sense that it was operating in a medium with intrinsically poor visual quality.

Many of the artistic successes of early television drama were the result of making an aesthetic virtue out of the inherent technical limitations of the form. One of the strongest influences on the course of British television drama, one which did much to define the particular nature of 'quality' work in the medium, was the work of the American writer Paddy Chayefsky. In the view of Alan Plater, 'Chayefsky observed that the greatest single asset of television was its simplicity and directness; the ability to watch a face in close-up . . . television drama should be the drama of the ordinary man or woman, revealing the extraordinary core of genius that rests in the heart of each individual' (Brandt 1981, p. 143). It was through Chayefsky's way of thinking that television drama oriented itself so centrally towards the subject matter of ordinary life and towards a naturalistic style. Chayefsky's work was a strong influence on Sydney Newman, a Canadian, who took over British commercial television's 'Armchair Theatre' in 1958, and then in 1963 moved to the BBC as its Head of Drama. In Canada, Newman had worked for John Grierson and the Griersonian tradition of plain style documentary realism runs deep in British television drama. Through the appointment of David Goddard as the ABC's first Head of Drama in 1965, an Englishman from the BBC in his turn greatly influenced by Newman, this style has influenced Australian television drama as well. Newman is much like Grierson in many respects: in his quest for documentary realism he professed a lack of interest in 'art' and yet he was the source of many striking stylistic pieces. Paralleling Grierson's attitude to film, Newman had a strong commitment to the 'mass' nature of television, that it should comment in a plain way on the world familiar to this mass audience. There is a story that he was greatly impressed seeing John Osborne's play *Look Back in Anger* at the Royal Court Theatre in London in the late 1950s and coined the phrase 'agitational contemporaneity' to describe its mode of operation (Self 1984, p. 49).

These two related strands of influence—the acceptance of the technical limitations of television, on the one hand, and the focus on ordinary life, coming from the influence of Chayefsky and Grierson, on the other—have been powerful shaping forces in that naturalism which has become television's dominant mode in England and Australia. Some of the most memorable pieces of television drama have been produced in its style, in regular spots like the BBC's 'Wednesday Play', which in 1970 became the 'Play for Today'. A team of fine writers, directors and producers worked in this period: one of the most famous of its productions is the story about a homeless family, 'Cathy Come Home', screened in 1966, with a script by Jeremy Sandford, produced by Tony Garnett, and directed by Ken Loach. Brandt's belief is that 'much of the history of British TV drama is tied up with this programme spot' (Brandt 1981, p. 17). Its hallmarks were contemporary settings and themes, often examined in an agitational way, a naturalistic style of presentation, and, despite the increasing use of film and a growing acceptance of the aesthetic of the film documentary, a high number of scripts written specifically for television.

This kind of 'issues' television has remained throughout a powerful presence in television drama. Some of the ABC's most popular and most critically successful series are squarely in the tradition: recent examples are 'Brides of Christ', which deals with changes in the Catholic Church in Australia in the 1960s, and the co-production with the BBC, 'The Leaving of Liverpool', which dramatises the cruel predicament of child migrants to Australia after the Second World War. Although set in the past, both series were seen to have an acute contemporary significance. In the case of the latter, in the true spirit of agitational contemporaneity, it was part of an international campaign to persuade the British government to release records affecting the families of those children who had migrated. Television awards frequently go to actors and directors involved in plays or series of this type, dramatising the most important (or most shocking) issues. In the popular mind, this is very much what good drama is. In 1993, the AFI awards for both best female and best male actor went to the ABC series 'G.P.': in the first case for an episode dealing with the traumatic aftermath to the accidental killing of a child, and in the second for an episode dealing with male anal rape. Sometimes the combination of powerful topic and documentary style seems to encourage disconcerting lapses of obliqueness. Following the success of 'Brides of Christ', Peter Couchman chaired a discussion on his program on the ABC about the changing role of the Catholic Church in Australian society, in which the series often seemed to be used as 'evidence'. Two of the stars of the series were members of the Couchman audience, took part in the discussion, and were photographed in such a way as to recall the parts they had played. This is a long way from Immanuel Kant.

'G.P.' is not produced for commercial television, nor is it, strictly speaking, 'soap opera'. However, it is marked by some of soap opera's most characteristic features, especially the features of what has been called 'quality soap'—in many ways a kind of popular counterpart on commercial television to 'issues television'. In Australia, this is partly the result of the influence of the Crawfords production company, which, rather than the ABC, has been, in the words of Albert Moran, 'the pioneer and nursery of Australian television drama' (Moran 1985, p. 89). One of the clearest examples of Australian quality soap is 'A Country Practice', produced for ATN 7 in Sydney by Jim Davern's company, JNP, and the subject of an extended study by John Tulloch and Albert Moran. Both Davern and his fellow producer, Lyn Bayonas, had worked for the ABC, Davern as its Head of Drama, 1976–78. 'A Country Practice' was carefully pitched between the quality associations of the ABC and the sort of audience that wanted to watch something like 'The Sullivans' at 7.30 pm. In this, 'A Country Practice' fitted well within the image Channel 7 had cultivated elsewhere as a sort of mid-point between Channel 9 and the ABC. It thereby reinforced the image of respectable quality commercialism of Channel 7's owners, the Fairfax group. This kind of mid-way positioning can be seen in other ways as well, through writers like Tony Morphett, but also through the great respect in which Crawfords were held by many of the people, both technical and artistic, who worked on the show.

In the interviews conducted for their study, Tulloch and Moran constantly draw attention to the many observations made by personnel about the quality nature of their work on 'A Country Practice'. In particular the writers testify to the unusual respect for 'authorship' in such a high-rating series and their greater contribution to the development of story-lines. The floor manager interviewed, Peter Conroy, said it had the highest technical quality of any series he had worked on. The director, Russell Webb, had credentials in film—this seemed to be an important conferrer of status—and tried to give the program a more filmic quality. Tulloch and Moran's comment is that 'the little "touches" working against the grain of the commercial two-hours-a-week routine came up again and again in discussion with *ACP* professionals' (Tulloch and Moran, 1986, p. 133).

Yet clearly this notion of television quality is a narrow one, and there is never any possibility of transcending the naturalism in which the program is grounded. Davern's original outline for the show had proposed a series which would be 'less long on superimposed melodrama' (Tulloch and Moran 1986, p. 29), but which would in effect have all the other hallmarks of naturalism: conflict, real values, strong emotion, characters with whom the audience could form an emotional relationship. One of the writers for the series, David Boutland, characterises the stories as 'real life compressed' and defines the place for 'A Country Practice' between 'the complexities, vagueness and confusion of real life (and "Art") and the "unreal" characterisation of soaps' (Tulloch and Moran 1986, p. 38). Whenever one aspect of the production process got too arty, it was quickly brought back into line. What makes 'A Country Practice' distinctive and gives it its quality is the depth of its professionalism and the seriousness with which it handles its themes and plots. Its art is a function of its 'values'; its creativity is 'nothing less than the negotiation of values (medical, feminist, sexist, soap, etc.) on behalf of "drama"' (Tulloch and Moran 1986, p. 95).

The possibilities for 'art' television

The strong influence of the 'Wednesday Play' style was not, and has not, subsequently, been greeted with universal support. Despite its ideological progressiveness, it was still seldom *formally* innovative or interesting in the manner of much of the theatre of the period. The dominance of the naturalistic style in television drama in a period when other art forms were struggling to detach themselves from it, was attacked at the time by the writer Troy Kennedy Martin, ironically one of its finest practitioners in series like 'Z-Cars'. Martin urged that television find new narrative styles and methods and ally itself more generally with cinema, not Hollywood which had led into such bad practices as an over-reliance on close-up, but the cinema of the European 'New Wave', represented particularly in the work of Alain Resnais (T. K. Martin 1964). A different line of criticism can be found in the work of Stuart Hall, who has seen the origins of the problem more deeply in the fundamental commitment of television to the communication of truth, of being 'faithful to reality'. While this may be an exemplary aesthetic for news and current affairs, dangerous simplicities are concealed in this approach. The process of editorialising in the construction of reality is ignored; there is a confusion between the hoped-for capture of a slice of life and the actual transmission of a 'message', coming ultimately from some particular group in an institution. This fosters a lack of reflection on the means by which reality is transmitted. In most 'good' television in the 1960s, the technical and practical aspects of representing reality were carefully hidden. In contrast, the best television drama for Hall has resulted where the boundaries between reality and fiction have been blurred (Hall 1976).

Taken as a whole, there has been very little television 'art'—not just good plays but plays which sought to redefine what the medium was capable of. Television has not created an exciting visual style of its own—and a critical discourse that goes with it—which can match film. John Caughie (1981a) has commented on television's relative lack of 'visual pleasure' and lamented the long-coming of what he has suggestively termed 'art television', with a rhetoric akin to the visual one of the cinema, to counter television's traditional dominance by the word, although he has warned, too, against the establishment of a simple dichotomy between the tradition of television naturalism and an oppositional television avant-garde with Dennis Potter at its head (Caughie 1981b). When one looks across the field of Australian television drama as a whole, a similar picture emerges, although it could be added further that we conspicuously lack a writer to fill the role that Potter filled in British television, or the kind of 'avant-garde realist', typified by Alan Bleasdale. Experimental drama in particular is meagrely represented not just on commercial television but on the ABC as well. Perhaps the nearest we come to it is the kind of 'surrealist melodrama' represented by productions like the ABC's 'Stark' (1993) and 'The Damnation of Harvey McHugh' (1994).

In almost all cases in Australia, 'quality' television drama has been found principally in the mini-series, which, since the early 1980s, seems to have taken over the 'flag-ship' role from feature film in the Australian industry. Its length and innovative scheduling methods allow for a greater fidelity to the source-texts—in Australia often adaptations of novels—than is characteristic of the classic Hollywood 'gutting' of a novel for its plot in the most basic and melodramatic of terms. To maintain an audience over successive nights, especially if targeting one overseas as well, the mini-series has to make a big visual and dramatic impact. The production values, accordingly, are high, invariably using film as shooting stock, with lavish (period) designs; they are widely promoted, often with Hollywood style spin-offs such as novelisations and programs about the making of the program. Stuart Cunningham (1993) has seen another manifestation of the quality of the mini-series in the way historical material is used. His study of mini-series based on historical events stresses their direct dealing with major historical figures and events rather than using them in the more conventional way, typical of soap opera, as a backdrop for stories built around fictional characters. Their view of history has been, in the main, serious and circumspect; even the most sensitive events in an Australian context are seen consistently from multiple perspectives. The story of the 'Cowra Breakout', for instance, makes extensive use of Japanese dialogue with subtitles; almost half the cricket controversy of 'Bodyline' is seen from the view of Douglas Jardine and the other English cricketers. Dealing with historical events in the style of dramatised documentary, an aspect of the strength of the naturalistic tradition in Australian television, has produced some of the best drama—Kennedy-Miller's 'The Dismissal', for instance, or the ABC's 'Scales of Justice'.

This is still a long way, however, from what I think Caughie implies by the term 'art television'. Something of the confusion can be seen from looking at a production which was widely received as art television, 'Edens Lost', an adaptation of Sumner Locke Elliott's novel of the same name, directed by Neil Armfield and produced for the ABC in 1988. A favourite marketing theme of the time was that it was Australia's *Brideshead Revisited.* Bearing out Cunningham's point about the conservatism of mini-series' adaptations, the screenplay of 'Edens Lost' is particularly faithful to the text of the novel, in terms not only of mood and historical setting, but also in characterisation, structure, and dialogue—as was John Mortimer's adaptation of Evelyn Waugh's *Brideshead Revisited.* Part of the reason for this is Elliott's own firm sense of the dramatic, structurally and textually. 'Edens Lost' is in some ways structurally more akin to a play than to a conventional novel. In the novel, Elliott departs from the chapter structure, preferring long 'parts' consisting of shorter scenes. There is a clear act/scene analogy here. The novel has a three-part structure, which lends itself very neatly, for example, to the three parts of the mini-series. Moreover, Elliott always seems to have a firm sense of the 'dramatic': the contrasting scenes in the Blue Mountains hotel before the war and the Long Island mansion in America after the war; the oppressive dinner table scenes with the 'Judge'; the scary ride on the 'funicular'; the revelation scene to Eve of her husband's reliance on Cissie; Eve's long climactic monologue explaining the history of the strange St. James family. In many ways, this sure sense of the workings of theatrical drama is not surprising. In fact, Elliott turned to novel writing very late for a major writer. His first novel, *Careful He Might Hear You* (made into a film in 1983), was not published until 1963, when he was forty six. His career was established on the stage, first in Sydney in the early years after the war, and then in America.

On the other hand, while there is no doubting that the series made good quality television drama in the traditional sense of the term, some of those same features (paradoxically) worked against it as a piece of 'art television'. In fact, Elliott's whole training in the theatre worked against this. One of the points that Caughie makes is that the traditional interdependency of theatre and television drama, its writers and actors moving freely between the two forms, has hindered the development of an 'art television', based more closely on links with film. In this, I disagree with Elizabeth Jacka's view that 'Edens Lost' neatly fits Caughie's criteria. In many ways, the series seems to me the very opposite of what Caughie means by the term. The high production values that Jacka identifies correctly—'beautiful images, stylish settings, lovely clothes and literate dialogue' (Jacka 1989, p. 20)—are more features of the high naturalism that is one of the things art television is trying to escape from. While visual pleasure is an important part of the film's appeal, and 'Edens Lost' is certainly a delight to watch, the distinguishing feature of art television—as Jacka says—is its visual rhetoric. Caughie sees art television as using the image, not simply as an object of beauty to contemplate, nor as a visual complement to what is said in the script, but as a discourse in its own right, sometimes an alternative discourse to the text in the script, able to develop its own themes and narrative. This is precisely, however, what the series never really develops. The beautiful scenes in the Blue Mountains really occupy only one of the three episodes. Even within the first episode, the one which most naturally lends itself to the kind of effect Jacka is looking for—with 'much of the content being conveyed through *mise-en-scène* devices rather than directly' (Jacka 1989, p. 21)—most of the action takes place indoors, for example the long dinner table scenes, with their arguments good-natured or otherwise, or the mock trial in the Judge's study.

These scenes are overwhelmingly 'wordy', many of them, indeed, revolve around word games. The St. James family plays a game of forfeit called 'Dull Generality or Trite Conclusion'; the mock trial in the Judge's study turns on verbal exactitude; 'D.K.', hiding behind her pen-name in episode 2, complains how no one has ever said exactly what they meant to her; even in episode 3, we are shown Stevie and her mother playing Scrabble. This is not, of course, some kind of 'fault' in the series. Dialogue is one of Elliott's strengths as a writer and the screenplay by Michael Gow, a playwright himself, is very impressive. Many of the most memorable moments of the plot turn on the recollection of particular phrases, such as Eve's 'come to us' which circumscribes the whole plot. The final revelation by Eve of the death of Heath, again turning on the significance of a particular phrase, 'Not you', is delivered as dramatic monologue, a classically theatrical rather than filmic form. While the background fades, Eve's speech moves to its shocking climax. Caughie makes much of the fact that television drama began as an outgrowth of radio drama and it is surely significant that the one dramatist present in the plot—Bea, or, to use her pen-name, D.K. Durfee—is a writer of radio plays.

A better case for a specific television high art can be made out, perhaps, for 'Bodysurfer' (1989), directed by Ian Barry and produced for the ABC, an adaptation of Robert Drewe's collection of short stories, *The Bodysurfers*, (1983). The problems in translating it to the screen were very different from 'Edens Lost', and fundamental to the process was the decision to re-mix the stories for adaptation to television. Alongside this, some of the stories were re-plotted, transferring roles between characters for instance, and finally much of the dialogue was rewritten. Different writers were used for different episodes of the four-part series. The whole process of screen-writing seems to have been the exact opposite of the conservatism of the adaptation of 'Edens Lost'. Something of the complexity of this process can be seen in the second episode which, in effect, combined three separate stories: 'Baby Oil' (number four of the collection), 'After Noumea' (number six), and 'Stingray' (number twelve). Nor was the re-mixing of the plot simply a matter of conflating the plots of the already existing stories. Stories which had previously only a loose connection by theme and a tenuous connection, if at all, by character, were integrated. The order of the stories in the collection, corresponding roughly to a chronological development between the mid-fifties and early sixties to the mid-eighties, was totally re-arranged. For example, the series effectively began with the ninth story and ended with a mixture of the first three.

This imaginative script-editing was part of a broader move away from that dominance of text which characterises the adaptation of 'Edens Lost'. The proportion of dialogue was cut and much of it was new. The visual style of the series was a studied departure from the naturalism that seems to be part of the ABC's house style. It was notable for its bold visual effects: the rapid cutting between scenes, the use of colour tones to differentiate mood and period, distancing and self-reflexive effects. Some of the visual images, such as the burning of the beach pavilion which opened episode one, appeared independently of any plot or dialogue, but developed thematic lives of their own, sometimes running counter to those developed in the dialogue. The image of destruction, so strikingly represented in that first scene, was not picked up by the plot until almost the very end of episode four, but it functioned continuously to undercut the whole discourse of building and creativity in the narrative of David's life as an architect. In a similar way, the theme of separation and conflict between the generations, while present in the verbal script, developed in its own way as well through the variations on the song 'After You've Gone', which occurred throughout the episodes and especially in the last one.

On the other hand, it needs to be said that these progressive stylistic moves away from naturalism, and the urge to restructure the stories in a new, distinctive visual style were paradoxically balanced by other tendencies in an opposite direction in the production. This was in large part a result of the greater concentration on one character, David Lang. While David is arguably the major character in the story collection, he does not dominate it and focus the action of the narrative in quite the way he does in the television series. The events of the stories are in fact distributed through a wide range of charac-ters, often though not always members of the Lang family. David's father, for instance, has a couple of stories in which he is an important character. Some of the members of the family find their way into the narrative, sometimes in very transitory ways. David's sister Anne, for instance, appears really only as the object of lust of the unidentified ex-crim fantasist of 'The View from the Sandhills'. The stormy love affair with Anthea in 'Baby Oil', which is the basis of episode two, involves not David but his brother Max. The second 'part' of the episode, the psychological deterioration of David at his beach house, involves neither David nor Max in the original story 'After Noumea', but Anthea's husband, Brian. It is only the last part of the episode, based on the final story, 'Stingray', that originally concerned David. With this went a trend, especially in the last episode, for the camera to see with David's eyes as it were. What we as viewers saw, and the interpretation we made of it, was more and more what David himself saw. In art television, for Caughie, on the other hand, the camera's 'look' is co-extensive, not with any particular character, especially not with the main character, but with the spectator. As the series progressed David became less and less the object of the camera's gaze and more and more its subject.

The reasons for making these changes are probably a mixture of stylistic and thematic. Perhaps the stories are a bit too short and elusive for coherent television narrative, at least one that wants to reach a popular audience. Certainly, the mini-series created a kind of meta-narrative of the story collection that was finally easier to follow. On the other hand, the gain in organic structure of the television plot was a loss of that sense of elusiveness and openness of significance that is one of the short story's, especially the story collection's, great strengths as a mode.

The decision to focus the stories around David was not, I suspect, solely the result of the exigencies of narrative structure. Rather, for all its touches of postmodernist visual style, there seems to have been a desire in the screen-writing especially, but also in other aspects of the production, to present a more traditional story, a modernist narrative of psychological disintegration. This seems to me the kind of message that the original collection most deliberately avoids. It is especially clear in the last two episodes. In episode three, Paul is made into that archetype of modern life, the misunderstood and under-valued artist, starving in a garret, possessing only his talent and a 'fatal attraction'—literally in the mini-series—to women. In one scene we see Paul steal the oil paints he cannot afford to buy. This is a very ornate elaboration of the short story, where Paul's interest in painting is mentioned only incidentally and then as yet another example of this shiftless teenager's inability to concentrate on the job in hand. David is transformed into the equally archetypal, uncomprehending father, trying to settle his son into a good career, if not accountancy exactly then his own profession of architecture. Paul's raincoat becomes less and less a sign of his fashion sense and more a sign of his alienation and poverty. As he climbs the stairs to Yvonne's flat, he is coughing like a consumptive—one wonders how common TB was amongst middle-class teenagers in Bondi in the 1980s. At the end, Paul does the only thing that such a character can do in such a story—he dies.

The mass media and high culture

Broadly speaking, the modern mass media—print journalism, cinema, broadcast radio and television—developed in the early twentieth century in a context of suspicion and hostility from the defenders of high culture. In essence, they represented for cultural critics as diverse as Adorno, the Leavises and (in our own time) Allan Bloom, what high art was not. A more complex picture emerged from the practitioners in these media, however, surprisingly early on. The practices of tabloid journalism had begun to transform the quality press as well by the 1920s, and by 1930 there was already a canon of (mainly European) film 'art' as well as a 'classic' popular cinema in Hollywood. Even more remarkable is the way that non-commercial public broadcasting in Britain and Australia established almost from its beginnings an alliance with high art: the early programming of the BBC represents an idealised version of middle-class literary and musical taste, quite unrelated, so far as one can gather, to what that same class actually wanted to read and hear. Although the 'wireless' was for the Leavises in the early 1930s one of the arch-conspirators in the war against high culture, for most people public broadcasting has seemed to be a major force in the opposite direction. The BBC emerged early on as a venerable cultural institution, like parliament. Radio, in particular, has retained this aura of prestige in both Britain and in Australia.

Television has never quite filled the same role as radio in public esteem—in comparison with film, it has always seemed a 'poor' medium in artistic and/or financial terms. Whereas radio drama was clearly a different means of communication from the theatre or the written word, television looked superficially rather like a poor man's film, and for years it was hamstrung by its technical limitations in comparison with film. Indeed, in many ways of course it still is:

videotape cannot match the subtlety of film as a recording medium, nor can the television set reproduce the audio-visual detail and immediacy of the impact of the big screen. The early successes of television drama made virtues out of these limitations, but there is only so much that can be done in that way. As Troy Kennedy Martin warned in the early 1960s, naturalism on its own cannot provide a flexible or sophisticated enough model for the development of a modern television art. Australian television, in particular, seems to have lacked this innovative artistic dimension. What one hears of the policy debates about the ABC confirms this view, and the general picture I have painted of its cultural ambience. While radio, perhaps because it is relatively cheap to finance, has gone its own way, its presenters often making a joke on air about how few people are probably listening, television seems to be endlessly troubled about the competing claims of minority and mass broadcasting. It is easy to appreciate the ABC's dilemma: if it caters too obviously to minority tastes, it infringes its chartered role as the national public broadcaster and jeopardises its funding; if it chases ratings, it loses its reason for a different kind of role from the commercial channels and also jeopardises its funding.

Even with the development of Media Studies and Cultural Studies in the 1980s, this situation has not really changed. If anything it has become more marked. There is very little writing about the self-consciously quality end of Australian television production in comparison with the boom in writing about popular television like soaps and quiz shows. It seems to be generally accepted from all sides that television is intrinsically a popular medium with little scope for 'art'; this may be either regretted or celebrated, depending on one's particular stance in the matter, but it does not seem widely questioned. It is surely one of the most glaring lacunae in the development of the disciplines of both Cultural Studies and English in Australia.

'ZONES OF CONTESTATION': ENGLISH AND CULTURAL STUDIES

Oppositional discourses

In the sphere of education, higher education in particular, one site of major conflict between popular culture and high culture has been in the relationship between the emergent field of 'Cultural Studies' and the older disciplines of the Humanities. In its simplest manifestation, this argument has taken the form that whereas the subject matter of the older disciplines, English especially, is grounded in the study of high culture, Cultural Studies is a study of the culture of the people, in particular the industry of the mass media and its texts, in the past so often an object of easy scorn for the practitioners of English. Moreover, Cultural Studies is not just a disinterested study of popular culture but a celebration of it.

The consequence of this is that when one looks at the development of Cultural Studies in Australia and elsewhere, although there is no shortage of work from academics holding appointments in departments of English, the actual subject of 'English'—especially English traditionally defined—seems to have no role to play. This is in spite of the fact that, from the opposite point of view, Cultural Studies has been widely touted as one of the ways in which the 'crisis' in literary studies or even in the Humanities as a whole might be averted or worked through. This is one of the themes of the symposia convened by the Australian Academy of the Humanities in 1989 (Gibbs 1990) and 1991 (Ruthven 1992). The second of the symposia, in particular, was convened to address the question of the future of the Humanities in the wake of the Dawkins reforms. Among the contributors was John Frow, Professor of English at Queensland University, who sees Cultural Studies as a logical outcome of thinking about the future of literary studies in a time of crisis: the project of Cultural Studies is part of 'the normal process of formation and reformation of the discipline of literary studies in response to real intellectual and social pressures: not with the scattering of a coherent discipline into incoherence' (Frow 1992, p. 22).

Yet there is very little reciprocity in this relationship between the older disciplines of the Humanities, English especially, and Cultural Studies. This is perhaps one of the differences between the Australian Academy's symposia. In the first collection of papers (Gibbs 1990), most of the speakers are concerned to justify the contribution which the Humanities, by and large traditionally defined, continue to make to the national culture. The second collection (Ruthven 1992), given two years later by a group of people prominent in Cultural Studies, but none of whom, as the editor points out, was a fellow of the Academy, seems to assume—although without ever quite saying it—that the traditional English discipline will have little or nothing to contribute to the 'New Humanities' in comparison with (to use the subject headings from the book) Multicultural Studies, Feminist/Gender Studies, Post-Colonial /Subaltern Studies, or even Legal Studies. While it is not to be expected that a symposium convened to address future developments in the Humanities should spend a great deal of space on *apologiae* for the way things have been done in the past, it is still surprising that there is not an essay in the entire collection which begins to argue for a *renewed* English or which seeks to find new ways in which what is increasingly dismissed as mere high culture might find a role to play in this new subject.

A similar picture can be observed in the Cultural Studies readers which have begun to appear in recent years—a sign of how well established the subject is becoming. In addition to the recently published volume of *Australian Cultural Studies*, edited by John Frow and Meaghan Morris (1993), Australians seem to be major players in the development of Cultural Studies worldwide. The reader published in England by Routledge, *The Cultural Studies Reader* (1993), is edited by Simon During, an Australian academic; there is also a substantial contribution by Australian academics to *Cultural Studies* (1992), edited by Lawrence Grossberg et al., the volume of papers from the conference on 'Cultural Studies Now and in the Future', held in America at the University of Illinois at Urbana-Champaign in April 1990. In none of these collections, destined I suspect to be influential in the development and teaching of the subject, is English or high culture a topic of the slightest moment. This is not to say that the editors do not pay a kind of lip-service to the notion that the study of culture (spelled with or without a capital C) should include the consideration of high culture. Grossberg, for example, says that it is a 'common misconception' that Cultural Studies is 'primarily concerned with' popular culture only (Grossberg et al. 1992, p. 11), and cites articles in the collection—very good articles, incidentally—by Ian Hunter on aesthetics and Cultural Studies, Peter Stallybrass on individualism in Shakespeare and Janet Wolff on fine art. The overall nature of the collection, however, can serve only to reinforce this misconception. The three articles cited by Grossberg are in fact the only three, out of a collection of thirty-nine (the volume is 788 pages long), that are concerned with high culture in some way. Much the same pattern emerges on the Australian scene. For example, in his paper on Cultural Studies delivered to the Australian Academy of the Humanities symposium in 1991, John Frow (1992) saw Cultural Studies as having to exclude literary studies, at least for the time being, for 'strategic reasons' of self-protection, presumably until it had defined and established itself more securely. While Frow could envisage a time when this strategy might be abandoned and Cultural Studies could move into areas traditionally the concern of the older Humanities disciplines—he does not seem to consider movement in the other direction—that time was not yet ripe. Nor had it arrived by the time he co-authored the introduction to *Australian Cultural Studies*, published in 1993. The introduction reinforces the idea that, in the last few years, the word 'culture' has been used by Australians in a sense 'that seems far removed from anything to do with literary texts' (Frow and Morris 1993, p. vii). While it is again pointed out that Cultural Studies is not restricted to popular culture and mention is made of 'several' essays in the collection on high culture—a presence that I find a little hard to detect—only an 'overlap . . . to the (limited) extent' (Frow and Morris 1993, p. xxii) is envisaged between literary studies and Cultural Studies, despite the general sense that one of the most exciting things about the new discipline is its eclectic choice of subject matter and its pluralism of methodologies and critical discourses. For both Frow/Morris and During, Cultural Studies is essentially the study of contemporary culture: 'Cultural Studies is, of course, the study of culture, or more particularly, the study of *contemporary* culture' (author's emphasis), as Simon During says in the introduction to his reader (During 1993, p. 1). In some ways this of itself serves to establish an antithetical relationship to the traditional disciplines of the Humanities, not because they have not dealt with contemporary literature or history or whatever, but because by and large they have adopted an historical methodology and structure for their curricula. The traditional English course has often been characterised as '*Beowulf* to Virginia Woolf'. During's volume does acknowledge, however, that while the subject of Cultural Studies may be restricted to contemporary culture, the discipline itself has evolved historically: he includes essays written as far back as the 1940s and quite a lot of work from the 1960s and 1970s. Frow and Morris's book, on the other hand, is alarmingly lacking in historical depth, either in terms of its texts discussed or in terms of its articles. There is no essay in the collection written before 1983 and most of the articles were produced in the last few years.

In many discussions of Cultural Studies something stronger than lack of interest in English can be detected: a note of real hostility, a sense that English (in particular) and Cultural Studies are oppositional discourses. This is more than a matter of the Humanities being in perpetual crisis on the one hand—not necessarily a bad thing for a discipline like English which is centrally concerned with criticism, as Chris Baldick (1983) has pointed out—and Cultural Studies being by its nature a discourse of 'oppositionality'[1] on the other, towards the powerful Leavisite strand in literary criticism and towards high culture in general. One feels sometimes not only that English can make no contribution to Cultural Studies or that Cultural Studies can afford to ignore it, but that English has to be killed off in order that Cultural Studies can flourish, like the high priest in the Sacred Wood who has to be murdered by his successor.

This oppositionality takes several forms. One is a guilt about the supposedly tainted and dishonourable history of English, that it is linked with British nationalism before the First World War,[2] that high culture is the culture of the upper class, and that, as a consequence, the continued existence of English is like the class war carried on by other means. In his inaugural lecture as Professor of English at Queensland University, John Frow referred to the formation of the discipline of English 'in a context of political and cultural colonialism, and of the teaching of a high culture which was specifically that of the English ruling class' (Frow 1990, pp. 358–9). While I could agree with the first statement, the second seems to me tendentious. In what ways exactly are Dickens's novels the culture of the upper class, especially the ruling class of Australia? Or the Earl of Rochester's poetry for that matter? But even if it were true then, why should it matter to us now? In the criticism of mass culture it is a commonplace to distinguish between the production of a text and its reception; the meaning constructed by the consumers of a text need not be the one intended by its producers, indeed it may well turn out to be the opposite. It seems odd that this kind of principle cannot be extended to high cultural texts.

Another form is that the reality of the modern world is its basis in communication through a technology that English and high culture simply cannot address. In this scheme, it is absurd for high culture, the culture of a minority, redundant in many ways, to act as if it had the leadership and agenda-setting role. High culture should accept its minority status, not just quantitatively as in the traditional modernist manner, but also qualitatively as well. This argument is put consistently by writers like McKenzie Wark, in his column in the *Australian* and in other journals. For example, in the article 'After literature', which discusses Tony Bennett's book, *Outside Literature*, he argues not just that literature has no privileged status among discourses, but that it has no claim to being anything more than 'a minor branch of the study of the media' if, as he takes Bennett to be arguing, we stop making claims for literature's intrinsic worth compared with other forms of writing (Wark 1992, p. 684). The pugnacious tone of much of his writing about literature, a subject in which he claims in the same article that he has no interest, is well caught in this kind of statement: 'media are the principal sites of contestation in and of the modern—and criticism had better get used to it' (Wark 1992, p. 683). Wark's writing is a part of that strand in Cultural Studies which Jim McGuigan has identified as 'Cultural Populism': '*the intellectual assumption, made by some students of popular culture, that the symbolic experiences and practices of ordinary people are more important analytically and politically than Culture with a Capital C*' (McGuigan 1992, p. 4, author's emphasis). While McGuigan is critical of some elements in this school of criticism he does not disagree with its fundamental drift. Cultural Studies for him is defined by the populist sentiment at its heart; a non-populist Cultural Studies is a contradiction in terms, 'an academic game which might do better calling itself something else' (McGuigan 1992, p. 13).

The parallel histories of English and Cultural Studies

The kind of stand-off between English and Cultural Studies represented in the remarks above is, on the whole, mystifying to anyone who investigates the history of the disciplines, although it is, arguably, more readily explicable in Australia and America than in Britain.

Like most new disciplines, the development of Cultural Studies was a mixture of two things: on the one hand, an awareness of new fields of knowledge and methods of enquiry and, on the other, dissatisfaction with already existing disciplinary and institutional structures. In Australia and America, more so than in England, the new fields of enquiry were Communications and Media Studies. Both these fields, the former in particular, had strong institutional infrastructures in place in Australia by the 1980s, principally in what used to be called, before the changes brought in by the Labor government in the late 1980s, the 'college' sector of higher education. In the universities, on the other hand, departments or even courses in Communications were uncommon, although one or two universities had departments or sub-departments of *Mass* Communications, one or two university English departments had courses in film, and in the Social Sciences the media had become an increasingly important area of study. Graeme Turner has traced the development of Cultural Studies in Australia to a split within this field of Communications study in the colleges (Turner 1989a). On the whole, Australian universities, especially Arts disciplines in universities, came to the party rather late, arguably when the parameters of the field had already become too established to be easily changed.[3] Furthermore, Meaghan Morris has consistently emphasised the importance of writers on Cultural Studies in Australia who have worked (at least for the majority of their lives) outside the university system, writers such as Sylvia Lawson and John Docker—she might also cite her own case, of course. One of the early texts of Australian Cultural Studies, Donald Horne's *The Lucky Country*, published in 1964, was the work of someone who at that time was a journalist, and who only subsequently became an academic, and then in a department of Political Science rather than one of the Arts.

In contrast, most of the people involved in the early development of Cultural Studies in Britain, unlike Australia, were from a background in university departments of English: notably both Richard Hoggart and Stuart Hall (despite Hall's current tenure of a Chair in

Sociology), as well as Raymond Williams. These people were neither ignorant of the high cultural traditions of English (in both the textual and institutional senses) nor ideologically opposed in some way to its basic concerns. Indeed, as Hall has pointed out, almost all of the people involved in the early work of the Centre for Contemporary Cultural Studies at Birmingham University had been formed in the Leavisite ethos of the post-war university English department (Hall 1990). It has often been pointed out that early work in British Cultural Studies grew out of 'left Leavisism', a late version of Cambridge English. Hall, for instance, sees Williams's seminal *Culture and Society* as a re-reading of the 'English Moralists' paper at Cambridge, a 'core' course required by all English students. Early work in Cultural Studies was defined, like Cambridge English, by its historical and cultural placement: 'An attempt to address the manifest break-up of traditional culture . . . registering the impact of the new forms of affluence and consumer society . . . Trying to come to terms with the fluidity and the undermining impact of the mass media' (Hall 1990, p. 12). Put like this the project sounds very like Leavis's own.

This is not to say that the establishment of the influential Centre at Birmingham University in 1963, with Hoggart as its Director and Hall as its Research Fellow, was viewed with equanimity in all quarters. Hall has recalled the bitter opposition to the work of the Centre from older disciplines at Birmingham like English and Sociology, despite the fact (or perhaps it should be because of it) that Hoggart actually held the Chair of English in the University. On the first day of the Centre's existence he received a letter from members of the Sociology department attacking the aims and methods of the Centre in the most basic terms.[4] Yet the intellectual project of the Birmingham Centre was clearly not the dethronement of art or high culture but the quest, to use Michael Green's phrase, for 'routes out' of established knowledges (Green 1982). Necessarily, the route out took cognisance of the road in. The route out of English took the form of the study of popular culture, of 'textuality' in a broader sense than that allowed by the traditional 'Language and Literature' matrix, the analysis of the construction of that class of the literary, what it excluded and why; a new History was to be written from below, focusing on oral history and popular memory; Sociology moved in the direction of ethnomethodology. Thus, from its origins, Cultural Studies was 'resolutely impure' (Green 1982, p. 83). At the same time, Green can see the underlying pattern in this collection of disaffected disciplines. In all of them there was an abiding interest in lived experience (something I shall return to later), and in those twin concerns of the new theory coming into the English-speaking world from the late 1960s, textuality and social structure.

The inter-connection between English and Cultural Studies goes far deeper than this, however, and not just in the British context. The similarities between the impulses which led to the formation of both disciplines are very striking. This is true not only of the similarities between Cultural Studies and that influential brand of the study of English which developed at Cambridge after the First World War, but it can even be seen in the similarities between the project of Cultural Studies and the work of Matthew Arnold in the nineteenth century.

Almost all descriptions of Cultural Studies speak of the text in its context: Grossberg's way of putting what he calls this 'impossible but necessary project' is that Cultural Studies 'entails the study of all the relations between all the elements in a whole way of life' (Grossberg et al., p. 14). This is hardly a new idea, however: the very term 'whole way of life', although it comes into Cultural Studies through the work of Raymond Williams, is fundamentally an Arnoldian concept. Moreover, it was Arnold's work which, in the words of Chris Baldick, founded 'modern' literary criticism by effecting its readjustment towards the social function of literature and criticism. The title of Baldick's book about the early years of English in the university is *The Social Mission of English Criticism* (1983).

At the time when Arnold wrote, there were few departments of English, and to all intents and purposes none of what we would think of as English literature. There was nevertheless a long tradition of writing about English literature outside the framework of academic study: a mixture of criticism, reviewing, *belles lettres* etc. on the one hand, and literary scholarship, Tyrwhitt's great edition of Chaucer in the 1770s for example, on the other. The revolutionary nature of Arnold's writing about literature and culture was 'a bold extension of its claim to *social* importance' (Baldick 1983, p. 59, my emphasis). This claim to extended social importance affected not only creative writing but also writing about literature. It is the second which is perhaps in the long run the more innovatory. In *Study of Poetry* (1880), for example, Arnold urged that we reconceive the status of poetry and its centrality to our experience in much more elevated terms. In the modern world it must function as a replacement for both religion and philosophy. Not all writing of course fits the bill; creative writing must be of great stature to carry this lofty responsibility. At the same time writing *about* this literature equally has new demands made upon it: 'it assigns to literary criticism responsibilities no less awesome than those of poetry, introducing into English critical writing a new sense of self-consciousness, a new sensitivity to the wider social and cultural duties befitting its special guardianship' (Baldick 1983, p. 19).

One key conditioning factor of Arnold's work is that he was not speaking on these matters from the inside as it were. Like the founders of Cultural Studies nearly a century later, he was not an academic in the conventional sense—the professorship of Poetry at Oxford which he held for a short time was not a teaching or research post in any way. Nor was he a professional 'man of letters' in the Victorian manner. As he told the Royal Academy in 1875: 'My life is not that of a man of letters but of an Inspector of schools' (Arnold 1960–77, vol. 8 p. 374). The source of his work, outside both the academy and the world of 'letters', gives it not only unusual breadth of reference and significance, especially social significance, but is the underpinning of its deep 'practicality', its sense that literature and writing about literature really matter to our lives now. Arnold's life as an Inspector of schools gave him a strong sense of art as a broad educational force. In his daily work for thirty-five years he saw the complex interplay between literature, culture and cultural policy, education, the State and the Church. As Baldick has suggested, his use of the word 'culture' is often well-translated by the German word *Bildung*, meaning education, training, 'growing-up'. In many ways his work is an adumbration of the 'Cultural Policy Studies' strand within the development of Cultural Studies. It is a terrible irony that Arnold's work should so commonly be seen as laying the foundations for a literary criticism of a purely formalist kind—the 'well-wrought urn' type of American New Criticism.

From the 1880s, the development of English as a school and university subject was closely bound up with projects for the renewal of English national life. English did not just embody the study of the high art of a social élite, but also in some mystical way the national character: 'the discipline came to be promoted as uniquely suited to a mission of national cultivation' (Doyle 1989, p. 12). English was larger than mere knowledge, it was to do with the imagination and spirit of the national culture as a whole. This sense of English as the central pedagogic instrument of a mission of national cultural renewal emerged as the foundation of the *Newbolt Report* of 1921, intended as a blueprint for the reform of the national education system. While it is hard to resist smiling (or worse) at its missionary zeal and jingoism, there is yet a kind of high-mindedness and imaginative breadth about it which is rather moving, particularly in our utilitarian times.

The departments of English literature that grew up throughout the world in the wake of the Cambridge English school in the 1920s and after were built upon precisely this readjustment towards the social that Baldick describes. Nor should the strong historical element—social history as well as linguistic history—in the English language departments formed on the Oxford model from the 1880s be ignored. Although their work is routinely minimised in the legendary history of the university English discipline, their real presence was profound, and their conception of the subject anything but the kind of pure, formalist contemplation of the high cultural artefact which English is often caricatured as in accounts written from the Cultural Studies perspective. It is a grave error to see this kind of American New Criticism—developed after the Second World War under the influence of I. A. Richards after he had left Cambridge for America—as the fundamental paradigm of English. Most departments of English throughout the world, even now, owe far more to the early Richards, before he left Cambridge. They are a bastard, yet cosmopolitan mixture of American New Criticism, English Culturalism, and (latterly) French critical theory.

The similarities between early work in literary criticism and the development of Cultural Studies can also be seen in the foundation of English as a university course in the late nineteenth century and the moves to spread the teaching of English in schools as well as universities after the First World War. The real pressure for the study of both Cultural Studies and English came originally from outside the academy. We have become used to this in the case of Cultural Studies. It is well known how the 'founding fathers' were marginal figures to the university world of the time. Both Hoggart and Williams had working-class backgrounds. In Williams's case he came from the 'border' country of South Wales as well. Both men, as well as E. P. Thompson, spent formative years teaching in adult education in extra-mural departments, peripheral to the mainstream work of the universities. In one of his last essays, published posthumously, Williams drew attention as well to the work of people in all forms of mass education and extension work, usually unsung and mostly unpublished, including for example army education during the war, long *before* the famous texts of Cultural Studies began to appear in the late 1950s (Williams 1989a). Jim McGuigan has pointed out how it has continued to be an unofficial discourse, a congenial site of activity for people from the margins, defined in various ways by class, ethnicity and gender.

This situation is not really very different, however, from the founding of English in the universities, and the similarities are more than those features which characterise the arrival of all new disciplines in institutions. The social position of its members for instance is comparable. Although few of the practitioners of Cambridge English after the First World War were of working-class origin, they were still marginal in important ways to the social world of their predecessors. Sir Arthur Quiller-Couch ('Q'), the legendary Professor of English at Cambridge from 1912, was a Cornish squire, but most of the people who defined the nature of Cambridge English were from very different social backgrounds. I. A. Richards was the son of a works manager from the north of England. F. R. Leavis, although Cambridge born and bred, was not from a don's family, but from the 'town', his father being a musical instruments dealer. His wife, Q. D. Leavis, was the daughter of an orthodox Jewish draper from north London.

More importantly, the pressures for English came likewise not only from outside the universities themselves but from similar quarters as Cultural Studies. Ian Hunter (1989, p. 3) has seen the earliest origins of literary education not in what he terms the 'aesthetico-ethical practice of a minority caste' writing about culture or aesthetic experience, but in the very practical changes made in *popular* education in the early nineteenth century by social reformers aghast at the nature of life in an industrialised but morally unformed and undisciplined society. Baldick has identified the most important areas of pressure in the later nineteenth century as coming from working men, from the colonies of the British empire, and from women. English literature was always a prominent part of the teaching of the Workers' Educational Association (WEA), founded in 1903. It prospered (somewhat unexpectedly and not without irony considering the attitudes of some of the members of later university English departments) in an environment where there was momentum for teaching 'practical' or scientific subjects, like technical colleges of one sort or another. It filled the perceived need for a Humanities presence better than Latin or (especially) Greek. For one thing it did not need the heavy investment of time and teaching in the elementary acquisition of the language. In that sense it rode on the back of the technological revolution of Victorian England, despite preaching values which were often openly inimical to it. Batsleer et al. see English literature as a school subject as having been born in mission schools overseas, in Africa and India, as part of a drive for linguistic standardisation and conformity.[5] English, like History and Modern Languages, was also one of the few subjects that women could study at university, and their presence was vital to the shaky status of the new disciplines in their formative years. In the first five years of the English department at Oxford, founded in 1893, women provided the overwhelming majority of candidates for examinations, sixty-nine compared with only eighteen men. This situation continued up to the beginning of the First World War, and in many universities, the majority probably, the gender balance has worsened—if anything—in the years since. Although Quiller-Couch always began his lectures with 'Gentlemen . . .', it was mostly women he addressed. The danger of 'effeminacy' haunted the subject of English literature in its early years; Oxford men commonly referred to it as 'pink sunsets' (Doyle 1989, p. 3).

The real catalyst which led to the expansion of both Cultural Studies and English as university subjects was, however, the impulse for change and reconstruction after the two world wars. Stuart Hall has said that Cultural Studies 'really begins with the debate about the nature of social and cultural change in postwar Britain' (Hall 1990, p. 12). But the situation is even clearer with the development of the English school at Cambridge in the shadow of the First World War. The tripos in English Literature—in Cambridge parlance a 'tripos' is a course of study leading to a first degree—was approved in 1917 and many people, those who opposed it as well as those who supported it, noted the coincidence of dates. F. L. Lucas, one of the opponents, recalled how 'it was . . . in March 1917, while the

German armies were falling back to the Hindenberg Line, while Russia was tottering into Revolution and America preparing for war, that at Cambridge members of the Senate met to debate the formation of an English Tripos separate from Modern Languages' (Mulhern 1979, pp. 3–4). English had been taught before at Cambridge but in the context of a faculty of medieval and modern languages and in a manner that was essentially philological. What motivated the proposers of the English tripos was not just the need for independence—philology was strongly identified with German scholarship and there was a lot of jingoism in some aspects of the proposal—but the need felt for a new *kind* of subject born out of changed circumstances, a sense that those who came back from the war would not be content with business as usual and would be driven to try to understand the world in which they lived and what had happened to it in new ways. Their instincts were absolutely right. I. A. Richards, one of the first teachers in the new course, glowed about his first year of teaching it in 1919:

> That year was quite beyond anything you could imagine. It was World War I survivors come back to college . . . There was an atmosphere, such a dream, such a hope. They were just too good to be true; it was a joy to deal with those people; those who got back to Cambridge from all that slaughter were back *for reasons*. (Richards 1977, p. 257, author's emphasis)

Baldick points to the 'constant sense of timeliness in his writings; the conviction that the war had placed momentous responsibilities and choices before the survivors' (Baldick 1983, p. 136). Nor was this feeling about the subject unique to Cambridge. Caroline Spurgeon, great Shakespearean scholar, Professor of English at University College, London, and a writer in a very different tradition from that of Cambridge English, recalled likewise how teaching literature during the war constantly led her mind 'to fly back irresistibly like a released spring to . . . some question of ultimate values as seen afresh in the scorching and purifying light of war' (Spurgeon 1917, p. 3). After doubting what she was doing when the war began, she later came to feel that the war had demonstrated all over again how important literature was and how vital was the training of the sensibility needed to appreciate it. Baldick has collected examples from academics at other universities of the time which echo what he sees as 'this keen sense of the war as a real test of the value of literary study' (Baldick

1983, p. 91). This sense of both teachers and students drawn to the subject of English through a need to understand the world in which they were living is markedly similar to the recollections of early workers in the new field of Cultural Studies. At the Birmingham Centre, Stuart Hall did not like taking students who did not already have a strong sense of what mattered to them. He expected and received a high level of personal engagement:

> So, from the start we said [to our students]: 'What are you interested in? . . . What is it about the way in which British culture is now living through its kind of postcolonial, posthegemonic crisis that really bites into your experience?' (Hall 1990, p. 17)

Nor is it often enough remembered that the full title of the new tripos at Cambridge was English Literature, Life and Thought. From the beginning its project was not a narrow formalist study of literary icons but a study of English culture as a whole. The kind of research it encouraged at the postgraduate level was, according to Francis Mulhern, 'of an unprecedentedly elastic kind' (Mulhern 1979, p. 31). One recurring aspect of this work was the connection between high culture and various aspects of popular culture. Both the Leavises did doctoral work in this field. F. R. Leavis's PhD, supervised (uneasily at times) by Quiller-Couch, was written on the relationship between literature and journalism in the seventeenth century; Q. D. Leavis's work, inspired and supervised by I. A. Richards, and later published as *Fiction and the Reading Public*, extended a similar kind of enquiry into the audience of popular fiction in later centuries. Such bold and innovatory work in 'English' was not, however, welcomed by all. In the fragile early years of the English school, Q. D. Leavis's dissertation was subjected to what Mulhern describes as a 'brutally sarcastic' attack by F. L. Lucas, one of the conservative heavyweights of the university, in the quasi-official conspectus *University Studies* (Mulhern 1979, p. 30). Until the ratification of the degree course wholly in modern English in 1926–27, and the establishment of the autonomous faculty of English to govern it, the conditions of the English school recall the borderline status of the Birmingham Centre in its early years. Most of the early staff had come from other disciplines, only a few held full-time posts in it, a great deal of the teaching was done by poorly paid 'freelances'. F. R. Leavis was not elected to a fellowship at Cambridge until he was thirty-seven and his wife never held a full-time university post, at Cambridge or anywhere else.

It is at the undergraduate level, however, that the distinctive nature of Cambridge English can best be appreciated. Leavis's vision was never fully implemented anywhere, least of all in Cambridge itself, but reading his 'Sketch for an "English School"', first published in 1943, is still a heady experience. While part I of the English tripos was designed as a wide-ranging course in English literature from Chaucer to the present day, it was really in part II that Leavis planned his greatest reforms. One of his fundamental aims was to take seriously the 'Life and Thought' aspects of the tripos which he saw by the 1940s as recognised in only a formal way. Part II would contain study in literature in languages other than English—he envisaged papers in both French literature and Italian literature—but at its heart would be a new paper on the seventeenth century, the period to be studied 'not merely in literature, but as a whole; the Seventeenth Century as a key phase, or passage, in the history of civilisation' (F. R. Leavis 1948, p. 48). Topics covered in the paper would include such areas as: Calvinism to Puritan individualism, tolerance, the rise of capitalism, Popular Culture. A fundamental aspect of the project was to try and understand how the seventeenth century turned into the England of the present day. Throughout, it seems to be assumed that the 'literary mind' would work extensively on non-literary materials.

Differences between English and Cultural Studies

It would be fatuous, however, to argue that Cultural Studies and English (even Cambridge English) are really the same thing and to ignore the broad differences between Cultural Studies and English which developed and grew with the passage of time. In particular, while both Cambridge English and Cultural Studies were predicated on the need to study culture from a broad base and perspective, major differences appeared in the understanding of how that broad culture is composed and what its values are. One important difference emerged early on in Williams's apophthegm that 'culture is ordinary'.[6] While Williams is clearly speaking of culture in its anthropological sense, it is impossible not to feel the barb in it, a thrust against the fundamental contention of Cambridge English as a whole and of

Leavis in particular, that culture is the province of a tiny minority in all periods, and that the distinctiveness of modern society is the direct assault on these minority values by a mass of people, who, while civilised, are not cultured. For Leavis, the period since the Industrial Revolution had witnessed a calamitous split in literary culture, between high art on the one hand, its traditions going back in English language and history to Chaucer, and a debased popular literature, mass-produced for cheap thrills and escapism in moments of lassitude, on the other. Before the emergence of this debased literary culture the people had two choices: either to accept the rigorous training necessary to access the high culture or to live in the (albeit highly valued) *oral* culture of the folk. High culture—literary culture—is an integral and unified phenomenon. There are no two ways about it. Williams's project in the late 1950s and early 1960s was fundamentally to reject this dichotomy, in particular to sever the link between oral culture and the culture of the people and, in the process, to valorise popular culture. A similar intellectual drift can be seen in the historical work of E. P. Thompson, tracing the history of working-class radicalism through popular movements and their pamphleteering. As Hall has said, not only did Thompson's work make it plain that the history of the period 1790–1830 could not be written without a sustained account of its 'culture', but that one could not speak of English culture in the singular, but only of cultures in the plural. Nor are these cultures given in some essentialist way but are fluid and multiplex structures, the result of conscious processes of self-formation and construction: there are 'struggles between "ways of life" rather than the evolution of "*a* way of life"' (Hall 1980, p. 20).

This acceptance of the Leavisite stress on 'culture', on the one hand, but lack of ease if not outright rejection of its narrow definition, on the other, is very much the temper of work produced in the early days of the Birmingham Centre under the directorship of Richard Hoggart. Hoggart's epoch-making book, *The Uses of Literacy* (1957), written before the Centre was founded, is in many ways a work of divided consciousness. The first part is a powerful and wistful picture of his own growing-up, evoking in loving detail the rich working-class culture of a northern industrial city in the 1920s and early 1930s. It is hard not to see this as a riposte to the gloomy and pessimistic rendition of industrial life so common not just in the work of Leavis and his circle at Cambridge, but of the whole modernist strand in English cultural life. The second part of the book, however, which Hoggart originally wanted to call the 'abuses' of literacy, is a ringing condemnation of the destructive effects of the importation of American-produced mass culture, wholly in keeping with that Leavisite-modernist view of culture which seems to be rejected in the first part. Hoggart's inaugural lecture at the Centre spoke of the concern of Cultural Studies with those aspects of popular culture and the media which had hitherto been neglected. But one of the themes of the extension of interest to these previously bypassed cultural materials was an extension to them of 'literary criticism', of evaluation of a still very Leavisite kind.[7] The influential collection, *The Popular Arts* (1964), edited by Stuart Hall and Paddy Whannell, extended this evaluative practice to areas of culture which had been demonised by the Cambridge school, but it was still strongly discriminatory—jazz, for instance, was admitted to the ranks of serious culture, but rock music was excluded. It was only with the work on 'subcultures', associated with the later tenure of Hall as director of the Centre in the 1970s, that this kind of patronising evaluation of popular culture from a lofty perspective disappeared and the ghost of Richards and Leavis's fearful view of popular culture was laid to rest.

Another area of difference that emerged between English and Cultural Studies was in the question of the political stance of the cultural critic to the world being studied. To put it crudely, while most work in Cultural Studies, at least within the British and Australian traditions, has originated on the political left, there is a recurrent conservative political stance in much work which comes out of the Arnoldian tradition in English, although it is easy both to exaggerate it and to misunderstand it. Simon During has identified the strong tradition in Cultural Studies of work which is 'engaged' and subjective, emerging out of strong personal experience (During 1993).

Something of the origins of this political quietism or conservatism in much of the work in English can be tracked down in Arnold's paradoxical view of the relationship of the critic to society. For all that his daily life constantly put him in mind of the interrelationship in culture between literature, education and the state, and his shift of literary criticism towards the social, he believed also that the critic's job could only be done from a position of 'disinterestedness'. Above all, while the individual critic will necessarily have political views, in the exercise of criticism itself the critic must not write from a standpoint of direct political partisanship. The kind of zealotry that partisanship implies is essentially at odds with those aspects in culture of gentleness, harmony and integrity which Arnold is at pains to identify. For all his practical work, there is yet in Arnold's writings a fear of the merely practical or of ideas being put into practice prematurely, especially when they affect the lives of the mass of the people. This conservatism and classicism can be seen in the work of Arnold's descendants, in Eliot's ideas of order and tradition for example. In Richards's work this develops into a kind of neo-Confucianism—Richards was in fact strongly interested in far Eastern culture. There is for Richards a close connection between the chaos of the post-war world, which he identifies like so many of the writers of the time, and social class. The lower class lives in a world of chaos, and this social chaos finds an analogy in the chaotic thinking of disorganised minds. Great writers, by contrast, attain a supreme level of self-control and understanding. The aim of literary education is to cultivate a kind of mental poise, capable of ordering the disparate impulses of modern life into a coherent whole. The secret of poetry and of the arts in general is this ability to produce wholeness of mind. This, in its turn, will be the only way in which a resolution of the general social and cultural crisis can be found. In Leavis's writing there is a slightly different picture. He was not politically conservative in the manner of Eliot. Several times in his work in the 1930s he seems to have viewed what he saw as the inevitable coming of a socialist planned economy with equanimity, but he was never convinced by socialist theories of culture, especially those of the more crudely economically determinist kind which were common in some quarters at the time. Of the work of socialist cultural theorists in the continental tradition, he seems, like more or less everyone else in England at the time, to have been ignorant.

English, both in its pure Leavisite form or in the kind of pragmatic mixture of practical criticism and literary history that came to be its dominant incarnation in English departments throughout the world, is often portrayed as an untheorised or openly anti-theoretical discipline. By contrast, Cultural Studies was, from its earliest days, marked by negotiation with a wide range of cultural and literary theories: Marxist cultural theory, the work of Althusser and Gramsci, structuralism, semiotics, theory of subcultures, communication theory, feminism, Lacanian psychoanalysis. Indeed, when one looks at the recently produced Cultural Studies readers, 'Cultural Studies' seems to be for many people a site where the 'theory' battles of the 1980s can be continued by other means.

There is some truth in both sides of this formulation. As a new discipline with a marginal status in the academy, Cultural Studies was arguably better placed to respond to the rapidly changing theoretical scene of the 1970s and 1980s. It was not burdened with quite the same weight of tradition as the older Humanities disciplines; the people who worked in it were more likely to have come from a range of intellectual backgrounds. On the other side, there is a kind of hostility in literary study to fully articulated theoretical positions—as distinct from more practical ways of discussing what writers do in general—and in some ways it is implicit in the whole tradition of aesthetics which underpins literary criticism's evaluative project. At the same time that the perception of beauty must be more than a purely subjective statement of individual taste, Kant had denied the possibility of formulating rules for it: 'the *beautiful* is that which pleases universally without a concept' (Kant 1957, p. 392). That phrase 'without a concept' seems to ring through the history of literary criticism like a bell. For different reasons, but with a similar kind of effect, Arnold had a thorough dislike of what he called 'systematic' judgements. The source of true literary criticism is neither in theory nor in 'facts' of one sort or another about books, but in an unmediated, empirical contact with the object itself. With this belief, literary criticism is in a position to appeal for the authority of its judgements over the head of various specialisms. Baldick puts this very well:

> his radical curtailment of theoretical argument or explanation protects the urgency of empirical demonstration ('*there*') from closer scrutiny, while the evacuated realm of theory thereby becomes vulnerable to reinvasion by cruder substitutes: first a certain vitalism, evident in Arnold's constant appeals to the authority of '*life*' or to the 'instinct of self-preservation in humanity' and its various radically determined manifestations. (Baldick 1983, p. 41)

The most notorious case study of traditional English's inability to deal with theory is the argument between F. R. Leavis and René Wellek in which Leavis scorned the notion of a theory of literature and consistently refused to discuss his own theoretical position.[8] As if to compound the felony, Leavis shared with Arnold a proud belief in the superior intellectual and indeed moral status of literary criticism, appealing like Arnold over the head of specialisms to the object itself or to self-justifying references to 'life', and offending potential allies in other disciplines by insisting on the leadership role of English in the Faculty of Arts over other subjects like History and Philosophy. While concepts of language and textuality have increasingly come to dominate all sorts of discourses in the Humanities, English literature as a discipline has paradoxically lost this sense of intellectual leadership in recent years. If anything, literature now feels itself in the junior position to philosophy and history, and the development of Cultural Studies has been bound up with this dramatic reversal.

At the same time, although Leavis and English in general were drastically weak on theory compared to Cultural Studies, nobody could accuse Leavis in particular of not knowing what it was that he was trying to do in the study and teaching of English, or of being unable to articulate it. In 'Sketch of an "English School"' there is a crystalline purity of vision and unity of purpose. The goals and methods of the study of English can be expressed in a couple of sentences. Thus, the intellectual discipline of English is literary criticism. Its uniqueness and special value is that it trains both the intelligence and the sensibility together and at the same time. Despite the imperative to study the culture of English society in a broad context of its social significance, the number of literary works which exemplify English Culture is very small—and thus is very amenable to syllabus formation. Few areas of the academy have been able to articulate their social value, their intellectual project and the delimited and manageable nature of their subject matter with such force or clarity.

Certainly Cultural Studies has not been able to: definition, especially in the literal sense of marking the boundaries, has seemed an impossible dream. In the first paper in Ruthven's collection on the New Humanities, Meaghan Morris characterises Cultural Studies as 'a difficult field to present in a summary way, and an impossible field to present in overview' (Morris 1992, p. 2). For John Frow in the same collection, the theoretical object of Cultural Studies is 'the culture of everyday life . . . the full range of practices and representations in which meanings and personal and group identities are formed' (Frow 1992, p. 25). This is Williams's 'whole way of life' of a society *plus* the renewed and greatly expanded study of the mechanism of representation and symbolisation that has evolved in the last twenty-five years. The only thing that seems to be left out is what most non-academics think of when they hear the world 'culture', the literary studies, for instance, which he suggests should be omitted for the moment for reasons of strategy and self-protection. It is not just the subject matter of Cultural Studies which seems such a baggy monster but the discipline seems to lack any defined methodology, certainly nothing resembling Leavis's conviction about the special nature of literary criticism. For During, Cultural Studies is not a discipline like any other: 'it possesses neither a well-defined methodology nor clearly demarcated fields for investigation' (During 1993, p. 1).

Most descriptions of work in Cultural Studies have sought to emphasise the distinctiveness, to build a definition in a sense, out of this very absence of clearly identifiable topics and methodologies. Hall has stressed that Cultural Studies has always been 'an adaptation to its terrain . . . a conjunctural practice' (Hall 1990, p. 11). In another context, he coined the phrase about culture as 'zones of contestation' and although the geographical nature of the metaphor has proved very fertile it has, paradoxically, brought us no closer to being able to identify exactly the place where this activity is being carried out. For Frow and Morris, Cultural Studies is a kind of place also, a site, a 'point of intersection and negotiation of radically different kinds of determination and semiosis' (Frow and Morris 1993, p. xv). The metaphor of the point of intersection suggests definition but the 'radically different kinds of determination' seems to pull in the opposite direction. I am not sure that one can have it both ways. Whether we call Cultural Studies a place or, more ambitiously, a 'point', it is hard not to feel that the upshot for the development of the discipline is a debilitating vagueness about what it is studying and how it is studying it. In Ruthven's collection, Tony Bennett points to the danger of the discipline becoming '[so] potentially all-embracing that to describe something as an example of Cultural Studies may, in the end, be saying very little about it' (Bennett 1992, p. 37). Bennett's response has been to shift his own work in the field into the more readily definable area of 'Cultural *Policy* Studies'.

The downfall of the Leavisite brand of Cambridge English was, paradoxically, its narrowness. Although the course itself was devised as a broad study of English culture, there seemed to be an ever-shrinking cadre of literary texts which witnessed to the transmission of it—the infamous Leavisite 'Great Tradition', which in the case of the novel, for instance, included Henry James but excluded Charles Dickens, and supposedly reached its culmination in the work of D. H. Lawrence. For all its compactness and coherence, at least in the minds of believers, ultimately it nearly strangled the discipline. Few academics, even those who thought themselves squarely within the tradition of English, could tolerate its exclusiveness, based on principles which had long since hardened into prejudice and bigotry and come to seem merely eccentric. In particular, the course seemed incapable of comprehending change or difference. Not just individual works or authors were excluded but whole areas of literary culture. Leavis's hostility to American literature, for instance, was notorious. Literature in English from other areas, like the British Commonwealth as it then was, received no consideration at all, not even in those universities in the Commonwealth which had departments of English of a Leavisite persuasion. The indifference and even open hostility towards Australian literature in those departments in Australia which were the last bastions of Leavisism in the 1960s is a matter of record. When it came to dealing with texts that were not 'literature' at all in the usual sense, non-literary texts like film and television, the texts of popular culture, Leavisite English could not cope at all. Ultimately it was doomed by that very sharpness of focus which had given it such power in the 1920s and 1930s.

Cultural Studies has clearly proceeded in the opposite manner. Its breadth of context and openness to innovation and difference have been a source of its intellectual strength and, in the 1990s, it has seemed to be in tune with a new spirit of global pluralism. But that is not to say that it does not have its own forms of narrowness, worryingly evident in some of its products. One aspect of the publication of Readers in Cultural Studies is that they tend to define the subject too clearly, legitimising some kinds of study and not others. This is the opposite of helpful in a subject which is still trying to find its feet. More alarming still is the authentication process whereby certain writers in the field are 'accredited' to the project and others not. This is something more than the inevitable consequences of making a selection from a large field in any area. All three of the

Readers that I have discussed use the design motif on the cover of a list of contributors. The covers of the collections edited by During and Grossberg et al., both published by Routledge, are remarkably similar in this: essentially the only design is the list of contributors on one side of the front cover and the editors' names on the other. The collection of *Australian Cultural Studies*, edited by Frow and Morris for Allen & Unwin, while it has a more imaginative front cover, likewise follows the same motif of listing the contributors on the back, topped by the editors' names and a rubric of 'Questions in Cultural Studies'. The effect for me is not unlike the family Bible, a sort of dynasty with the parents at the top and their legitimate offspring ranged beneath. This would be less worrying if there were not a conspicuous overlap between the volumes in their contributors. In the case of the Frow and Morris collection, not only are most of the articles reprints of work already published elsewhere—not of itself a bad thing and indeed inevitable in an anthology—but some of the articles have already been *anthologised* elsewhere as well. Stuart Cunningham's essay on the Australian mini-series, for instance, has had several incarnations, including publication in two different journals and a place in Tulloch and Turner's (1989) collection of essays on Australian television. The only differences that I can spot between the versions in the anthologies are in the title and the subheadings. Another essay, John Hartley's 'Invisible fictions', originally published in *Textual Practice*, was recently collected in a whole volume dedicated to his work on television published by Routledge.[9] The picture that this conveys, of Cultural Studies as a well-marked and small pond inhabited by a few large fish, well-established enough to have seminal essays, is a curious one for a discipline which has proclaimed its commitment to innovation and difference and which, by its very nature, is predicated on breadth of interest.

Moving beyond the high–popular conflict

The parallel histories of English and Cultural Studies ought to warn us of the dangers of locking them into intellectual and institutional struggles to the death. This is more than a naive plea for tolerance and a bland hope for intellectual pluralism—for live and let live in the academy. In some ways, we would do well to keep an open mind about the most ubiquitous concepts in this sphere, such as the whole question of the opposition between the so-called 'aesthetic' view of culture (culture with a capital C) and its alternative, culture understood in an anthropological sense. This particular binary has become a bit like the second law of thermodynamics, so basic a truth of Cultural Studies—and traditional English for that matter—as to require no discussion. Yet Q. D. Leavis thought that her work was 'anthropological' too. On a more weighty note, some anthropologists have suggested that the distinctiveness between the two views of culture may not be as clear as is often assumed. James Clifford, for example, has pointed to the coincidence of dates: modern anthropology dates its origins to the same period in which Arnold was writing *Culture and Anarchy*. In writings which describe other cultures, he constantly sees what he calls 'a straining towards aesthetic form and autonomy' (Clifford 1993, p. 62). Since the nineteenth century, those elements in other cultures which have been valued are things like their depth, their coherence, and the driving impulse in examining them has been to see 'it whole rather than disrupted, torn, intertextual, or syncretic' (Clifford 1993, p. 62)—and a bit like a modernist poem, one might add. He quotes the view of George Stocking to the effect that modern anthropology owes as much to Matthew Arnold as it does to its official founding father, E. B. Tylor. In the early twentieth century, as anthropologists investigated more and more societies (cultures in the anthropological sense), so more and more of their products came to be viewed as 'art' (culture in the aesthetic sense). The major contribution of primitive art to modernism, for instance, is a particularly well-documented case of this.

Many critics have seen the need for literary criticism to move out of the privileged domain of high art into other aspects of culture—indeed, much of Cambridge English is predicated on just such an idea. Leavis himself certainly saw a training in literary criticism as a kind of enabling discipline for studying other aspects of culture. In Hoggart's early work at the Birmingham Centre, there is a similar view that reading cultures requires a kind of literary sensibility: 'without appreciating good literature, no one will really understand the nature of society, . . . [and] literary critical analysis can be applied to certain social phenomena other than "academically respectable" literature' (Hoggart 1966, p. 277). The work of Barthes and McLuhan operates in a similar way, using the techniques of literary analysis on non-literary material, although Barthes, in particular, was not concerned with evaluation in the way that Hoggart, grounded in the Leavisite tradition of English, was.

The need to move beyond the high culture–popular culture polarity has also been urged from the perspective of the study of popular culture. For Tony Bennett, popular culture can only be defined by reference to what it is not—folk culture, élite culture, etc. The loss of consensus about what high culture is has removed a crucial point of reference from which popular culture could be distinguished. What seems to be left is a fairly loose sense of popular culture as a space constituted by an 'historically specific alignment between the culture and ideology of the dominant classes and the culture of the subordinated classes' (Bennett 1980, p. 28). Obviously, as these historically specific alignments change over time, the nature of the space they produce and the texts they comprehend will change. It is a matter of common observation that different texts or practices fill different roles in culture at different times, that the popular work of one period becomes the high art of another, and vice versa. For this reason alone it seems important that the categorisation of culture should not be reified. One of the things that Cultural Studies should surely focus upon is that very process of transformation and move-ment in culture, the setting up of boundaries and their transgression. Raymond Williams put it well, as usual, in one of his late works when he spoke of the need to keep different traditions of reading in mind and to examine the conjunction of the 'most common ordinary meanings' with the 'finest individual meanings' (Williams 1989b, p. 4).

If the early days of the disciplines of English and Cultural Studies show great similarities, it is to be hoped that their latter days might be different, and that Cultural Studies might learn from some of the mistakes of English. Cambridge English began as an intellectual project on the margins of the academic establishment, driven to understand the nature of a new world, and its relation to the old one which had faced annihilation and had undergone profound transfor-mation. That this broad humane project should have degenerated into sectarianism and political correctness is part of its tragic fall, but it should not be allowed to irremediably taint the discipline as a whole. Cultural Studies, likewise, began on the fringe, concerned that traditional intellectual structures—especially those of the English discipline—were inadequate and too narrow to address a changing society. Hoggart was a professor of English, but he wanted to take up those things which orthodox English missed or deliberately excluded. I hope that Cultural Studies does not fall into the same trap as English. The flaw in English's understanding of Culture was that it had little understanding of, and even less sympathy with, culture with a small *c*. In the mass society of the modern world, this was a terrible handicap, a recipe for irrelevance and powerlessness. Nor was it good enough any more simply to 'assert' the values of a different society, especially when some of those values were often either unexamined, or intellectually and/or morally indefensible, or simply non-existent. Certainly, few writers now would see the accrediting of value to be as unproblematic as it seemed in the work of Cambridge English. Terry Eagleton, for instance, has attacked traditional English's self-limiting to high culture because the mechanism by which value is accorded is not disinterested: 'literary criticism cannot justify its self-limiting to certain works by appeal to their "value" [because it is] part of a literary institution which constitutes these works as valuable in the first place' (Eagleton 1983, p. 202). Eagleton goes on in his study to urge a shift in the direction of English away from literature towards the larger project of a study of 'discursive or signifying practice', in which literature would have a place but not an automatically privileged role. Similar views can be found in other kinds of post-Althusserian textual study which, like Macherey's work for example, urge a focus on the text as a unit of social production. Bennett (1979, 1990) has consistently proposed the wholesale abandonment of the idea of the aesthetic. One avenue would seem to be to retain the concept of 'literature' but to apply it much more narrowly and systematically to a specific, definable body of writing—the European tradition of *belles-lettres* since the eighteenth century, for example—perhaps definable in non-aesthetic terms as well, rather than to use it across the board as if there were some collection of attributes, transcending space and time, which constituted it.

By the same token, though, a 'Cultural' Studies which feels it is able to ignore high art, Culture with a capital *C*, even if only temporarily and for strategic reasons, seems to me to be a fatally compromised project. While the notion of a study of texts, unworried and undifferentiated by any notions about quality, in their broad discursive contexts, has much to recommend it, one must point out, at the same time, what is lost in the abandonment of the aesthetic dimension in the study of the text. René Wellek, a voice from an earlier generation of literary theory, has more recently insisted that this denial of the notion of quality 'runs counter to the whole long history of the term "literature" and the concept' (Wellek 1982, p. 12). It is hard not to feel that there is something a little mealy-mouthed about those kinds of formulation of Cultural Studies which speak of it in such terms as offering 'a training in arts of mediation that can make navigating difference possible' (Morris 1992, p. 21). It seems a worthy project, but what does it really amount to? Nor is this simply a problem in the discipline which used to see high culture as its focus. Issues of quality lie at the heart of the study of popular culture as well. In a collection of essays about the question of quality in television, John Ellis shows how the debate seems divided between, on the one hand, the most unreconstructed paternalism of the concept of Public Service Broadcasting with its fear of 'ordinary people and their values' and, on the other hand, the abdication of concerns with quality in favour of a notion of 'diversity' (Ellis 1990, p. 34). While this sounds all right it offers no mechanisms by which plans can be laid or priorities listed beyond the, very laudable, principle that 'everyone should have a chance to see their particular interests . . . represented on their TV screens' (Ellis 1990, p. 34). At the Edinburgh Television Festival in 1989, Rupert Murdoch attacked the defenders of quality television as no more than an élite class defending an élitist culture. But, as Jim McGuigan concludes, 'the study of culture is nothing if it is not about values' and that 'if we cannot say that the *Sun* has told lies on behalf of oppressive power we are in trouble' (McGuigan 1992, pp. 173, 180). Who is now undertaking that training in sensibility which F. R. Leavis saw as indispensable to the work of the English school?

I do not think myself that Cultural Studies will be able to develop while locked in a kind of vulgar poststructuralism, as if one kind of text is pretty much the same as any other, acting as if 'art'—the special nature of the performed text, whether devised for or accessed by a mass or élite audience—does not exist, and that the discrimination of values, that inevitably goes with it, is some kind of bottomless philosophical imponderable. Artists themselves, after all—actors in soap operas, painters, rock musicians, writers, or whatever—make decisions about the quality of their work, in a context of specialist professional expectation as well as success with audiences, on a daily basis. It is hard to imagine that they could conduct their professional lives in any other way. If Cultural Studies thinks this is beyond its competence, then as a discipline it will simply become another name for Sociology—but a Sociology diluted and confused by the influx of all sorts of material and ideas that were formerly the province of other specialist disciplines. Good subjects are defined as much by what they leave out as what they include. Undifferentiated and undefined 'culture' for me is simply an ungraspable topic—what could possibly be excluded from it?—at the very least it is an unteachable one. The worst scenario is, of course, that in this mêlée, Cultural Studies will seek definition and sharpness of focus by leaving out 'Culture', the one thing which really holds it together as a project, decreeing that it is only popular culture or the mass media which belongs in this branch of study. Already, this seems to me—despite protestations to the contrary by their editors—the drift of the main Cultural Studies readers on the market. If an obsession with the exclusiveness of high art proved the undoing of English, I hope that an antithetical populism does not bring about the downfall of Cultural Studies.

ENDNOTES

Chapter 1

1 See the work of Peter Burke, for example 'The discovery of popular culture' in *People's History and Socialist Theory*, ed. Raphael Samuel, Routledge & Kegan Paul, London, 1981, pp. 216–26.

2 Quoted in Pierre Bourdieu, *Distinction: A Social Critique of the Judgement of Taste*, trans. Richard Nice, Harvard University Press, Cambridge, Massachusetts, 1984 (originally published in French in 1979), p. 245.

3 See José Ortega y Gasset, *The Revolt of the Masses*, translator unknown, W.W. Norton, New York, 1932 (originally published in Spanish in 1930).

4 This famous quotation is often taken out of context. Arnold is not in fact celebrating the centrality of reading to Victorian daily life, and by implication the spread of literacy, but in a way the opposite, that reading has to stand in for a whole range of cultural experience that has vanished during the industrialisation of England.

5 This seems to be the common view, but it should be pointed out that this kind of genealogy of the subject of 'English', traced back to Arnold's speculations about culture, is challenged by Ian Hunter in his book, *Culture and Government*, Macmillan, London, 1988. He sees the origins of modern literary education in the educational reforms of the earlier nineteenth century.

6 This view is implicit in Williams's writing about culture from *Culture and Society* on.

Chapter 2

1 Critical responses to Douglas can be found in Jane P. Tompkins, 'Sentimental power: *Uncle Tom's Cabin* and the politics of literary history', *Glyph 8*, Johns Hopkins University Press, Baltimore, 1981, pp. 79–102, and in Tania Modleski, *Feminism Without Women: Culture*

and Criticism in a 'Postfeminist' Age, Routledge, New York and London, 1991, pp. 24–6.

2   D. H. Lawrence, letter to his sister-in-law, 1922, quoted in Manning Clark, 'Rewriting Australian history', *Occasional Writings and Speeches*, Fontana, Melbourne, 1980, p. 5.

3   Frederic Eggleston, 'Two great Australians', *New Statesman*, 29 May 1929, quoted in Rowse, *Australian Liberalism*, p. 108.

4   For a discussion of these various categorisations see Herbert J. Gans, *Popular Culture and High Culture: an Analysis and Evaluation of Taste*, Basic Books, New York, 1974.

5   See the essay 'How to look at television', originally published in 1954, in *The Culture Industry*, ed. J. Bernstein, pp. 136–53.

6   See Tony Bennett, *Formalism and Marxism*, Methuen, London and New York, 1979.

7   See for example the work of John Tulloch and Manuel Alvarado on the complex industrial history and textuality of 'Doctor Who' in *Doctor Who: The Unfolding Text*, Macmillan, London, 1983.

8   See J. M. Bernstein, introduction to Theodor W. Adorno, *The Culture Industry: Selected Essays on Mass Culture* ed. J. M. Bernstein, Routledge, London, 1991, pp. 1–25.

Chapter 3

1   See Margaret A. Rose, *The Post-Modern and the Post-Industrial: a Critical Analysis*, Cambridge University Press, Cambridge, 1991.

2   For a discussion of Jencks's work in the context of theories of the postmodern, see Rose, *The Post-Modern and the Post-Industrial: a Critical Analysis*.

3   Figures from *Superculture: American Popular Culture and Europe*, ed. C. W. E. Bigsby, Bowling Green Popular Press, Bowling Green, Ohio, 1975, p. 3.

4   See, for example, Patton & Johnston, *In the Shadow of the Silent Majorities*.

Chapter 4

1   James Tuckey, lieutenant on the ship which brought convicts to Port Phillip Bay and Hobart Town in 1803–4, quoted in Geoffrey Serle, *From Deserts the Prophets Come: the Creative Spirit in Australia, 1788–1972*, Heinemann, Melbourne, 1973, p. 1.

2   See Vance Palmer, *The Legend of the Nineties*, Currey O'Neil, Melbourne, 1954, pp. 26–29 passim.

3   For a late example of this see D. H. Lawrence's novel, *The Boy in the Bush* (1924).

4   The phrase, 'a new Britannia', comes from his poem, 'Australasia' (1823).

5   The article by Marilyn Lake, 'The politics of respectability: identifying the masculinist context', which can be found reprinted in *Debutante Nation: Feminism Contests the 1890s*, eds S. Magarey, S. Rowley & S. Sheridan, Allen & Unwin, Sydney, 1993, pp. 1–15, is perhaps the most complete statement of this argument. There is a critique of it by John Docker in the same volume.

6   See, for example, his 'Towards an Australian literature', *Meanjin*, vol. 18, 1959, pp. 59–68, which stresses the importance of forming a canon of Australian writers.

7   Figures based on Margaret Simons, 'The Medici complex', the *Weekend Australian*, 13–14 February 1993, p. 21.

8   Report in the *Australian*, 24 August 1993.

Chapter 5

1   These figures and much of the information in the early part of this chapter is derived from D. L. LeMahieu, *A Culture for Democracy: Mass Communication and the Cultivated Mind in Britain Between the Wars*, Clarendon Press, Oxford, 1988.

2   These figures and those that follow are derived from John Carey, *The Intellectuals and the Masses: Pride and Prejudice among the Literary Intelligentsia, 1880–1939*, Faber, London, 1992.

3   Part 4 of the report was published in 'Television and culture', *Sight and Sound*, vol. 45, 1976, pp. 246–52.

4   See, for example, the report by Wanda Jamrozik in the *Sydney Morning Herald* of 28 September 1992 about tempestuous arguments over a perceived populist shift in the management.

Chapter 6

1   The word is used by Lesley Johnson in her contribution to Ruthven's volume, 'A shared project? Cultural studies and cultural policy studies', *Beyond the Disciplines*, pp. 45–56.

2   See Brian Doyle, *English and Englishness*, Routledge, London and New York, 1989.

3   The work of John Tulloch and the status of the Mass Communications discipline within the School of English and Linguistics (now renamed English, Linguistics, and Media) at Macquarie University is a notable exception to the general picture I am drawing.

4   Hall's narrative of the foundation of the Birmingham Centre can be found in several places, perhaps most grippingly told in 'The emergence of cultural studies'.

5   See Janet Batsleer et al., *Rewriting English*, Methuen, London and New York, 1985.

6   Used in Raymond Williams, *The Long Revolution*, 1961.

7   The lecture can be found reprinted as 'Schools of English and contemporary society' in Richard Hoggart, *Speaking to Each Other*, vol. 2, Chatto & Windus, 1971, pp. 246–59.

8   The argument was originally conducted in the pages of the journal *Scrutiny*, but some of it can be found in F. R. Leavis, *The Common Pursuit*, Pelican Books, 1976, pp. 211–22.

9   John Hartley 1992, *Teleology: Studies in Television*, Routledge, London, pp. 101–18.

BIBLIOGRAPHY

Adams, Francis 1893, *The Australians: a Social Sketch*, T. Fisher Unwin, London

Adorno, Theodor W. 1991, *The Culture Industry: Selected Essays on Mass Culture*, ed. J. M Bernstein, Routledge, London

Adorno, Theodor W. & Max Horkheimer 1973, *Dialectic of Enlightenment*, trans. John Cumming, Allen Lane, London

Anderson, John 1952, 'Democratic Illusions', *Hermes*, pp. 16–18.

Anderson, Patricia 1991, *The Printed Image and the Transformation of Popular Culture: 1790–1860*, Clarendon Press, Oxford

Arnold, Matthew 1960, *Culture and Anarchy*, ed. John Dover Wilson, Cambridge University Press, Cambridge (originally published 1869)

——1960–77, *Complete Prose Works of Matthew Arnold*, ed. R. H. Super, Ann Arbor, Michigan, 1960–77

Bakhtin, Mikhail 1968, *Rabelais and His World*, trans. Helene Iswolsky, MIT Press, Cambridge, Mass.

Baldick, Chris 1983, *The Social Mission of English Criticism: 1848–1932*, Clarendon Press, Oxford

Banham, Rayner 1960, *Theory and Design in the First Machine Age*, Architectural Press, London

Barthes, Roland 1973, *Mythologies*, trans. Annette Lavers, Paladin, London

Batsleer, Janet et al. 1985, *Rewriting English*, Methuen, London and New York

Baudrillard, Jean 1983, *In the Shadow of the Silent Majorities*, trans. Paul Foss, Paul Patton & John Johnston, Semiotext(e), New York

Bell, Clive 1928, *Civilization: an Essay*, Chatto & Windus, London

Benjamin, Walter 1969, 'The work of art in the age of mechanical reproduction', *Illuminations: Essays and Reflections*, ed. Hannah Arendt, Schocken, New York, pp. 217–51

Bennett, Tony 1979, *Formalism and Marxism*, Methuen, London and New York

——1980, 'Popular culture: a "teaching object"', *Screen Education*, vol. 34, pp. 17–29

——ed. 1981, *Popular Television and Film*, BFI, London

——1990, *Outside Literature*, Routledge, London and New York

——1992, 'Coming out of English', in *Beyond the Disciplines*, ed. K. K. Ruthven, Australian Academy of the Humanities, Canberra, pp. 33–44

Bennett, Tony & Janet Woollacott 1987, *Bond and Beyond: the Political Career of a Popular Hero*, Macmillan, London

Bigsby, C. W. E. ed. 1975, *Superculture: American Popular Culture and Europe*, Bowling Green Popular Press, Bowling Green, Ohio

——ed. 1976, *Approaches to Popular Culture*, Edward Arnold, London

Bloom, Allan 1987, *The Closing of the American Mind: How Higher Education Failed Democracy and Impoverished the Souls of Today's Students*, Simon & Schuster, New York

Bogle, Deborah 1992, 'The great divide', the *Weekend Australian*, 12–13 September, p. 23

——1994, 'Art gossips turn radio active', the *Australian*, 11 February, p. 10

Bolton, Geoffrey 1967, *Dick Boyer: an Australian Humanist*, Australian National University, Canberra

Bordwell, David, Janet Staiger & Kristin Thompson 1985, *The Classical Hollywood Cinema: Film, Style and Mode of Production to 1960*, Routledge & Kegan Paul, London

Bourdieu, Pierre 1980, 'The aristocracy of culture', *Media, Culture and Society*, vol. 2, pp. 225–54

——1984, *Distinction: a social critique of the Judgement of Taste*, trans. Richard Nice, Harvard University Press, Cambridge, MA, (originally published in French, 1979)

Brandt, George W. ed. 1981, *British Television Drama*, Cambridge University Press, Cambridge

Brooks, Peter 1976, *The Melodramatic Imagination: Balzac, Henry James, Melodrama and the Mode of Excess*, Yale University Press, New Haven

Buckley, Vincent 1957, 'The image of man in Australian poetry', in *Essays in Poetry, Mainly Australian*, Melbourne University Press, Melbourne

——1959a, 'Towards an Australian literature', *Meanjin*, vol. 18, pp. 59–68

——1959b, 'Utopianism and vitalism in Australian literature', *Quadrant*, vol 3, no. 2, pp. 39–51

Bürger, Peter 1984, *Theory of the Avant-Garde*, trans. Michael Shaw, University of Minnesota Press, Minneapolis

Burgmann, Verity & Jenny Lee eds 1988, *Constructing a Culture*, McPhee Gribble/Penguin, Melbourne

Burke, Peter 1981, 'The discovery of popular culture' in *People's History and Socialist Theory*, ed. Raphael Samuel, Routledge & Kegan Paul, London

Carey, John 1992, *The Intellectuals and the Masses: Pride and Prejudice among the Literary Intelligentsia, 1880–1939*, Faber, London

Carroll, John ed. 1992, *Intruders in the Bush: the Australian Quest for Identity*, 2nd edn, Oxford University Press, Melbourne

Caughie, John 1981a, 'Rhetoric, pleasure and "art television"', *Screen*, vol. 22, pp. 9–31

——1981b, 'Progressive television and documentary drama', in *Popular Television and Film*, eds Tony Bennett et al., BFI, London, pp. 327–52

Clark, Manning 1962, *A History of Australia*, vol. 1, Melbourne University Press, Melbourne

——1980, 'Rewriting Australian history', *Occasional Writings and Speeches*, Fontana, Melbourne (originally published in 1956)

Cleary, W. J. 1992, 'Developing the musical cultural life', in *Stay Tuned*, ed. Moran, pp. 59–62

Clifford, James 1993, 'On collecting art and culture', in *The Cultural Studies Reader*, ed. S. During, Routledge, London and New York pp. 49–73

Coleman, Peter, ed. 1962, *Australian Civilization*, F. W. Cheshire, Melbourne

Coleman, Peter 1962, 'Introduction: the new Australia', in *Australian Civilization*, ed. P. Coleman, pp. 1–11

Coleridge, Samuel Taylor 1856, *Seven Lectures on Shakespeare and Milton*, Chapman and Hall, London

Connell, R. W. 1968, 'Images of Australia', *Quadrant*, vol.12, pp. 9–19

Creative Nation: Commonwealth Cultural Policy October 1994, Commonwealth of Australia, Canberra

Cunningham, Peter 1827, *Two Years in New South Wales*, 2 vols., H. Colburn, London

Cunningham, Stuart 1992, *Framing Culture: Criticism and Policy in Australia*, Allen & Unwin, Sydney

——1993, 'Style, form and history in Australian mini-series', in *Australian Cultural Studies: a Reader*, eds J. Tulloch & G. Turner, Allen & Unwin, Sydney, pp 117–32

Darwin, Charles 1985, *The Origin of Species*, ed. J. W. Burrow, Penguin, Harmondsworth (originally published 1859)

Davidson, Martin 1992, *The Consumerist Manifesto: Advertising in Postmodern Times*, Routledge, London

Davison, Graeme 1992, 'Sydney and the Bush, in *Intruders in the Bush*, ed. J. Carroll, pp. 109–30

De Certeau, Michel 1988, *The Practice of Everyday Life*, trans. Steven Rendall, University of California Press, Berkeley (first published in French 1974)

Dempsey, Kenneth 1992, 'Mateship in country towns', in *Intruders in the Bush*, ed. J. Carroll, pp. 131–42

Denoon, Donald 1983, *Settler Capitalism: the Dynamics of Dependent Development in the Southern Hemisphere*, Clarendon Press, Oxford

Dermody, Susan, John Docker & Drusilla Modjeska 1982, eds *Nellie Melba,*

Ginger Meggs and Friends: Essays in Australian Cultural History, Kibble Books, Malmsbury, Victoria

Dixon, John 1991, *A Schooling in 'English': Critical Episodes in the Struggle to Shape Literary and Cultural Studies,* Open University Press, Milton Keynes and Philadelphia

Docker, John 1974, *Australian Cultural Élites: Intellectual Traditions in Sydney and Melbourne,* Angus & Robertson, Sydney

——1984, *In a Critical Condition: Reading Australian Literature,* Penguin, Ringwood

Douglas, Ann 1978, *The Feminization of American Culture,* Alfred A. Knopf, New York

Douglas, Mary 1982, 'Goods as a system of communication', in *The Active Voice,* ed. Mary Douglas, Routledge & Kegan Paul, London

Doyle, Brian 1989, *English and Englishness,* Routledge, London and New York

Drewe, Robert 1989, *The Bodysurfers,* Pan, Sydney (first published in 1983)

During, Simon ed. 1993, *The Cultural Studies Reader,* Routledge, London and New York

——1993, 'Introduction', in *The Cultural Studies Reader,* ed. S. During pp. 1–25

Eagleton, Terry 1983, *Literary Theory: an Introduction,* Blackwell, Oxford

——1984, *The Function of Criticism: From 'The Spectator' to Post-Structuralism,* Verso, London

——1990, *The Ideology of the Aesthetic,* Blackwell, Oxford

Easthope, Antony 1991, *Literary into Cultural Studies,* Routledge, London

Eco, Umberto 1979, *The Role of the Reader: Explorations in the Semiotics of Texts,* Indiana University Press, Bloomington

Eliot, T. S. 1919, 'Tradition and the individual talent', in *Selected Essays,* 3rd edn, Faber & Faber, London, 1951, pp. 13–22

——1949, *Notes Towards the Definition of Culture,* Harcourt, Brace & Co., New York

Elliott, Sumner Locke 1970, *Edens Lost,* Michael Joseph, London

Ellis, John 1978, 'Art, culture and quality: terms for a cinema in the forties and seventies', *Screen,* vol.19, pp. 9–49

——1990, 'What's the point?', in *The Question of Quality,* ed. Geoff Mulgan, The Broadcasting Debate, 6, BFI, London, pp. 33–42

Empson, William 1930, *Seven Types of Ambiguity,* Chatto & Windus, London

Evans, Caroline & Minna Thornton 1989, *Women and Fashion,* Quartet, London

Feuer, Jane et al., eds 1984, *MTM: 'Quality Television',* BFI, London

Fiedler, Leslie 1964, 'Death of avant-garde literature', in *The Collected Essays of Leslie Fiedler,* Stein & Day, New York, 1971, vol. 2, pp. 454–60

——1975, 'Towards a definition of popular literature', in *Superculture: American Popular Culture and Europe*, ed. C. W. E. Bigsby, Bowling Green Popular Press, Bowling Green, Ohio, pp. 28–42

Fiske, John 1989, 'Everyday quizzes, everyday life', in *Australian Television: Programs, Pleasures and Politics*, ed. John Tulloch & Graeme Turner, Allen & Unwin, Sydney, pp. 72–87

——1992, 'Cultural studies and the culture of everyday life', in Grossberg et al. *Cultural Studies*, pp. 154–73

Fiske, John, Bob Hodge & Graeme Turner 1987, *Myths of Oz: Readings in Australian Popular Culture*, Allen & Unwin, Sydney

Foster, Hal ed. 1983, *The Anti-Aesthetic: Essays on Postmodern Culture*, Bay Press, Port Townsent, Washington

Forster, E. M. 1910, *Howard's End*, Edward Arnold, London

Freud, Sigmund 1921, *Group Psychology and the Analysis of the Ego*, in The Pelican Freud Library, Penguin, Harmondsworth, vol. 12, pp. 91–178

Friedan, Betty 1963, *The Feminine Mystique*, Gollancz, London

Frith, Simon 1992, 'The cultural study of popular music', in *Cultural Studies*, eds Grossberg et al., Routledge, New York and London, pp. 174–86

Frith, Simon & Jon Savage 1993, 'Pearls and swine: the intellectuals and the mass media', *New Left Review*, vol. 198, pp. 107–16

Frow, John 1990, 'The social production of knowledge and the discipline of English', *Meanjin*, vol. 49, pp. 353–67

——1992, 'Beyond the disciplines: cultural studies', in *Beyond the Disciplines*, ed. K. K. Ruthven, Australian Academy of the Humanities, Canberra pp. 22–8

Frow, John & Meaghan Morris, eds 1993, *Australian Cultural Studies: A Reader*, Allen & Unwin, Sydney

——1993, 'Introduction', *Australian Cultural Studies*, ed. Frow & Morris, pp. vii–xxxii

Gans, Herbert J. 1974, *Popular Culture and High Culture: an Analysis and Evaluation of Taste*, Basic Books, New York

Gibbs, A. M. ed. 1990, *The Relevance of the Humanities*, Australian Academy of the Humanities, Canberra

Goodwin, Andrew 1993, 'Fatal distractions: MTV meets postmodern theory', in *Sound and Vision: the Music Video Reader*, eds Simon Frith, Andrew Goodwin & Lawrence Grossberg, Routledge, London and New York, pp. 45–66

Gorman, Clem ed. 1990, *The Larrikin Streak: Australian Writers Look at the Legend*, Sun Books, South Melbourne

Green, Michael 1982, 'The centre for contemporary cultural studies', in *Re-Reading English*, ed. Peter Widdowson, Methuen, London and New York, pp. 77–90

Grossberg, Lawrence, Cary Nelson & Paula Treichler, eds 1992, *Cultural Studies*, Routledge, New York and London

Hall, Stuart 1976, 'Television and culture', *Sight and Sound*, vol. 45, pp. 246–52

——1990, 'The emergence of cultural studies and the crisis of the humanities', *October*, vol. 53, pp. 11–23

Hall, Stuart & Martin Jacques, eds 1989, *New Times: the Changing Face of Politics in the 1990s*, Lawrence & Wishart, London

Hall, Stuart & Paddy Whannell 1964, *The Popular Arts*, Penguin, Harmondsworth

Hancock, W. K. *Australia*, 1961, Jacaranda Press, Brisbane (first published in 1930)

Hartley, John 1992, 'Continuous Pleasures in Marginal Places', in *Teleology: Studies in Television*, Routledge, London, pp. 158–80

Hawkins, Harriet 1990, *Classics and Trash: Traditions and Taboos in High Literature and Popular Modern Genres*, Harvester Wheatsheaf, London

Head, Brian & James Walter, eds 1988, *Intellectual Movements and Australian Society*, Oxford University Press, Melbourne

Heseltine, H. P. 1960–61, 'Saint Henry—our Apostle of mateship', *Quadrant*, vol. 17, no. 1, pp. 5–11

——1962, 'Australian Image, The Literary Heritage', *Meanjin*, vol. 21, pp. 35–49

Hirst, J. B. 1992, 'The pioneer legend', in *Intruders in the Bush*, ed. J. Carroll, pp. 14–37

Hodges, Eleanor 1992, 'The bushman legend', in *Intruders in the Bush*, ed. J. Carroll, pp. 3–13

Hoggart, Richard 1966, 'Literature and Society', *The American Scholar*, vol. 35, 1966, pp. 277–89

——1971, 'Schools of English and contemporary society', in *Speaking to Each Other*, vol. 2, Chatto & Windus, London, pp. 246–59

——1977, *The Uses of Literacy: Aspects of Working-class Life with Special Reference to Publications and Entertainments*, Penguin, Harmondsworth (first published in 1957)

Horne, Donald 1971, *The Lucky Country*, 3rd revised edn, Penguin, Melbourne (first published in 1964)

——1989, *Ideas for a Nation*, Pan, Sydney

Hunter, Ian 1988, *Culture and Government: the Emergence of Literary Education*, Macmillan, London

Huyssen, Andreas 1986, *After the Great Divide: Modernism, Mass Culture, Postmodernism*, Indiana University Press, Indianapolis

Inglis, Fred 1993, *Cultural Studies*, Blackwell, Oxford UK and Cambridge USA

Inglis, K. S. 1983, *This is the ABC: the Australian Broadcasting Commission, 1932–1983*, Melbourne University Press, Melbourne

Jacka, Elizabeth 1989, 'Feast of Edens', *Cinema Papers*, no. 75, pp. 20–24

——1991, *The ABC of Drama: 1975–1990*, AFTRS, North Ryde

Jameson, Fredric 1983, 'Postmodernism and consumer society', in *The Anti-Aesthetic: Essays on Postmodern Culture*, ed. Hal Foster, Bay Press, Port Townsent, Washington, pp. 111–25

Jaspers, Karl 1959, *Man in the Modern Age*, trans. Eden and Cedar Pane, Routledge & Kegan Paul, London (first published in German in 1931)

Jencks, Charles 1978, *The Language of Post-Modern Architecture*, revised and enlarged edn, Academy, London

Johnson, Lesley 1992, 'A shared project? Cultural studies and cultural policy studies', *Beyond the Disciplines*, ed. K. K. Ruthven, pp. 45–56

——1993, *The Modern Girl: Childhood and Growing Up*, Open University Press, Buckingham and Philadelphia

Kant, Immanuel 1957, 'The Critique of Judgement', in *Selections*, ed. Theodore Meyer Greene, Scribner, New York (first published in German in 1790)

Kaplan, E. Ann 1987, *Rocking Around the Clock: Music Television, Postmodernism, and Consumer Culture*, Routledge, New York and London

Kermode, Frank 1975, *The Classic*, Faber, London

——1988, *History and Value*, Clarendon Press, Oxford

King, Noel & Tim Rowse 1990, '"Typical Aussies": television and populism in Australia', in *The Media Reader*, ed. Manuel Alvarado & John O. Thompson, BFI, London, pp. 36–49

Kipnis, Laura 1986, '"Refunctioning" reconsidered: towards a left popular culture', in *High Theory/Low Culture*, ed. Colin MacCabe, Manchester University Press, Manchester, pp. 11–36

Kramer, Leonie ed. 1981, *Oxford History of Australian Literature*, Oxford University Press, Melbourne

Kroker, Arthur 1992, *The Possessed Individual: Technology and the French Postmodern*, St Martin's Press, New York

Lake, Marilyn 1993, 'The politics of respectability: identifying the masculinist context', in *Debutante Nation: Feminism Contests the 1890s*, eds Susan Magarey, Sue Rowley & Susan Sheridan, Allen & Unwin, Sydney, pp. 1–15

Lawrence, D. H. 1924, *The Boy in the Bush*, M. Secker, London

——, 1923, *Kangaroo* M. Secker, London

Lawson, Sylvia 1983, *The Archibald Paradox: a Strange Case of Authorship*, Allan Lane, Melbourne

Le Bon, Gustave 1977, *The Crowd*, Penguin, Harmondsworth (first published in French in 1895)

Leavis, F. R. 1930, *Mass Civilization and Minority Culture*, The Minority Press, Cambridge

——1948, *Education and the University*, Chatto & Windus, London

——1976, *The Common Pursuit*, Pelican Books, London

Leavis, F. R. & Denys Thompson 1962, *Culture and Environment: the Training of Critical Awareness*, Chatto & Windus, London

Leavis, Q. D. 1965, *Fiction and the Reading Public*, Chatto & Windus, London

LeMahieu, D. L. 1988, *A Culture for Democracy: Mass Communication and the Cultivated Mind in Britain Between the Wars*, Clarendon Press, Oxford

Levine, Lawrence W. 1988, *Highbrow/Lowbrow: the Emergence of Cultural Hierarchy in America*, Harvard University Press, Cambridge, MA

Lowenthal, Leo 1988, *Literature, Popular Culture, and Society*, Pacific Books, Palo Alto, CA

Lukács, Georg 1963, *The Meaning of Contemporary Realism*, trans. John & Necke Mander, Merlin Press, London (first published in German in 1957)

MacCabe, Colin ed. 1986, *High Theory/Low Culture*, Manchester University Press, Manchester

McDonald, Dwight 1957, 'A theory of mass culture' in *Mass Culture: The Popular Arts in America*, eds B. Rosenberg & D. M. White, The Free Press of Glencoe, London, pp. 59–73

McFarlane, Brian & Geoff Mayer 1992, *New Australian Cinema: Sources and Parallels in American and British Film*, Cambridge University Press, Cambridge

McGuigan, Jim 1992, *Cultural Populism*, Routledge, London and New York

McLuhan, Marshall 1967, *The Mechanical Bride: Folklore of Industrial Man*, Routledge & Kegan Paul, London

McQueen, Humphrey 1970, *A New Britannia: an Argument Concerning the Social Origins of Australian Radicalism and Nationalism*, Penguin, Harmondsworth

——1977, *Australia's Media Monopolies*, Widescope, Melbourne

Marcuse, Herbert 1964, *One Dimensional Man: Studies in the Ideology of Advanced Industrial Society*, Routledge & Kegan Paul, London

Martin, Adrian 1993, 'In the name of popular culture', in *Australian Cultural Studies: a Reader*, eds Frow and Morris, pp. 133–45

Martin, Troy Kennedy 1964, '"Nats Go Home": first statement of a new drama for television', *Encore*, no. 48, March/April

Megaw, Ruth 1985, 'American influence on Australian cinema management, 1896–1923', in *An Australian Film Reader*, eds A. Moran & T. O'Regan, Currency Press, Sydney, pp. 24–33

Milner, Andrew 1991, *Contemporary Cultural Theory: an Introduction*, Allen & Unwin, Sydney

——1993, *Cultural Materialism*, Melbourne University Press, Carlton

Mitchell, W. J. T. 1986, *Iconology*, Chicago University Press, London

Modleski, Tania 1991, *Feminism Without Women: Culture and Criticism in a 'Postfeminist' Age*, Routledge, New York and London

Moran, Albert 1985, *Images and Industry: Television Drama Production in Australia*, Currency Press, Sydney

——1992, 'ABC radio networking and programming, 1932–1963', in *Stay Tuned: the Australian Broadcasting Reader*, ed. Albert Moran, Allen & Unwin, Sydney, pp. 49–58

——ed. 1992 *Stay Tuned: the Australian Broadcasting Reader*, Allen & Unwin, Sydney

Morris, Meaghan 1988, *The Pirate's Fiancée: Feminism, Reading, Postmodernism*, Verso, London and New York

——1990, 'Banality in cultural studies', in *Logics of Television: Essays in Cultural Criticism*, ed. Patricia Mellencamp, Indiana University Press, Bloomington and Indianapolis, pp. 14–43

——1992, 'Cultural studies' in *Beyond the Disciplines*, ed. K. K. Ruthven, pp. 1–21

Mulgan, Geoff ed. 1990, *The Question of Quality*, The Broadcasting Debate, 6, BFI, London

Mulhern, Frances 1979, *The Moment of Scrutiny*, NLB, London

Mulvey, Laura 1986, 'Melodrama in and out of the Home', in *High Theory/Low Culture*, ed. Colin MacCabe, Manchester University Press, Manchester, pp. 80–100

Myers, Kathy 1986, *Understains*, Routledge, London

Ortega y Gasset, José 1932, *The Revolt of the Masses*, translator unknown, W.W. Norton, New York (first published in Spanish in 1930)

Orwell, George 1979, *The Road to Wigan Pier*, Penguin, Harmondsworth (first published in 1937)

Palmer, Vance 1954, *The Legend of the Nineties*, Currey O'Neil, Melbourne

Patton, Paul & John Johnston 1983, trans Paul Foss, *In the Shadow of the Silent Majorities*, Semiotext(e), New York

Phillips, Arthur 1966, *The Australian Tradition: Studies in a Colonial Culture*, 2nd edn, Cheshire-Landsdowne, London and Melbourne

Price, Jonathan 1978, *The Best Thing on TV: Commercials*, Penguin, Harmondsworth

Pringle, John Douglas 1958, *Australian Accent*, Chatto & Windus, London

Richards, I. A. 1926, *Principles of Literary Criticism*, 2nd edn, Routledge & Kegan Paul, London

——1977, 'An Interview Conducted by B. A. Boucher and J. P. Russo',

Complementarities, ed. J. P. Russo, Manchester, Carcanet New Press, pp. 254–69

Rose, Margaret A. 1991, *The Post-Modern and the Post-Industrial: a Critical Analysis,* Cambridge University Press, Cambridge

Rosenberg, Bernard & David M. White eds 1957, *Mass Culture: The Popular Arts in America,* The Free Press, Glencoe, Illinois

Ross, Andrew 1989, *No Respect: Intellectuals and Popular Culture,* Routledge, London and New York

Rotha, Paul 1949, *The Film Till Now: a Survey of World Cinema,* rev. edn, Vision, London

Rowse, Tim 1978, *Australian Liberalism and National Character,* Kibble Books, Melbourne

——1985, *Arguing the Arts: the Funding of the Arts in Australia,* Penguin, Ringwood, Victoria

Rowse, Tim & Albert Moran 1984, '"Peculiarly Australian"—The political construction of cultural identity', in *Australian Society,* 4th edn, ed. Sol Encel & Lois Bryson, Longman Cheshire, Melbourne

Ruthven, K. K. ed. 1992, *Beyond the Disciplines: the New Humanities,* Australian Academy of the Humanities, Canberra

Schedvin, M. B. & C. B. 1992, 'The nomadic Tribes of urban Britain: a prelude to Botany Bay', in *Intruders in the Bush,* ed. J. Carroll, pp. 82–108

Scruton, Roger 1982, *Kant,* Oxford University Press, Oxford

Self, David 1984, *Television Drama: an Introduction,* Macmillan, London

Semmler, Clement 1963, *For the Uncanny Man: Essays Mainly Literary,* Cheshire, Melbourne

——1984, 'The arts and the ABC', *Artforce,* vol. 45, pp. 16, 28

——1991, 'The (abysmal) state of Australian television', *Quadrant,* April 1991, pp. 10–21

Serle, Geoffrey 1973, *From Deserts the Prophets Come: the Creative Spirit in Australia, 1788–1972,* Heinemann, Melbourne

Simons, Margaret 1993, 'The Medici complex', the *Weekend Australian,* 13–14 February, p. 21

Smith, Bernard 1945, *Place, Taste and Tradition: a Study of Australian Art since 1788,* Ure Smith, Sydney

Sontag, Susan 1986, 'Against interpretation', in *Against Interpretation: and Other Essays,* Farrar Strauss Giroux, New York, pp. 3–14

——1986, 'Notes on "Camp"', in *Against Interpretation: and Other Essays,* pp. 275–92

Spengler, Oswald 1954, *The Decline of the West,* trans. C. F. Atkinson, Allen & Unwin, London (first published in German in 1922)

Spurgeon, C. F. E. 1917, 'Poetry in the Light of War', English Association pamphlet, London

Stallybrass, Peter & Allon White 1986, *The Politics and Poetics of Transgression*, Methuen, London

Thompson, Denys ed. 1964, *Discrimination and Popular Culture*, Penguin, Harmondsworth

Thompson, Elaine 1994, *Fair Enough: Egalitarianism in Australia*, New South Wales University Press, Kensington

Tocqueville, Alexis de 1946, *Democracy in America*, trans. Henry Reeve, Oxford University Press, London (originally published in French 1840, 1855)

Tompkins, Jane P. 1981, 'Sentimental power: *Uncle Tom's Cabin* and the politics of literary history', *Glyph 8*, Johns Hopkins University Press, Baltimore, pp. 79–102

Tulloch, John 1981, *Legends on the Screen: the Australian Narrative Cinema, 1919–1929*, Currency Press, Sydney

Tulloch, John & Manuel Alvarado 1983, *Doctor Who: The Unfolding Text*, Macmillan, London

Tulloch, John & Albert Moran 1986, *A Country Practice: 'Quality Soap'*, Currency Press, Sydney

Tulloch, John & Graeme Turner eds 1989, *Australian Television: Programs, Pleasures and Politics*, Allen & Unwin, Sydney

Turner, Graeme 1989a, 'Dilemmas of a cultural critic: Australian cultural studies today', *Australian Journal of Communication*, vol. 16, pp. 1–12

——1989b, 'Transgressive TV: from *In Melbourne Tonight* to *Perfect Match*', in *Australian Television: Programs, Pleasures and Politics*, ed. John Tulloch & Graeme Turner, Allen & Unwin, Sydney, 1989, pp. 25–38

——1990, *British Cultural Studies: an Introduction*, Unwin Hyman, Boston

——1993, ed. *Nation, Culture, Text*, Routledge, London

Turner, Ian 1968, *The Australian Dream: a Collection of Anticipations about Australia from Captain Cook to the Present Day*, Sun Books, Melbourne

Twitchell, James B. 1992, *Carnival Culture: the Trashing of Taste in America*, Columbia University Press, New York

Walker, David 1976, *Dream and Disillusion: a Search for Australian Cultural Identity*, Australian National University Press, Canberra

Ward, Russel 1965, *The Australian Legend*, 2nd edn, Oxford University Press, Melbourne

Wark, McKenzie 1992, 'After literature: culture, policy, theory and beyond', *Meanjin*, vol. 51, pp. 677–90

Waugh, Evelyn 1928, *Decline and Fall*, Chapman & Hall, London

Wellek, René 1982, *The Attack on Literature and Other Essays*, Harvester Press, Brighton

Wells, H. G. 1933, *The Shape of Things to Come*, Hutchinson, London

——1905, *A Modern Utopia*, Collins, London

White, Patrick 1958, 'The Prodigal Son', *Australian Letters*, vol. 1, no. 3, April, pp. 37–40

White, Richard 1981, *Inventing Australia*, George Allen & Unwin, Sydney

Wilkes, G. A. 1962, 'The Eighteen Nineties', *Arts I*, 1958, reprinted in *Australian Literary Criticism*, ed. Grahame Johnston, Oxford University Press, Melbourne, pp. 30–40

——1981, *The Stockyard and the Croquet Lawn: Literary Evidence for Australia's Cultural Development*, Edward Arnold (Australia), Melbourne

Williams, Raymond 1987, *Culture and Society: Coleridge to Orwell*, Hogarth Press, London (first published in 1958)

——1965, *The Long Revolution*, Pelican, Harmondsworth (first published in 1961)

——1981, *Culture*, Fontana, London

——1989a, 'The future of cultural studies', in *The Politics of Modernism: Against the New Conformists*, ed. Tony Pinkney, Verso, London, 1989, pp. 151–62

——1989b, *Resources of Hope: Culture, Democracy, Socialism*, ed. Robin Gable, Verso, London and New York

INDEX